Date Due

POLITICAL LIBERTY

POLITICAL LIBERTY

A HISTORY OF THE CONCEPTION
IN THE MIDDLE AGES AND
MODERN TIMES

BY

A. J. CARLYLE

FRANK CASS & CO. LTD.

1963

First published by
The Oxford University Press in 1941

This edition published by Frank Cass & Co. Ltd.
10 Woburn Walk, London W.C.1

First published 1941
New impression 1963

Printed by Charles Birchall & Sons Limited
Liverpool and London

CONTENTS

PART IV

INTRODUCTION

THERE is a vulgar opinion that the conception of Political Liberty, however important it may have been in Athens and Republican Rome, disappeared in the period of the Roman Empire and in the Middle Ages, and has only been recovered in the last two centuries.

There are even some who think that the pursuit of Political Liberty is only a passing phase, an abnormal development, and that all that is needed for the development of civilization is authority and force. Whatever may be the place of authority and force in a rational order, to any serious student of human nature and human history, the notion that it is mere force which has created, and which holds together human society is an absurdity, an irrational and stupid absurdity. And the notion that the pursuit of liberty is a merely passing phase of Western Civilization is equally absurd.

Some men have found themselves unable to admit that we can trace any clearly marked progress in European civilization, any normal line of development. To myself it seems evident that the history of civilization during the last two thousand years is primarily the history of the development of liberty, interrupted indeed on its political side by a curious but passing phase of absolutism in the seventeenth and eighteenth centuries, but this fell to pieces under the weight of its inherent absurdity and incompetence.

In another work my brother and I have endeavoured to write a history of Political Theory in the Middle Ages, and while, in doing this, we had little if any conscious intention of writing the history of the theory of Political Liberty in those centuries, yet that is what we have actually done. This work is primarily an attempt, but on a much smaller scale, to set out the continuity of the development of the conception of Political Liberty during the Middle Ages and the seventeenth and eighteenth centuries—the development, but even more, the continuity of the development, for this has been inadequately appreciated.

It is, however, true that it is impossible to deal with the

conception of Political Freedom without some reference to the meaning of the larger and more complex subject of Individual Freedom, not indeed in the more strictly philosophical sense, but in the sense of the relation of the authority of the political society to the individual; for it is clear that anyone who considers the history of political authority finds himself confronted with the question how political and individual freedom are related to each other.

We must therefore begin by taking account of the fact that, while we shall be occupied primarily with the history of the European conception of Political Liberty in Medieval and Modern Times, a great development in the conception of the relation of the individual to the society had been taking place in the centuries which preceded the fall of the Roman Empire in the West. I find it impossible to think that this development of the conception of the equal personality of human beings had no relation to the development of the conception of Political Liberty.

PART I

INDIVIDUAL AND POLITICAL LIBERTY IN THE MIDDLE AGES

I

INDIVIDUALITY, EQUALITY, AND PERSONAL LIBERTY

THERE are few contrasts in literature more impressive or more suggestive of some profound change in the temper of men than that between the words of the Second Commandment and those of the prophet Ezekiel.

'I the Lord thy God am a jealous God, visiting the iniquity of the fathers upon the children, upon the third and upon the fourth generation of them that hate me.'[1]

These are the words of Exodus, while Ezekiel says:

'The word of the Lord came unto me again saying, What mean ye that ye use this proverb concerning the land of Israel, saying, The fathers have eaten sour grapes, and the children's teeth are set on edge? As I live, saith the Lord, ye shall not have occasion any more to use this proverb in Israel. Behold all souls are mine; as the soul of the father, so also the soul of the son is mine, the soul that sinneth, it shall die. . . . The soul that sinneth, it shall die, the son shall not bear the iniquity of the father, neither shall the father bear the iniquity of the son; the righteousness of the righteous shall be upon him, and the wickedness of the wicked upon him.'[2]

The contrast is impressive and arresting, the one represents the conviction of the solidarity of the continuous group, the other the distinctiveness of the individual, and his moral responsibility. This is only the more arresting when we observe that, after our first almost instinctive feeling that Ezekiel's words correspond with our judgement of what would be right, we go on to remember, uneasily perhaps, that the words of the Second Commandment are after all strangely near the facts of our human experience. For we may think that the individual and he alone should experience

[1] Exodus xx. 5.   [2] Ezekiel xviii. 1–4, 20.

the consequences of his good deeds, of his mistakes, or wrong doings, but we know that in the world as it is, it is not so, but that the good or evil that men do lives after them. And, if we think a little more deeply, we know that we would not have it otherwise. We know that we do not live in solitude and in isolation, but in and through each other, that we are bound to each other by ties which we would not break if we could. It is not merely the ties of a hard necessity which bind us to each other, but the ties of that love which is the greatest quality of human nature.

We must, however, fix our attention upon the fact that the words of Ezekiel represent with an impressive force one aspect of the great change which we are considering, the disintegration of the group, and the recognition of the individual, as the primary unit of human life.

It would be unbecoming in me to pretend to deal with the Platonic or Aristotelian conception of personality, for indeed I am in no way competent to do this, but it is not difficult to recognize the significance of the extreme and even fantastic individualism of a Roman Stoic like Seneca. Where Aristotle had set out with admirable justice and force the impotence and incompleteness of the solitary man, Seneca asserts with a certain magnificent recklessness the self-sufficiency of the truly wise man. No one, he says in one treatise,[1] can either injure or benefit the wise man, there is nothing which the wise man would care to receive. Just as the divine order can neither be helped nor injured, so is it with the wise man; he is indeed, except for his mortality, like God himself; or, as Seneca puts it elsewhere, it is only in some general, outward, and loose sense that the wise man can be said to receive a benefit.[2] There is indeed a certain magnificence in such an individualism, however exaggerated and overstated it may be, but at least his words will serve to illustrate the fact of an immense change in the conception of the relation of the individual personality to the group.

We shall not, however, be able to appreciate the whole significance of this, unless we also take account of the parallel development which had taken place in the western conception of human equality and freedom. Aristotle had

[1] *De Constantia Sapientis,* viii.   [2] *De Beneficiis,* vii. 4.

defended slavery by arguments which, if his premisses had been well founded, would have constituted a profoundly moral and rational justification of slavery. He had contended that slavery was a natural and reasonable institution, because there was a fundamental difference and inequality among men. Some, he said, were capable of determining their lives to some rational end, while others were only possessed of reason enough to be able to apprehend it in others. The first were by nature free men, the second were naturally slaves, for it was better to be under the control of reason, even if it were that of a master, than to be without the guidance of reason—evidently a profound defence of slavery.[1]

Cicero, on the other hand, who obviously knew the system of Aristotle's political ideas, in his treatise on 'The Laws', elaborately and dogmatically contradicts this theory of inequality in human nature, and sets out the principle of equality. There is no resemblance in nature so great, he says, no equality so complete, as that which exists among men, there is therefore only one possible definition of human nature; for that reason, by which men are superior to the mere animals, is common to all, men differ indeed in learning, but they are equal in the faculty of learning; there is no man or race of men who cannot attain to virtue. Nature has given to all men reason, and therefore law which is right reason commanding and forbidding.[2]

What Cicero said in the century preceding the Christian era was restated in equally emphatic terms in the century which followed. The slave is of the same nature as his master, says Seneca, virtue can be attained by all, the slave or the free man, the slave may be just, brave, and magnanimous; we have all the same beginnings, we are all descended from one common parent, the world, no one in truth is nobler than another, except so far as his temper is more upright, his character better developed. It is fortune that makes a man a slave, slavery is only external, it only affects the body of a man, the body may belong to a master, the mind is its own, it cannot be given into slavery.[3]

---

[1] Aristotle, *Politics*, i. 5.
[2] Cicero, *De Legibus*, i. 10, 12.
[3] Seneca, *De Beneficiis*, iii. 19, 20, 28.

4 INDIVIDUALITY, EQUALITY, AND PERSONAL LIBERTY

It is above all significant that Cicero and Seneca both find the foundations of their doctrine of equality just where Aristotle found the principle of inequality; that is in the mind and reason, which are the distinctive and common prerogatives of human nature, and which separate man from the merely animal. Men are possessed of reason and capable of virtue, therefore they are both equal and free.

It may perhaps be suggested that these are only rhetorical phrases, abstract and unpractical declamations far removed from the actual and practical world, and that they had little relation to the actual conditions and movements of contemporary society. This would be merely an example of that ignorance which is so characteristic of some persons who think themselves practical. For in the first place these are the doctrines not only of literary men and philosophers, but also of the great jurists of the Roman Empire. We find that in their works the Aristotelian conception that slavery was founded upon some essential inequality has disappeared, and that it is looked upon as a conventional incident of war. Slaves, Florentinus says, are so called because those who are captured in war are kept alive and sold, while they might have been slain. Slavery is an institution of the Law of Nations, under which men are subjected to the lordship of others, and this is contrary to Nature.[1] And Ulpian in a more famous passage says that by the civil law slaves are indeed reckoned as *nulli*, but this is not so by the natural law, for by it all men are equal.[2]

In the second place, it is obvious to any student of the Roman jurisprudence that during the first and second centuries these legal theories were finding a practical form in a change in the legal position of the slave. Gaius, one of the most eminent of the jurists of the second century, begins indeed his treatment of slavery by saying that slaves are *in potestate dominorum*, and that among all nations the master has the power of life and death over his slaves, and that whatever the slave may acquire belongs to his master. He goes on, however, to say that this is no longer the case, but that neither the Roman citizen nor any other subject of the Roman Empire is permitted to treat his slaves with im-

[1] *Digest*, i. 5. 4. [2] Ibid. l. 17. 32.

moderate and groundless cruelty (*supra modum et sine causa in servos suos saevire*); and that, by a law of the Emperor Antoninus, the man who kills his slave without cause is held accountable to the law, just as much as the man who kills the slave of another master; and that masters should be compelled to sell their slaves whom they had treated with intolerable cruelty, and who had fled to the temples of the Gods, or to the statues of the emperor.[1] Another jurist of the same century, Modestinus, tells us that in the first century the Emperor Claudius had decreed that if a slave were deserted by his master on account of grave illness, he should be free.[2] And, what is perhaps more remarkable still, Ulpian says that the Emperor Hadrian banished for five years an Umbrian lady, who on slight grounds had outrageously ill-treated her slave women.[3]

The careless person may still think that these were small and unimportant matters, but that is the opposite of the truth, for they really mean nothing less than the beginning of the practical recognition of the legal personality of the slave. It was not incorrectly that Bulgarus, one of the great civilians of the twelfth century, interpreted the Roman law, in spite of its apparent denial of the *persona* of the slave, as recognizing that the slave was really possessed of some rights against his master which would be recognized in the Law Courts.[4]

It is with the impression of these great changes in the philosophical and legal conceptions of human nature in our minds that we can understand the place of the Christian religion in the development of the conception of the equality of men.

To St. Paul, as represented in the Acts of the Apostles, like Cicero, all men are alike. '(God) made of one every nation of men for to dwell on all the face of the earth, . . . that they should seek God, if haply they might feel after him and find him, . . . for in him we live and move and have our being; as certain even of your own poets have said, "For we are also his offspring" '.[5] Men are all alike, for they are all the children of the one divine nature, and they are all

---

[1] Gaius, *Institutes*, i. 53.   [2] *Digest*, xl. 8. 2.   [3] Ibid. i. 6. 2.
[4] Bulgarus, *Comm. on Digest*, l. 17. 107.   [5] Acts xvii. 26–8.

capable of the highest, and are all made for the same divine end, the communion of the soul with God. It is the same principle again which St. Paul sets out against the nationalism of the Hebrews, and the pride of the Greeks, in his letter to the Galatians, 'Ye are all sons of God, through faith in Christ Jesus. For as many of you as were baptized into Christ, did put on Christ. There can be neither Jew nor Greek, there can be neither bond nor free, there can be no male and female, for ye are all one in Christ Jesus.'[1] It is indeed evident, and beyond the need of detailed exposition, that the Christian Society set out in the world with the same conception of the equality of man as had been developed in the post-Aristotelian philosophy; and the principle was never wholly forgotten. It is also clear that while the Christian faith accepted and ratified the principle, it was from the pre-Christian and non-Christian writers that the Christian Fathers derived the terms in which they expressed it.

Minucius Felix, in the little work known as the *Octavius*, says that all human beings without difference of sex and race are born with the capacity of reason and feeling, and obtain wisdom not by fortune but by nature.[2] Lactantius, in the beginning of the fourth century, discussing the nature of justice, says that the second part of justice is *aequabilitas*, that is the temper which teaches a man to put himself on an equality with his fellow men. God who brings forth and inspires men wished all to be equal. He made them all for wisdom, and promised them all immortality; no one in God's sight is a slave or a master. He is the father of all men, and we are all free.[3] Lactantius, not very felicitously, goes on to criticize the character of contemporary non-Christian society as not expressing these principles, but he might have remembered that it was from the Roman writers that he borrowed the terms in which to express his principles; and, had he been able to look forward for one or two generations, he would have seen that the Christian Empire was not much more adequate in its application of these great human principles than the pre-Christian.

[1] Gal. iii. 26–9. [2] *Octavius*, xvi.
[3] Lactantius, *Divine Institutes*, v. 14.

The principles of the equality and the natural liberty of men are indeed the common judgement of all the Christian Fathers. I only cite one or two more of the most important, but the principles are common to them all.

Perhaps it is St. Ambrose who developed the conception most fully; the slave, he says, may be the superior in character of his master, no condition of life is incapable of justice, the body may be enslaved, the mind is free. The slave may be more free than the master; it is sin which renders a man truly a slave, innocence is free.[1] Some of these words remind one very forcibly of those of Seneca, and they are only reinforced by the more strictly Christian conceptions. Slaves or freemen, we are all one in Christ; slavery can take nothing from a man, nor freedom add anything to him.[2] The words of Gregory the Great are probably the best known. He admonishes masters to remember that their slaves are of the same nature as themselves, and equal to them; and in another place he bids great men remember that by nature we are all equal (*omnes namque homines natura aequales sumus*).[3] These words are probably derived from those of Ulpian, but they are not the less significant and important.

It was no doubt through the Christian Fathers that in the main the principles of the natural equality of men passed into the literature of the Middle Ages. The writers of the ninth century repeat the words especially of Gregory the Great. Ionas of Orleans warns Christian men not to mistake the differences of worldly dignity and wealth for a real difference in nature, for in nature men are all equal; and he warns the powerful and wealthy that they must not allow themselves to be carried away by passion and fury to the illtreatment of their slaves.[4] Agobard of Lyons, Hrabanus of Strassburg and the great Hincmar of Rheims also repeat this affirmation of human equality.[5]

It is partly from the Christian tradition, partly from that

[1] St. Ambrose, *De Joseph Patriarcha*, iv.

[2] Ibid., *Exhortatio Virginitatis*, i. 3.

[3] Gregory the Great, *Liber Pastoralis*, Part III. 5, and *Expositio Moralis in Job*, xxi. 15.

[4] Ionas of Orleans, *De Institutione Laicali*, ii. 22.

[5] Agobard, Ep. VII; Hrabanus, *In Genesim*, ii. 8; Hincmar, *De Regis Persona*, 3.

of the Roman jurists, that the great legal works of the thirteenth century derived their very interesting and important treatment of slavery and equality. There is a remarkable passage in the *Sachsenspiegel*, the most important German law book of the thirteenth century, in which the author, Eike von Repkow, contrasts the Christian principles with the actual conditions of his time. God, he says, made all men in his own likeness, and redeemed them by his passion, the poor as well as the rich; there were no slaves, when our forefathers first settled in the land, slavery began by capture and unrighteous force, and it is not in accordance with the truth that one man should belong to another.[1] The greatest of French feudal lawyers of that century sets out the same principles though in slightly different terms. Though there are now various conditions of men, he says, in the beginning all were free, slavery has arisen in various ways, some men were forced into it by the violence of the 'Seigneurs', but by natural law all men are free.[2] Bracton says that God accepts no distinction between slaves and free, before Him the greater may be the lesser; and it is only among men that there are such distinctions.[3] To these great medieval jurists slavery and inequality rested upon conventional, and not upon natural, distinctions.

It may seem that I have been dwelling at unnecessary length on these developments, remote as some may think from our actual temper and problems, but I have done this deliberately and intentionally, for I cannot but feel that a good many well-meaning, but not very well-informed persons, even in our time, seem to think that they can play fast and loose with these questions, can discuss them as though they were merely modern speculations belonging, as they perhaps think, to the first enthusiasm of the French Revolution, while the real truth is that it is upon these assumptions of individuality and equality that the whole fabric of our legal civilization is founded.

If there are some who are unable to understand the immense complexities of our political order, and there are

---

[1] *Sachsenspiegel*, iii. 42.
[2] Beaumanoir, *Les Coustumes du Beauvoisis*, xlv. 1453.
[3] Bracton, *De Legibus*, i. 8. 1.

such persons in England, to say nothing of some continental countries, I should only ask them to consider the simpler characteristics of our whole legal system. I do not mean to suggest that this is simple, only that it is much simpler than our political system. If they will do this they cannot fail to see that the foundations upon which it is built are the principles of the individual and equal personality of men, their equality before the law, that equality which rests upon the assumption that all men are rational creatures, and are therefore to be held accountable for their actions. In our legal system the solidarity of the primitive group has disappeared, and with it the conception of some fundamental inequality, and its place is taken by the individual, the individual who is equal and rational.

We are indeed well aware that this legal assumption of the individual responsibility is in a certain sense an abstraction, an abstraction which is very far from the whole truth. For it remains true, and we know it, that we are what we are, not merely in virtue of our individual characters, but in virtue of our environment and education. We are not wholly responsible for our actions, and yet it is upon the quality of our rational and self-determining personality that the legal structure of modern society is founded, and rightly, for it is the function of society not to constrain but to emancipate our personality, the human world is not a world of predetermined and blind movements, but a world of equal personalities moving towards freedom.

Enough has been said to make it plain that if we are to think of any interruption in the continuity of Western Civilization, it is here that we find it, that is in the development of the conception of the equality or rational human nature. As I have already said, I find it impossible to think that there was no relation between this conception and the development of the conception of political liberty, as we shall see it in the Middle Ages.

It is true no doubt that the new development of the conception of individuality coincided in time with the disappearance of political liberty in the West. The freedom of the Greek city-states had been lost; and, with the establishment of the Empire in Rome, while some of the forms of political freedom remained, the reality was disappearing. 'Quod cunque principi placuit, legis habet vigorem,'[1] Ulpian said; and four centuries later Justinian claimed that the emperor alone had the authority to make and to interpret the laws. 'Si enim in praesenti leges condere soli imperatori concessum est, et leges interpretari solum dignum imperio esse oportet.'[2]

It might seem that the conception of the authority of the community had disappeared and given place to the authority of the prince. And yet this is not the whole truth.

It was in the last days of the Republican constitution of Rome that Cicero made an observation on the true nature of a free government which seems to indicate a profound and penetrating conception of the nature of political liberty.

Cicero had clearly been brought up in the Aristotelian tradition that the distinction between good and bad government was determined by its end or purpose, that a government was good if it was directed to the well-being of the whole community, evil if it pursued the good of the ruler or ruling class. But Cicero was not wholly satisfied with this. The three forms of government, the Monarchy, the Aristocracy, the Democracy, are, he says, only tolerable. The least satisfactory was to him that in which the whole power was in the hands of the people, but he was equally dissatisfied with the mere aristocracy or monarchy, and it was here that his conception assumed a new significance. The most just aristocracy, or the most just monarchy was to him unsatisfactory, for under such forms of government there was a certain appearance of slavery, and the multitude under such governments can scarcely be said to possess liberty.[3]

This criticism was indeed profound and far-reaching. It would seem to be founded upon the principle that men are in their proper nature equal, for they are possessed of reason, and are capable of virtue, and therefore a government that takes no account of these qualities cannot be wholly good. Cicero seems to assume that without a share in political authority men cannot be properly said to possess liberty. He is therefore dissatisfied with the three simple forms of

[1] Code I. 141. 12.
[2] *Digest*, i. 4. 1.
[3] Cicero, *De Republica*, i. 26. 27.

government and is in favour of a fourth, a mixed form, compounded of the three simple ones.

Here it would seem that we find a relation in principle to the conception of the natural equality and freedom of the human personality. It would seem to me also reasonable to add to this, that the conception of the source of all political authority which the great jurists of Rome handed down to the Middle Ages and the modern world was, that there is no other source of political authority except the community itself; neither the authority of God, nor the intrinsic superiority of the ruler, but the will of the community. Few passages in the *Digest* are more familiar than the saying of Ulpian, 'Quod principi placuit, legis habet vigorem'; a statement of an absolute legislative authority of the prince, but it is sometimes forgotten that Ulpian continued: 'utpote cum lege regia, quae de imperio eius lata est, populus, ei, et in eum omne suum imperium et potestatem conferat.'[1] The emperor has indeed an unlimited legislative authority, but only because the people (i.e. the whole community) confers this upon him. Ulpian's words sum up in a single phrase the theory of all the great Roman jurists from Ulpian at the end of the second century to the Emperor Justinian himself towards the end of the sixth.[2] This has indeed no direct reference to the principle of human personality and equality, but it may be said that it represents what we may call a reasonable deduction from it. Political freedom implies that all political authority is derived from the community, the community which is composed of men who are capable of directing and controlling their public as well as private lives to ends determined by themselves.

---

[1] *Digest*, i. 4. 1.
[2] I would venture to refer to a detailed discussion of this matter in our *History of Medieval Political Theory* (vol. i, chap. vi).

II

THE CONCEPTION OF POLITICAL LIBERTY IN THE MIDDLE AGES

THE first and most fundamental aspect of political thought in the Middle Ages was the principle that all political authority was the expression of justice; as some jurists put it, all civil and positive laws flow from justice, as a stream flows from its source;[1] or, as it may be put in other terms, there is behind the positive law of the State a greater and more august law, the Law of Nature. This Law of Nature may indeed have been in some points modified by the transition from the state of nature to the conventional order of society, but in its proper character it is divine and unchangeable, and cannot be abrogated by Positive Law.

This principle, that all merely human authority is limited, was derived immediately from the Roman law, and was of the greatest importance in medieval thought and sentiment, for it meant that there neither was nor could be any such thing as an absolute political authority. It was St. Thomas Aquinas himself who said that while sedition was a mortal sin, it was not sedition to resist an unjust authority.[2] Even Bodin in the sixteenth century, who has sometimes been thought the first who explicitly maintained the conception of the sovereignty of the State, recognized that even his absolute king was subject to the natural and divine laws. It was not till Hobbes in the seventeenth century that anyone ventured to maintain the rather absurd doctrine of the complete and absolute sovereignty of the State.

The second great principle of political theory, which came as we have seen to the Middle Ages from the Roman law, was that there could be only one immediate source of political authority, and this was the community itself, that there was no other source, neither the personal qualities of the prince, his greater wisdom and intelligence, nor force,

[1] *Fragmentum Pragense,* iii. 9, in H. Fitting, *Juristische Schriften des früheren Mittelalters.*
[2] *Summa Theologica,* 2. 2. 42. 2.

nor, normally, the direct appointment of God, but only the community.

To those not acquainted with the Roman law it may seem paradoxical to say this, for the *Corpus Juris Civilis* belongs to the time when the Roman Commonwealth was governed by emperors, who had an authority which at first sight, at any rate, looks absolute, and who were themselves the source of law. It is true that, as we have seen, Ulpian, one of the great jurists of the latter part of the second century, said in a famous passage that what the prince wills has the force of laws ('Quod principi placuit, legis habet vigorem'),[1] but it was, and is sometimes forgotten, that he added that this was so because by the 'Lex Regia' the Roman people conferred its *imperium* and *potestas* upon him.

The authority of the Roman prince was derived from the people. This was the doctrine of all the Roman jurists of the Empire. It is by a law of the Roman people that the emperor receives the *imperium*.[2] Pomponius, in his discussion of the sources and development of Roman law, says that when it was found necessary that one man should take charge of the affairs of the commonwealth, a prince was created, and he was given authority that what he established should be held valid (i.e. as law).[3] What is perhaps even more significant is that this was also the judgement expressed by the emperors themselves. Theodosius II and Valentinian II, in a famous passage in the Code, of the year 429, say that the prince is bound by the laws, for his authority is drawn from the law,[4] and Justinian himself in the sixth century refers explicitly to the ancient law by which the Roman people transferred all their authority and power to the emperors.[5] These two great principles of political civilization the Middle Ages inherited from the ancient world, and directly from the Roman law.

When, however, we consider the general character of the political order of the Middle Ages we find ourselves in a very different world from that of the Ancient Empire. It is not the prince who is supreme, but the law, and the law was during the Middle Ages primarily the custom of the com-

[1] *Digest*, i. 4. 1.   [2] Gaius, *Institutes*, i. 2. 7.
[3] *Digest*, i. 2. 2.   [4] *Cod.* i. 14. 4.   [5] Ibid. i. 17. 1. 7.

munity. It is no doubt true that we can see that to the great
jurists of the *Digest*, behind the declared will of the commonwealth, there lay the authority of custom,[1] but in fact their
legislative authority was normally delegated to the prince.
To the jurists of the Middle Ages the positive law was not
normally made, but was the expression of the custom of the
community. Gratian, the first great systematic canonist, sets
out in his *Decretum* in the middle of the twelfth century the
principle that mankind is ruled by natural law, or by
custom; all positive law is to him, properly speaking,
custom.[2] In another place he says that laws are established
when they are promulgated, but they must be confirmed by
the custom of those who live under them.[3] This broad and
sweeping judgement that, properly speaking, positive law
is nothing but the custom of the community may seem to
those who are not acquainted with medieval history, extravagant, but it is the dogmatically expressed judgement not
only of Gratian, but of two of the greatest jurists of the
thirteenth century, Bracton in England and Beaumanoir in
France. Bracton indeed, with a somewhat characteristic
English ignorance of the world across the Channel, says
that while other countries used written law, England alone
used unwritten law and custom.[4] Bracton had probably a
vague impression that the Roman law prevailed on the
Continent. His great contemporary in France, Beaumanoir,
about the same time, wrote: 'All pleas are determined by the
Customs. . . . The king is bound to keep, and to cause to be
kept, the Customs of his country.'[5]

The truth is that Gratian and Bracton and Beaumanoir
were only putting down in explicit terms the normal character of medieval law, as we can see it in all the earlier collec-
tions of laws. These are not 'laws' if to be a 'law' implies
being made by some definite person or persons, they are the
records of the customs of various countries and provinces.
The original and normal conception of medieval law was

[1] Cf. *Digest*, i. 3. 32 and 35.
[2] Gratian, *Decretum*, i, D. 1.
[3] *Moribus utentium*, ibid. D. 4 after chap. 3.
[4] Bracton, *De Legibus*, i. 1. 2.
[5] Beaumanoir, *Les Coustumes du Beauvoisis*, xxiv. 682.

thus very different from the normal conception of the law of the Roman emperor. It was not the expression primarily of the will and command of the king or prince, but of the habits of life of the community; and it is very important to observe that the determination of what was, or was not, the customary law was a matter to be decided not by the king or lord, but by the community, or in the feudal court, by the vassals. No doubt in the later Middle Ages this place was to a great extent taken by the king's court and the king's judges, but the court was in principle an impartial body, not subject to the king's personal will and commands, and was expected to carry out the law even against the king's will. This is evident as late as the fifteenth and sixteenth centuries in England in Fortescue, in France in Gerson, De Seyssel, and Machiavelli.[1]

The first and most important form of the conception of political liberty in the Middle Ages was then the supremacy of law, not as made by the prince, or any other legislator, but as expressing the habit and custom of life of the community; it is this that makes the notion that the law was in the Middle Ages made by the king's will a mere absurdity, held by no one except some Roman lawyers, so absorbed in the study of the *Corpus Juris* that they forgot the world in which they lived.

It was this principle of political society which was so well expressed by Bracton in his famous words that the king had two superiors, the one was God, and the other the law. The king he meant was not over the law, but subject to it, he was not the master of the law, but the servant. Where there is no law there is no king.[2] The same principle is admirably expressed by the compiler of the Assizes of the Court of Burgesses in Jerusalem in the twelfth century, when he said that the Lord or Lady, is Lord only of Right, he is not Lord to do wrong.[3] (The word *Droit* means what we call right or justice, as well as what we call law.) The same blending of

---

[1] Fortescue, *De Natura Legis Naturae*, i. 16; Gerson, *Sermo pro viagio Regis Romanorum*; De Seyssel, *Grant Monarchie de France*, i. 10; Machiavelli, *Discorsi sopra la prima Deca di Tito Livio*, i. 126.

[2] Bracton, *De Legibus*, i. 8. 5.

[3] *Assizes of the Court of Burgesses*, 26.

the conception of justice and law is admirably illustrated in another passage in Bracton. The authority of the king is the authority of law (or right) and not of wrong. He should exercise the authority of law, as being the vicar and servant of God on earth, for this alone is the authority of God, the .authority to do wrong belongs to the devil, and the king is the servant of him whose work he does, when he does justice, he is the vicar of the eternal king, but the servant of the devil when he turns away to do wrong. Let him therefore restrain his authority by the law which is the bridle of authority, let him live according to law.[1] Bracton's words represent admirably that combination, which was so characteristic of the Middle Ages, of a profound reverence for the office of the king, with a drastic judgement of the man.

No doubt as time passed, and the complexities of life increased, some deliberate changes, or at least some modifications of customary law were required. These were for a long time effected by the almost insensible changes of custom by which a living community adjusts itself to new conditions in its environment. It is, however, true that as early as the ninth century, in some degree, and certainly by the twelfth and thirteenth centuries, the conception of a definite legislative authority, and action, began to take shape. This gradually developed into the conception of an authority greater than that of the law, which in popular opinion both makes laws and abrogates them. (I do not mean that this is a very complete or rational conception of law.)

We must therefore ask, when in course of time men began to think of law, not merely as immemorial custom, but as being made by some definite authority, by whom did they think it was made? The answer is simple and clear, the law of the community was made by the community. The Roman emperor derived his authority from the people, but he made laws without any necessary consultation with it, while the medieval king or emperor, who at first did little more than declare the customs of the community, when something like deliberate legislation began, made laws indeed, but properly only with the advice and consent of those who stood for the community.

---

[1] Bracton, *De Legibus*, iii. 9. 3.

This was admirably expressed in principle in the ninth century by Hincmar of Rheims, the most important ecclesiastical statesman of the time in northern Europe, when he said that kings must govern their people by the laws of their ancestors, which were promulgated with the general consent of their faithful men (*generali consensu fidelium suorum*).[1] That this was no mere *obiter dictum* of Hincmar is clear, when we examine the formulas of legislation in the *Capitularies* of the ninth century. These were made by the emperor or prince with the consent of the great men and all his faithful subjects. The famous words of the *Edictum Pistense* of A.D. 864, 'Quoniam lex consensu populi et constitutione regis fit', only sum up the general principles and practice of the time.

This is indeed a very different principle and practice from that of the ancient Roman Empire, as expressed for instance by Justinian, when he claimed that the emperor was the sole legislator.[2] The medieval emperor or king had indeed the first place in legislation, but he could only exercise this power in conjunction with those who in some sense stood for the community. If this is clear in the Carolingian Empire of the ninth century it became clearer still in the later Middle Ages. As we have seen, Bracton in England and Beaumanoir in France still, in the thirteenth century, looked upon law as expressing primarily the custom of the community, but Bracton also describes English law as being made by the king with the counsel and consent of the great men, and the approval of the commonwealth,[3] and in another place he contrasts this with the doctrine of the Roman law, with which, by the thirteenth century, the jurists even of northern Europe were familiar—that what the prince pleases has the force of law,[4] while in England the king made laws with the counsel of his great men.[5] Perhaps the most interesting illustration of the normal medieval doctrine that the prince could not legislate alone, is to be found in the fact that even some of the most important of the Bologna civilians of the

[1] Hincmar of Rheims, *De Ordine Palatii*, 8.
[2] *Cod.* i. 14. 12.
[3] Bracton, *De Legibus*, i. 1. 2.
[4] *Digest*, i. 4. 1.
[5] Bracton, *De Legibus*, iii. 9. 3.

twelfth and thirteenth centuries maintained that laws should be made by the prince after consultation with the 'Proceres' (the magnates) and the Senate. This is the judgement of the *Summa Trecensis*,[1] of Roger,[2] and of Azo.[3] We cannot indeed always be sure when these civilians were merely commenting on the *Corpus Juris Civilis* and when they are stating principles which belonged to their own time; but the *Summa Trecensis* at least is clearly laying down the contemporary rule, 'Aliter enim hodie leges confici non debent' (Laws are not to be made otherwise to-day).[4] Clearly the author is not merely interpreting the ancient Roman law, but is laying down what he understood to be the rule of contemporary practice. It really needs no detailed argument to prove that the method of legislation described by Bracton corresponded with the general practice of the Middle Ages. The notion that the medieval emperor or king could legislate alone is an illusion.

The supremacy of the law, the law which expressed first the custom, and then the counsel and consent of the community, was the first element in the conception of political liberty in the Middle Ages, for this meant that the king or prince held an authority, august indeed, but limited, not absolute. We must consider this a little further and under other terms.

There runs through the whole political literature of the Middle Ages from the seventh century to the end of the sixteenth a distinction between the king and the tyrant, which was not merely rhetorical, and found expression not merely in the literature but in the actions of men. The king was to the Middle Ages one who ruled according to the law, while the tyrant was one who ignored or violated the laws.[5] It is this principle which found a practical and formal expression in the great constitutional doctrine of western Europe in the Middle Ages that the king cannot take any action against the person or property of any of his subjects except by process of law. This is expressed not only in the famous clause

[1] i. 14. 3.   [2] Roger, *Summa Codicis*, i. 12.
[3] Azo, Ibid. i. 14. 2.
[4] *Summa Trecensis*, i. 14. 3.
[5] John of Salisbury, *Policraticus*, iv. 1; viii. 17.

of Magna Carta (39) but in the equally important and emphatic and constantly reiterated statement of the principles of law in Spain. At the Cortes of Leon in 1188 Alfonso IX swore that he would not take action against any man except by judgement of the court, and in the Cortes of Valladolid in 1299 it was decreed that no one was to be killed or deprived of his property till his case had been heard by *fuero* and Law.[1] This was also the constitutional law of France as testified by Gerson in the fifteenth century, and by De Seyssel and Machiavelli in the sixteenth; cases between the king of France and a private person were subject to the jurisdiction of the *Parlemens*.[2] This was the normal legal rule of the Middle Ages, and it is only the more significant when contrasted with the alien and intrusive conception of some Italian civilians of the fifteenth century who interpreted the words of Ulpian in the *Digest*,[3] 'Princeps legibus solutus est', as meaning that the prince was not bound by the law, but could do anything *supra jus, et contra jus, et extra jus* (above the law and against the law and outside the law).[4] It is interesting to notice that Cujas, the greatest French civilian of the sixteenth century, maintained that this was a wrong interpretation of Ulpian.[5]

Political liberty in the Middle Ages then meant primarily the supremacy of law, law which was the expression of the habit of life of the community and also of the will of the community, but this was not all. For it was in the Middle Ages that there was developed a form or method for the expression of the will of the community, that is the system of representation, adapted not merely to small communities, but to the national states which were slowly taking form.

It is indeed true that the development of the municipal liberties of the cities of Italy was of immense importance,

[1] *Colleccion de Cortes de los reinos de Leon y de Castiella,* vol. i, 7. 2; 25. 1; 26. 3.

[2] Gerson, *Sermo pro viagio Regis Romanorum*; De Seyssel, *Grant Monarchie de France,* i. 10; Machiavelli, *Discorsi sopra la prima Deca di Tito Livio,* iii. 1.

[3] i. 3. 31.

[4] Jason de Mayno, *Comm. on Digest,* i. 4. 1.

[5] Cujas, *Comm. on Code,* vii. 23. 3.

related no doubt to economic developments, but expressing immense and vital energies of the human spirit. It was indeed in the great cities of Italy, Germany, and the Low Countries that at least from the twelfth and thirteenth centuries the recovery of civilization was most rapid.

It is, however, true that, when we look back over the history of these centuries, it was the discovery of a form or method of political freedom for the great national communities which we feel to have been the most important achievement of medieval political civilization. This was not, as some seem to think, peculiar to England, it belonged to all the countries of central and western Europe; and naturally, for it arose out of conditions and conceptions of life which were common to them all. It was indeed in Spain that the representatives of the towns were first summoned to the great councils of the kingdoms, more than a hundred years before the Parliament of 1295 in England,[1] and in the thirteenth and fourteenth centuries we find something of the kind in almost all parts of Europe. It is indeed sometimes suggested that these early representative bodies had little relation to anything but the imposition of taxes by a common authority, and it is no doubt true that the principle that the prince could not take a man's property except by legal process, was so firmly fixed in men's minds that without the development of some system of representation it would have been impossible to obtain the financial resources which the developing organization and policy of the various countries required. It is, however, a mere absurdity to suggest that these representative councils were called into being for merely financial purposes; it is clear that they were concerned with all important national affairs, with legislation and general policy as well as finance. The famous words of the English Parliament of 1322, whatever may have been their original significance, that "all those matters which were to be established for the kingdom and people were to be treated, agreed upon, and determined in Parliament by the king, with the assent of the Prelates, Counts, Barons and the whole Commonalty of the kingdom"[2] are closely parallel to

---

[1] *Colleccion de Cortes,* i. 7.
[2] *Statutes of the Realm,* vol. i, p. 189.

the provisions of the Cortes of Bribiesca in 1387, which laid down that royal briefs contrary to custom or law were to be treated as null and void, and that laws and ordinances were not to be annulled except in Cortes.[1] The words of the little English treatise, entitled *Modus tenendi Parliamentum*, which belongs probably to the earlier part of the fourteenth century, and in which the proper order of business in Parliament is discussed, are very significant of the functions of Parliament. The author puts, first, questions of war, and the affairs of the king and his family, second, the common affairs of the kingdom, the amendment of laws, &c., and third, the affairs of private persons and petitions.[2]

The principles of political liberty had then developed in the Middle Ages first under the terms of the supremacy of law, not as something imposed on the community from outside, but as representing first the character and habit of life of the community, and then the deliberate will of the community. A free community was one which lived by its own laws, and under the terms of the supremacy of the community itself, not only in its law, but in its control over all matters which concerned its life.

There are some words of Nicholas of Cusa in the fifteenth century which may serve to illustrate the fundamental convictions of men in the Middle Ages as to the proper nature of government and law. Every ordered empire and kingdom, he says, takes its origin from election, all authority is recognized as divine when it arises from the common agreement of the subjects. The laws of a country should indeed be devised by wise men chosen for the purpose, but these wise men have no coercive power over the unwilling. Governments can only arise from the free consent of the subjects, just as laws can only be made by their consent.[3]

These conceptions found their expression in almost all the serious political thought of central and western Europe until the end of the sixteenth century, indeed they were more

[1] *Colleccion de Cortes*, vol. ii. 28, Tercero Tractado, 9.

[2] Cf. the very valuable work on the *Modus tenendi Parliamentum* by Miss Maud Clarke of Somerville College, whose premature death has been a great loss to English historical work.

[3] Nicholas of Cusa, *De Concordantia Catholica*, iii. 4 and ii. 14.

clearly and confidently expressed in the sixteenth century than before. The Renaissance and the Reformation had indeed no distinctive influence upon them, it can only be said that the violent conflicts which were incidental to the Reformation were the occasion, but not the cause, of their developed assertion. This will be clear to anyone who will be at pains to examine and compare the political theory of George Buchanan in Scotland with that of a great Jesuit political thinker like Mariana in Spain. These writers, however profoundly they might differ on theological or ecclesiastical questions, were agreed upon the source and nature of political authority, that it came from the community, and was normally under the control of the community, subject indeed to the higher authority of the divine and natural laws, and the principles of justice.

PART II
THE CONCEPTION OF POLITICAL LIBERTY IN THE SEVENTEENTH CENTURY

I

THE DEVELOPMENT OF THE THEORY OF ABSOLUTISM IN THE SIXTEENTH AND SEVENTEENTH CENTURIES

WE have pointed out, in the preceding chapter, that, while the forms of political society in the Middle Ages were very different from those of to-day, the principles of political liberty were very highly developed, especially under the terms of the supremacy of the law over the ruler, the law which was the expression not of the will of the ruler, but of the habit of life of the political community.

We have now to ask how it came about that in the course of the seventeenth and eighteenth centuries, this conception was almost wholly lost over a great part of Europe, and was replaced by a theory of the absolute authority of the prince; or rather, for this work is not a constitutional history of Europe, under what terms was this somewhat irrational conception expressed?

It would be absurd to attempt to find a short and adequate answer to the question why this happened, but it is possible to point out some of the elements which would find their place in such an inquiry. We may begin by observing that in one great country of Europe political liberty had in large measure perished as early as the fourteenth century. The great Italian jurist Bartolus of Sassoferrato had no illusions about a tyranny, to him it was the worst of all evil forms of government. The government by the few over the multitude was corrupt when it pursued its own good, and not that of the whole, but it was not so far removed from the common good as that of the one man who governed for his own profit, that is the tyrant, but 'Italy is to-day full of Tyrants'.[1] Two

[1] Bartolus, *De Regimine Civitatis*, 27. 29.

centuries later Machiavelli said that nothing could restore liberty to Milan or Naples, this could be seen in the fact that, when Filippo Maria Visconti died, Milan desired to recover its liberty, but it was impossible, for the corruption of the people had gone too far.[1] The judgement was just, though Florence was still, after Machiavelli wrote, to make a last effort to regain its liberty, and it was not only by its own fault that it failed, but because of the unscrupulous ambition of the Medici, and because Italy had become the battleground of the equally unscrupulous ambitions of the great European powers, as it remained for many centuries. Machiavelli's judgement was no doubt just. We may put it in other terms, and say that it was the intolerable anarchy of the conflicting factions in the great and small cities which destroyed the possibility of liberty.

It seems true to say that it was a cause of the same kind which destroyed political liberty in some of the great countries of Europe, and France furnishes us with an excellent example. It was the anarchical and unscrupulous foolishness of the French princes and nobles to which we may fairly attribute the disappearance of political freedom in France. Not even the English invasions of the fourteenth and fifteenth centuries could teach them to subordinate their individual passions and ambitions to the interests of their country. It is this which palliates, if it does not justify, the unscrupulous craft and violence of Louis XI in the fifteenth century.

Two centuries later Richelieu said in the *Mémoires de l'État* (attributed to him) that when he came to power he found that the Huguenots divided the government of the State with the Crown, that the great nobles behaved as though they were not subjects, and the governors of the provinces as though they were sovereigns.[2] It may be doubted whether the unscrupulous incompetence of a powerful class has ever been as forcibly illustrated as in the anarchical foolishness of the great nobles of France in the Fronde, surely the most ludicrous of all attempts at revolution.

Machiavelli had said with reference to the Italian terri-

---

[1] Machiavelli, *Discorsi sopra la prima Deca di Tito Livio*, i. 17.
[2] Richelieu, *Mémoires de l'État*, ed. 1764, vol. i, p. 1.

torial nobility, that the very existence of such a class was incompatible with any true political order of life (*vivere politico*) for such a class of men were the enemies of all civilized life (*nimici d'ogni civiltà*),[1] and he went on to say that, where this class existed, there was no way out but by submission to an absolute king. The history of continental Europe in the seventeenth and eighteenth centuries provides an excellent commentary on his words.

We may perhaps think that the happier fortune of England was in large measure due to the destruction of the feudal Baronage in those faction fights which we call the Wars of the Roses, for the new nobility created by the Tudors never possessed the local authority of the old Baronage.

We may perhaps find another cause of the decline of the political liberty of the Middle Ages in the influence of the study of the Roman law, which gradually spread over continental Europe, in the later Middle Ages. The Roman law had indeed, as we have seen, handed on to the Middle Ages the dogmatic judgement that all political authority was derived from the people, that is the community, but the *Corpus Juris Civilis* was after all the Law Book of Imperial, not of Republican Rome, and assumed that the Roman people had transferred to the prince that authority which had belonged to them. The Roman law, as known to the Middle Ages, had normally its immediate source in the prince; and further, the medieval civilians had learned from occasional references in the *Corpus Juris* that the prince was *legibus solutus*, a phrase which seemed to mean that the prince was not only the source of law but stood outside and above it. What had been the original meaning of these words, I confess, seems to me very doubtful, but that is a question too complex to be dealt with here, as is also the history of their interpretation by the medieval civilians.[2] These two conceptions, that is, that the prince, as distinguished from the community, was the source of law, and that the prince was free from the law and above it, were indeed wholly alien to

---

[1] Machiavelli, *Discorsi sopra la prima Deca di Tito Livio*, i. 55.

[2] I venture to refer those who may wish to know more about this last question to our *History of Medieval Political Theory*, especially vol. vi, part i, chaps. 2 and 5; part ii, chap. 2; part iii, chap. 5.

C

the normal principles of the Middle Ages, but it is probably true that they had begun to exercise some influence even before the sixteenth century.

There was yet another conception which goes back to an earlier time than the Middle Ages, and that was the conception that the authority of the prince was derived directly from God, and that the prince was answerable only to God. This was derived by Gregory the Great from some parts of the Old Testament. It had been practically set aside in the Middle Ages, but was revived in the sixteenth century. We shall have to deal with this immediately, as it is stated in certain writers of the sixteenth and seventeenth centuries.

However we may explain it, the fact is obvious, that the king in France, and gradually the kings and princes in other continental countries, came to be thought of in some quarters, in the sixteenth, seventeenth, and eighteenth centuries, as possessing an absolute authority; that is, there grew up a conception of political authority which was fundamentally different from that of the Middle Ages, for absolute monarchy was a new thing, an innovation which had no real relation to the past. It was indeed a revolutionary innovation, an experiment in government, which lasted two centuries and then failed.

The first form in which the theory of the absolute prince was expressed in the sixteenth century was, strangely enough, a theological one. The theory that political authority is derived from God, in such a sense that resistance to the prince is resistance to God, however unjust and tyrannical he may be, is traditionally known as the 'Divine Right of Kings', or as the doctrine of 'Non Resistance'. This doctrine was substantially derived from the East, from some passages in the Old Testament, and was first fully developed by Pope Gregory the Great at the end of the sixth century.[1] This doctrine passed on formally to the Middle Ages, but their real judgement was quite different. From Hincmar of Rheims and other writers of the ninth century to Hooker in the sixteenth, the great political thinkers maintained that the king was under the law and not over it, and that the

[1] Pope Gregory I, *Regulae Pastoralis*, iii. 41. Libri Moralium in Job xxii. 24.

authority of the king was divine only so far as it was the expression of justice. It was only a few, and those of no great political importance like Gregory of Catino in the twelfth century and Wycliffe in the fourteenth, who took the doctrine of Gregory the Great seriously. It was only in the sixteenth century that it began to have any importance, and it was in some of Luther's early work that we find its first important restatement. Luther, however, was taken in hand by some of the German jurists, and in the Declaration of Torgau he formally withdrew his earlier judgement, and in 1536 this recantation was repeated by Luther, Melanchthon, and others of the German Reformers.[1] The earlier theory of Luther had, however, passed into England in the work of Tyndale, *The Obedience of Christian Men*, published in 1525, and it is probable that it was from him that English divines like Bishop Bilson of Winchester learned the doctrine of the 'Divine Right'. Bilson's treatise, *The true difference between Christian Subjection and Unnatural Rebellion*, was published in 1586. We find the same doctrine set out by some French Roman Catholic writers like Pierre de Belloy and Peter Gregory of Toulouse in the later years of the sixteenth century.

We shall have much more to say about this conception as we see it in the seventeenth century.

The first important statement of the secular theory of absolutism was set out by the French writer Jean Bodin, who published his work *De la République* in French in 1576, but translated it into Latin and republished it in 1586.[2]

There are two conceptions of great importance which Bodin sets out, first the conception that there must be in every political society some supreme authority, which is outside of the positive law, and above it, for it is the source of positive law. It is to this authority that he gives the name of *Majestas*.[3] The second is that the best form of government is that of an absolute monarch in whom the *Majestas* is

---

[1] For a full discussion of Luther's position cf. K. Müller, 'Luther's "Äusserungen über das Recht des Widerstandes"' in: "*Sitzungsberichte der Bayer. Akad. der Wissenschaften*", 1915.

[2] It is to the second edition that references are here made.

[3] Bodin, *De Republica*, i. 2. 3. 8; iii. 5.

embodied, and Bodin maintained that this was the nature of the monarchy in France.

The first is what may be termed the theory of the Sovereignty of the State. It would be a mistake to say that this theory was wholly new, it was no doubt assumed in the treatment of the nature of the positive law by the great Roman jurists like Gaius;[1] and it is clear that the medieval jurists sometimes thought of the law as being made. It is true, however, that the general medieval conception was, that law was custom, the expression rather of the habit of life of the community than of a conscious and deliberate will.

When Bodin says that law is nothing but the command of the Supreme Power, the *Maiestas*, which is *legibus soluta*, he was not, I think, setting out an entirely new conception, but he was giving a definite form to one which had generally hitherto been vague and undefined.

We must, however, be careful to observe that this is not the same as the theory of Hobbes, to which we shall turn later, for Bodin dogmatically maintains that the supreme authority is itself subject to the authority of the natural and divine law, and the law of all nations.[2] The supreme power of the State is free from the positive law of the State, but there is a greater authority which it must obey.

This must not be confused with the second conception of Bodin. So far he was laying down the principle of the sovereignty of the State, not that of the prince, for this sovereignty may be vested in the whole people or in a few, or in one.[3] It is clear that it must be placed in one of them, for he maintains dogmatically that the supreme power is indivisible, that a mixed government is simply a *popularis status*.[4] The theory of the sovereignty of the State does not, to Bodin, necessarily imply an absolute prince.

Bodin's second important conception, however, and it is this which is for the moment the most important for us, is that the best form of government is that of an absolute monarch whose authority is not shared with the nobles or the

---

[1] Gaius, *Institutes*, i. 1.
[2] Bodin, *De republica*, i. 8.   [3] Ibid. ii. 7.
[4] Ibid. ii. 7.

people. This is the best not only for the prince, but for the community, any attempt to limit his authority, or to subject him to the assemblies of the people can only lead to a detestable anarchy, and any tyranny is better than the domination of the people.[1] It is curious to notice the reckless audacity with which in this passage Bodin ventures to appeal to the universal judgement of legislators, historians, philosophers, and theologians as holding that monarchy is the best form, and his neglect to ask what kind of monarchy it was that they had praised.

It was then the absolute monarchy, where the *maiestas*, that supreme authority, itself free from the law, resided in the prince, which Bodin conceived to be the best form of government. It can hardly be said that he developed any serious philosophical argument in justification of his contention, and the absence of this is the more noticeable when we observe that he justified his view neither by an appeal to history, nor to the actual and general conditions of political authority in Europe. Indeed, when he deals with the contemporary constitutions of European countries, he quite frankly recognized that it was difficult to find any examples of a true monarchy. In Spain and in England he admits that laws were made *rogatione Populi*, and could not be annulled except in the assemblies of the people; while of the contemporary Empire he says that the emperor swore to observe the laws of the Empire, and was bound by the laws and decrees of the princes.[2] In another place he frankly admits that the *maiestas* of the Empire resided in the assembly of the princes and the nobles, and that the emperor could not make laws or appoint officials without their consent. Indeed, in his judgement the Empire was not a monarchy but an aristocracy. In France alone did Bodin find a government which had the nature of a supreme or sovereign monarchy. The Estates could indeed present their petitions to the king, but he controlled all things at his will, and Bodin maintained that the coronation oath was not an oath to keep the laws, and that in France laws had often been abrogated without the meeting or consent of the Estates.[3]

[1] Bodin, De republica, vi. 4.
[2] Ibid. i. 8.　　　　[3] Ibid. ii. 1.

This is an explicit and thoroughgoing assertion of the principle of an absolute monarchy, and it is in violent contrast with the whole character of political civilization in the Middle Ages. The prince is absolute, it is from him that all laws proceed, and he is above the law. That Bodin really meant this is evident when we notice that in another place he says that, if the prince commands what is contrary to the laws, the inferior magistrate may indeed remonstrate, but if the prince repeats his commands the magistrate must obey.[1] It is true that with all this dogmatism there are some passages in Bodin's work which are different in tone or suggestion. The value of the States General and Provincial Estates,[2] the inviolability of private property,[3] the importance of the perpetual tenure of the judges as protecting their independence,[4] all these he insists upon in various places, and it is difficult to reconcile these with his general position, but there is no reason to doubt that Bodin thought that the absolute monarchy was the best form of government and that he maintained that it existed in France.

So far then we have seen the beginning of a theory of absolute monarchy in the sixteenth century, and we have found it in two forms, under the terms of the conception of the king as deriving his power from God in such a sense that resistance to the king is revolt against God; but also under the terms of the secular theory of Bodin. As we shall see, in the seventeenth century these conceptions are frequently combined, or at least lie side by side in the same works.

Our readers must bear in mind that we are not attempting to give a complete account of the absolutist literature but only endeavour to illustrate its character by a selection from the better known works.

The seventeenth century opened with a work entitled *De Regno et Regali Potestate*, published in 1600 by William Barclay, a Scotsman. He was educated first in Aberdeen, migrated like so many of his countrymen to France, studied in the great school of Roman law at Bourges, and became a professor of Roman law at Angers. This work was in large measure an attempt to reply to George Buchanan's *De Jure*

---

[1] Bodin, *De republica,* iii. 4.   [2] Ibid. iii. 7.
[3] Ibid. i. 8.   [4] Ibid. iv. 4.

Regni apud Scotos, the famous defence of the constitutional limitations of monarchy, and of the deposition of Mary Queen of Scots.

Barclay's contentions are threefold. He emphatically repudiates Buchanan's contention that either generally, or in Scotland, laws were made with the consent of the community, and he maintains that the king was not bound by the law.[1] He also defended the theory of the absolute authority of the king, by an appeal to the authority of the medieval Roman lawyers, that is really to those of the fourteenth and fifteenth centuries; for he passed over the great Bologna civilians of the thirteenth century, like Azo and Hugolinus, and found himself compelled to repudiate his great contemporary Cujas, and other French civilians of the sixteenth century.[2] So far for the secular arguments, but he also insisted that the king when lawfully instituted received from God an authority which was greater than that of the community, the king, however unjust his actions may be, is answerable only to God, and cannot be judged by the people; that is, he asserts the Divine Right of kings.[3] It is true that Barclay recognized some exceptions to the doctrine of non-resistance, for he was a good Scotsman, and remembered John Balliol and Edward I.[4] Barclay's work is not indeed of much intrinsic importance, but it had some reputation in its time.

It is, however, with a work of that strange and half-grotesque figure of James I of England that the revolutionary innovation of the upholders of the 'Divine Right', and of Bodin's absolute monarchy, began to have some relation to the actual conditions of political life.

It would be difficult to find in history a sharper contrast than that between the claims set out by James I in his little treatise entitled *The True Law of Free Monarchies* (published first in Scotland in 1598, but republished in England in 1603), and the terms of the Resolution of the Convention of 1689. 'That King James II having endeavoured to subvert the constitution of this kingdom by breaking the original contract between King and People, and by the

[1] Barclay, *De Regno*, i. and ii.   [2] Ibid. iii. 14, 15.
[3] Ibid. iii. 6.   [4] Ibid. iii. 8, and 16, and vi. 22.

advice of Jesuits and other wicked persons, having violated
the fundamental laws, and having withdrawn himself out
of the kingdom, has abdicated the government, and that
the throne is thereby vacant.'

It will therefore be well to examine briefly some of the
most important passages in James I's little book. He begins
indeed by expressing a formal deference for the principles
of the coronation oath, by which he had sworn to maintain
justice, the good laws of his predecessors, and the liberties
and privileges of his subjects.[1] This is, however, merely
formal, for he maintains that the kingdoms of Scotland and
England had been conquered by his ancestors.[2] The king
is the source of all law, and over all law, for he is 'maister
over every person that inhabiteth the same (countries) having
power of life and death over every one of them. For although
a just prince will not take the life of any one of his subjects
without a clear law, yet the same laws, whereby he taketh
them, are made by himself.'[3] Again he cites the speech of
Samuel on the nature of kingship (1 Sam. viii), and explains
what this implied.

'First he (Samuel) declares unto them what parts of justice and
equity their king will bear in his behaviour unto them. And next he
putteth them out of hope that, wearie as they will, they shall not
have leave to shake off that yoke, which God through their importuni-
ties hath laid upon them.'[4] Again he adds to these somewhat grotesque
conceptions of the nature of political order, the conception of the
'Divine Right' and, like Gregory the Great, cites the example of
David's submissive attitude to Saul, and concludes, 'Shortly then, to
take up in two or three sentences . . . the duty and allegiance of the
people to their lawful king, that obedience, I say, ought to be to him,
as to God's lieutenant upon earth, obeying his commands in all things,
except directly against God, as the commands of God's minister,
acknowledging him a Judge set by God over them, having power to
judge them, but to be judged onely by God, whom to onely he must
give count of his judgement . . . following and obeying his lawful commands, eschewing and flying his furie, in his unlawful, without resistance, but by sobs and teares to God.'[5]

James I had indeed heard of a contract between king and
people, but sets it aside:

[1] James I, *The True Law of Free Monarchs*, ed. 1603, B. 3. [2] Ibid. C.
[3] Ibid. D 1.   [4] Ibid. B.   [5] Ibid. C.

'As to this contract alledged, made at the coronation of the king, although I deny any such contract to be made then, especially containing such a clause irritant as they alledge, yet I confess that a King at his coronation or at the entry to his kingdome, willingly promiseth to his people to discharge honourably and truly the office given him by God over them. But presuming that thereafter he breake his promise unto them, never so inexcusable, the question is who should be judge of this breake, giving unto them this contract were made to them never so sicker, according to their alleageance.'[1]

We might indeed almost say that the whole conflict between the Stuart kings and the English people is represented in the contrast between the principles embodied in James I's little book, and the Resolution of the Convention of 1689. The subversion of the constitution, the appeal to fundamental laws, and to the original contract, these are continually recurring conceptions of the long conflict.

It is interesting to notice that a few years after the publication of James's *True Law* two works were produced in England which set out that the authority of the king in England had a double form; in the exercise of his ordinary authority he was bound by the law, but he was possessed also of an extraordinary authority, which was by some identified with the 'Prerogative' in which he was absolute and free from the authority of the law.

It was this conception which was set out by Albericus Gentilis in his work entitled *Regales Disputationes* in 1605, and by James Cowell in his *Interpreter* in 1607. Both of these were primarily Roman lawyers, the first had been a professor at Perugia, but adopting some kind of Reformed opinions escaped to England, and had been made Professor of 'Civil Law' in Oxford; while the second was Professor of 'Civil Law' in Cambridge.

The conception of a difference between the ordinary and the extraordinary authority of the prince, the first, which is normally subject to the Law, the second and absolute authority, which is not under the law, had been set out by Baldus of Perugia[2] in the fourteenth century, and the identification

---

[1] Ibid. ii.   [2] Baldus, *Comm. on Code*, i. 14. 4.

of the latter with the Prerogative of the king of England by Albericus Gentilis and Cowell lent some respectability to the revolutionary conception that the king of England was in some sense above the law. The constitutional or legal theory of Prerogative in England is, however, too complex a subject for the mere layman to deal with. We are concerned with it here mainly as illustrating a possible influence of Roman law in England in the seventeenth century.

It is, however, in the work of some Anglican and Gallican theologians that we find the most dogmatic statement of the theory of the absolute monarchy, and it is well to begin by considering this in its crudest form, that is in the work which is known as *Bishop Overall's Convocation Book*. This work was not published till 1690, but it professes to be a collection of 'Canons' drawn up by the Lower House of the Convocation of Canterbury in 1606, but also submitted to, and approved by, the Upper House. The most important principles laid down in these Canons are as follows.

Canon I. Chap. II: 'That the Son of God did give to Adam and the rest of the Patriarchs . . . Authority, Power and Dominion over their children and offspring to govern them . . . although it be not called either Patriarchal, Regal, or Imperial, yet we may truly say that it was in a sort "Potestas Regia"; as now, in a right and true construction "Potestas Regia" may justly be called "Potestas Patria".'

Canon II: 'If any man shall therefore affirm, that men at the first . . . acknowledging no superiority over another, until they were taught by experience the necessity of Government, and that therefore they chose some authority among themselves to order and rule the rest, giving them power and authority so to do, and that consequently all Civil Power, Jurisdiction, and Authority was first derived from the People, and disordered multitude, and either is originally still in them, or else deduced by their consents, naturally from them, and is not God's ordinance originally depending upon Him, he doth greatly err.'

Chap. VI. 'Noah lived after the Flood 350 years . . . he was the Patriarch and chief Governor over them . . . ruling and ordering them by virtue of that superiority, power, and authority of the sword of justice, which was given unto him by Almighty God, and was also warranted by the laws of Nature and Reason . . . also the extent of his authority was so large that he lawfully distributed the whole world unto his three sons and their posterity. So that his said three sons, after him, were by the ordinance of God . . . made three great Princes, and also the sons of these three great Princes were the Kings and Governors of the families and nations that descended from them, according to their tongues in the several countries.'

Canon XVI affirms that every form of disobedience to the prince was forbidden to the Jews in the Old Testament, but what is more remarkable is that Canon XXXI extends this principle to the relations of the Jews to their conquerors, like the kings of Babylon, and Persia, and Alexander the Great.

The conclusion therefore is drastic and unqualified, and is expressed in Canon XXXIII:

'If any man therefore shall affirm . . . that the rebellion against any King, absolute Prince, or Civil Magistrate, for any cause whatsoever, is not a sin very detestable against God . . . he doth greatly err.'

These statements of principle were not only crude and irrational, but it should be observed that they represent a complete ignorance or disregard of the conception of the nature of political society as it had been set out for some 1,600 years by the post-Aristotelian philosophers, by the Roman lawyers, and by the medieval thinkers. We can understand that Protestant Churchmen should refuse to recognize the authority of a great schoolman like St. Thomas Aquinas, when he said that resistance to an unjust and tyrannical authority was not the sin of sedition,[1] but it is curious that they should have been apparently so ignorant as to overlook Richard Hooker's treatment of the origin and nature of human government.[2]

There is one gleam of common sense in Canon XXVIII of the Convocation Book, where the authors perhaps remembered the very important statute of Henry VII, that no person could be convicted of treason on account of his obedience to the king *de facto*.[3] Canon XXVIII says:

'If any man therefore shall affirm either that the subjects when they shake off the yoke of obedience to the sovereign, and set up another form of government among themselves, after their own humour, do not therein very wickedly . . . or that when any such new form of

[1] *Summa Theologica*, 2. 2. 42. 2.   [2] *Ecclesiastical Polity*, i. 10.
[3] Statutes 4. Henry VII, c. 2.

government, begun by rebellion and after thoroughly settled, the authority in this is not of God . . . he doth greatly err.'

The Convocation Book certainly represents a very crude and unintelligent attitude on the part of some of the clergy, but the best-known English work on the 'Divine Right', that is Sir Robert Filmer's *Patriarcha*, while it contains other arguments for the absolute authority of kings, is in the first place a restatement of the conceptions set out in the Convocation Book, and it is reasonable to think that it implies some acquaintance with it, or some tradition of what it contained. It is not certainly known when it was written, but it must have been before 1653 when Filmer died; it was published in 1680.

Like the Convocation Book Filmer begins with the repudiation of the conception that men are naturally free, and at liberty to establish whatever form of government they please. He attributes the origin of this opinion to the 'School Divines', but admits that it was also accepted by the Reformers.[1] Against this he sets up the assertion that political authority was derived from that authority which God gave to Adam and the Patriarchs over their children and children's children, 'The three sons of Noah had the whole world divided amongst them by their father'; and again, 'most of the civilest nations of the earth labour to fetch their original from some one of the sons or nephews of Noah which were scattered abroad after the confusion of Babel. In this dispersion we must certainly find the establishment of regal power throughout the kingdoms of the world.'[2] A little later Filmer indeed adds: 'It is true all kings be not the natural parents of their subjects, yet they all either are, or are to be reputed, the next heirs to their progenitors who were at first the natural parents of the whole people, and in their right succeed to the exercise of supreme jurisdiction.'[3]

This is absurd enough, but Filmer was compelled to face the question: 'What becomes of the right of Fatherhood, in case the Crown does escheat for want of an heir, whether doth it not then devolve upon the people. The answer is:

[1] Filmer, *Patriarcha*, i. 1.   [2] Ibid. i. 5.
[3] Ibid. i. 8.

'It is but the negligence or ignorance of the people to lose the knowledge of the true heir, for an heir there always is.'[1] This, however, compels him to devise another way of establishing the prince. The supreme power does not devolve upon the multitude, but 'the kingly power escheats in such cases to the princes and independent heads of families . . . all such prime heads and fathers have power to consent in the uniting or conferring of their fatherly right of sovereign authority on whom they please; and he that is so elected claims not his power as being a donative from the people, but as being substituted properly by God.'[2]

Again, Filmer, remembering presumably, like the author of the *Convocation Book*, the Act of Henry VII, maintains that while rebellion or usurpation are damnable, yet the authority of the usurper is 'the only right and natural authority of a supreme Father'.[3]

Apart from this attempt to derive the authority of the king from that of Adam, the most important contention of the work is that the authority of the king is not subject to the law. 'It is necessary also to enquire whether human laws have a superiority over princes, because those that maintain the acquisition of royal jurisdiction from the people do subject the exercise of it to positive law. But in this also they err, for as kingly power is by the law of God, so it hath no inferior law to limit it.'[4] Filmer has the singular audacity to quote in support of this judgement the words of Bracton, that all men are under the king, and he under no one but God, while he omits Bracton's words that while the king is under no man he is under God and the law, for it is the law which makes the king.[5] Filmer continues 'although a King do frame all his actions to be according to the laws, yet he is not bound thereto but at his good will, and for good example, or so far forth as the general law of the safety of the commonweal doth naturally bind him'.[6] The coronation oath of the King to maintain his laws Filmer dismisses contemptuously; it is no more binding on him than private persons are bound

---

[1] Ibid. i. 9.   [2] Ibid. i. 9.
[3] Ibid. i. 10.   [4] Ibid. iii. 1.
[5] Ibid. iii. 3 (cf. Bracton, *De Legibus*, i. 8. 5).
[6] Ibid. iii. 6.

by their voluntary oath;[1] a somewhat singular defence of perjury.

It is, however, in his treatment of the famous words in which Samuel warns the Hebrews of the oppressive nature of a monarchy that Filmer touches the lowest depths of servility. He cites what he calls

'that majestical discourse of the true law of free monarchy [meaning probably that foolish tract of James I which we have already considered] wherein it is evidently shewn that the scope of Samuel was to teach the people a dutiful obedience to their King, even in those things which themselves did esteem mischievous and inconvenient; for by telling them what a king would do, he indeed instructs them what a subject must suffer, yet not so that it is right for kings to do injury, but that it is right for them to go unpunished by the people if they do it. So that in this point it is all one whether Samuel describes a king or a tyrant, for patient obedience is due to both; no remedy in the text against tyrants, but in crying and praying unto God in that day.'[2]

Certainly it would not seem that Filmer's tract deserved the detailed refutation which Locke gave it in the first of the *Two Treatises of Government*, but it would seem that in Locke's words 'it made such a noise at its coming abroad' that it was taken seriously by a good many people.

A few years later, an important Scots jurist, Sir George Mackenzie, published a work entitled *Jus Regium* in which he combined the absurdity of the Patriarchal Theory with an unscrupulous misrepresentation of the Roman law. His work is in large measure directed against George Buchanan's *De Jure Regni apud Scotos* and first against Buchanan's contention that kings derive their authority from the people. 'I lay down', he says, 'as my first position that our monarchs (i.e. in Scotland) derive not their right from the People, but are absolute Monarchs, deriving their Royal authority immediately from God Almighty.'[3] He has the effrontery to cite from the Code the words 'Deo auctore nostrum gubernante imperium quod nobis a caelesti maiestate traditum est', and to omit all reference to the words 'cum lege antiqua, quae regia nuncupatur, omne ius omnisque potestas populi

---

[1] Filmer *Patriarcha*, iii. 7   [2] Ibid. iii. 2.
[3] In George Mackenzie, *Jus Regium*, ed. 1684, p. 13.

Romani in imperatoriam translata sunt potestatem'.[1] He must have known that according to the Roman law all the powers of the Roman emperors were derived from the Roman people.

Mackenzie also affirmed the patriarchal origin of political authority, and repeats the contention of James I that the kings of Scotland derived their authority from conquest; and he cites Ulpian's dictum 'quod principi placuit, legis habet vigorem',[2] omitting Ulpian's statement that it was the Roman people who had given him this authority. He cites the unhappy saying of Grotius that a people like an individual could sell itself into slavery.[3] He maintains that a monarch must in his proper nature be absolute, must not be required to consult with nobles or people,[4] and he says that a tyrant is one who has no right to govern, not one who misgoverns.[5]

He does indeed feel himself compelled to say something in justification of the Revolt of the Protestants on the Continent, and argues that the king of Spain was not king of the Netherlands, but only duke of Burgundy, and did not hold the supreme power. The revolt of the Protestant princes in Germany, he says, was founded upon their rights as declared in the Golden Bull of Charles IV, while the civil wars of France in the sixteenth century were due to quarrels between the princes of the Blood and the Guises, but nothing in these would justify the risings in Scotland about religion.[6]

We have been considering the development of the theory of absolutism in the seventeenth century in England, but we must turn back to France where it was not merely defended in theory but was in the later part of the century established in fact. We take two examples of the defence of it in principle. The first by a jurist, Le Bret, who published a work entitled *De la Souveraineté du Roy* in 1632, the other by a great theologian and preacher, Bossuet, in his work entitled *Politique tirée des Propres Paroles de l'Écriture Sainte.*

[1] *Code,* i. 17. 1. 7.
[2] *Dig.* i. 41. 1.
[3] 'Ius Regium' p. 32.
[4] Ibid. p. 37.
[5] Ibid. p. 48.
[6] Ibid. pp. 117, 120.

The work of Le Bret has a special interest in that, unlike Barclay, he shows that he was acquainted with the older political system of France. At the same time he is clear and dogmatic in affirming the absolute authority of the king of France in his own time. He begins by setting out a definition of *Souveraineté* which is very significant.

A perfect and complete *Souveraineté*, he says, belongs to one who is subject only to God and his law.[1] We may conjecture that this is related to Bodin. Le Bret remembers indeed that Demosthenes and Papinian had described the law as *Communis Reipublicae Sponsio*[2] and that there had been a time when the people possessed the sovereign power; but from the time when God had set kings over them, they had lost this authority and now the only laws which men accepted were the commands and edicts of the prince, as Ulpian had said.[3] The king then has a complete and absolute legislative authority, and this extends even to the power to alter the customary law, but Le Bret added that this must be done with caution.[4] The king has also the supreme authority in interpreting the law, and he refers to the Code.[5] The king is thus the supreme legislator and can make and change the laws, for he is the only sovereign in his kingdom; though it is becoming even in a great king, to consult his 'Parlemens' and the principal officers of the law, and he refers to the rescript of Theodosius and Valentinian.[6]

Le Bret was indeed clear that if the king's laws were contrary to the law of God, men must not obey them, but he was clear that even if the king's commands were unjust, while his courts and officers should remonstrate, in the end they must submit and carry them out, whatever they were. The only exception which he seems to make is that the courts are not to pay any attention to a letter from the king with regard to any case concerning a private person which was already before them.[7] Le Bret was also clear that the king of France had now the power to impose taxes without the consent of

[1] Le Bret, *De la Souveraineté du Roy* (ed. Paris, 1632, i. 2 (p. 9)).
[2] *Dig.* i. 3. 1 and 2.   [3] Ibid. i. 4. 1 (p. 61).
[4] Ibid. i. 2 (p. 9).   [5] Ibid. i. 4. 12.
[6] Cod. i. 14. 8.
[7] Ibid. ii. 6 (pp. 188, 196, 198).

the people, and he adds that the theologians said that the people were bound in conscience to pay them.[1]

This is all very clear and dogmatic. Le Bret was contending that the king of France now had an absolute and sovereign power to make and unmake laws, and to impose taxation at his will; but we must be careful to notice that he was aware that this had not always been the case, but that the royal authority in this form was a new thing. Law was not originally in France simply a command of the king, the sovereign power had formerly belonged to the whole commonwealth and the people had authority to make laws;[2] and he was aware that in former times the king in France had never issued edicts without calling together and consultnig 'les plus gens de bien du Royaume'.[3] It is also important to observe that Le Bret thought highly of the value of the States General; they only met by the authority of the king, and could only present humble petitions to him and they were therefore not inconsistent with the sovereignty of the king, but he recognized their value.[4]

The truth is that while Le Bret affirms in dogmatic language the absolute sovereignty of the king, he was also aware of the fact that this was a modern thing and an innovation.

Le Bret is an important defender of the absolute authority of the king, but he dealt with it almost exclusively from a secular standpoint. Bossuet on the other hand defended it almost entirely from a theological standpoint, and indeed the title of his principal work on politics is *Politique tirée des Propres Paroles de L'Écriture Sainte.* Bossuet had been appointed Preceptor to the Dauphin, and this work was prepared primarily for the instruction of his pupil. This work is, as indeed its title implies, curiously limited in its scope. It takes practically no account of history, or of the great political thinkers of the ancient world, or of the Roman jurists, or of the canon law, or of the medieval political thinkers.

It is indeed a curious thing to see a great Catholic, but Gallican, divine thus restricting himself, and it is difficult to

---

[1] Ibid. iii. 7 (p. 395).   [2] Ibid. i. 9 (p. 61).
[3] Ibid. i. 9 (p. 71).   [4] Ibid. iv. 12 (p. 640).

avoid the suspicion that he was aware that the political principles not only of St. Thomas Aquinas, but of the great mass of medieval theological as well as secular writers were very different from those which he maintained.

We may begin by noticing some generalizations about the nature and source of political authority. In one place he lays down dogmatically that, while the prince is assisted by wise men, and the experience of former ages, the authority of the laws does not depend upon the consent of the people.[1] In another place he says that it is in the prince that there resides the whole 'power and will, and even the reason of the State'.[2] In another work he says that the *État populaire* is the worst of all forms of government.[3]

More important, however, than these are his dogmatic statements of the quasi-divine authority of the prince. The judgements of the sovereign, he says, are attributed to God himself, and men must therefore obey the Prince as one would obey justice itself. It is God only who can judge his judgements. The prince may amend himself when he knows that he has done evil, but there is no remedy against his authority except in his authority.[4] And again, princes must always be respected, always served, whether they are good or bad.[5] Princes should indeed listen to the complaints of the people, when they are made respectfully, and by lawful channels, but bitter complaints and murmurs have something of the nature of sedition, and should not be tolerated.[6]

This is all strange enough, but Bossuet, like Filmer, reached a lower depth of servility when he treated Samuel's warning of the misgovernment of the kings whom the Israelites had desired to have, not indeed as implying the approval of God, but as intimating that the king could do this with impunity, as far as human justice was concerned.[7] And he reaches the lowest depth of absurdity when he tries to explain away the revolt of the Maccabees against Antiochus.[8]

---

[1] Bossuet, *Politique tirée des Propres Paroles de l'Écriture Sainte*, i. 4. 6.
[2] Ibid. vi, Art I, Prop. 1 and 2.
[3] Ibid. *Avertissement aux Protestants*, Works, vol. xlix, p. 462.
[4] Ibid. iv. 1, Prop. 2.   [5] Ibid. vi. 2, Prop. 4.
[6] Ibid. vi. 2, Prop. 6.   [7] Ibid. iv. 1, Prop. 3.
[8] Ibid. vi. 3, Prop. 2.

So far then Bossuet's position would appear to be clear and unambiguous. The prince is absolute, answerable only to God, the sole source of law, and the only authority who can enforce it. It is, however, true that Bossuet makes a distinction between arbitrary government and absolute government, and we must consider the meaning of the distinction. This is best understood in his description of arbitrary government. First, he says, the people subject to it are slaves, there are no free men under it. Second, there is under it no such thing as private property, all *les fonds* belong to the prince. Third, the arbitrary prince has the right of disposing at his pleasure not only of the goods, but of the lives of his subjects. Fourth, under an arbitrary government there is no law except the will of the prince. Bossuet refuses to discuss the question whether such a government is *licite* or *illicite*; there are, he says, some peoples who seem to be satisfied with it (he refers presumably to some Oriental States). But, with what at last is some generous emotion, he says that it is 'barbarous and odious', such conditions of life are far removed from our customs. The 'Absolute' government is, he says, quite different, it is 'Absolute' in the sense that there is no power which can compel the sovereign, who is in this sense independent of all human authority. But it does not follow that this government is 'arbitrary', for besides that it is subject to the judgement of God, there are laws, the transgression of which is *nul de droit*.[1] 'Arbitrary' actions of the government, Bossuet says, are *nul de droit*, no one can possess anything in security *au préjudice des lois.*

These are admirable sentiments and represent the natural reactions of an honest Frenchman, but it is difficult to reconcile them with Bossuet's own previous statement that there is no remedy against the prince but in his own authority. It is indeed strange that a man of Bossuet's authority should have forgotten the principles of Gerson and De Seyssel on the relations of the royal authority to the courts of law.

Bossuet does not involve himself in the absurdities of the English *Convocation Book* and of Filmer's *Patriarcha* about the descent of the royal authority from Adam, and he has in some curiously confused way some sense of the authority of

[1] Ibid. viii. 2, Prop. 1.

law, but he was doing his best to train his pupil the Dauphin in the principles of absolute monarchy.

It is difficult to deny the justice of the severe criticism which the Count of Boulainvilliers passed on the political works of Bossuet in his *Lettres sur les Anciens Parlements de France*, published in 1727, where he said that every disinterested and enlightened man must look upon the *Système Politique* of the illustrious Bossuet as the most shameful evidence of the degradation of the times, and the corruption of men, for which neither learning nor enlightenment can compensate; and he goes on to say that nothing could show such bad faith as the continual abuse by Bossuet of passages from Holy Scripture for the purpose of forging new chains for the natural liberty of men, and of increasing the ostentation and harshness of the king.[1]

I have left to the last in this chapter the discussion of the position of Hobbes, because his treatment of the subject is very different from that of the political writers whom we have hitherto considered. Strictly speaking it is not a defence of the absolute monarch, but rather of the absolute State, a conception which is perhaps even more dangerous to liberty than the former.

The truth is that the moral philosophy of Hobbes is probably more important than his political theory, for it represents a complete breach with the conception of human nature as it had been generally accepted by philosophers, jurists, and theologians for many centuries.

Not indeed that his theory of morals was entirely new. It is clearly related to the theory which Cicero scornfully reports as being defended by Carneades, that laws are made simply because they are useful, that there is no such thing as natural law or justice. 'The notions of right and wrong, justice and injustice have there no place. Where there is no common power there is no law, where no law, no injustice'[2] (i.e. in the natural condition of man).

It is this conception which separates the political theory

---

[1] Boulainvilliers, *Lettres sur les Anciens Parlements de France*, ed. 1727, Lettre III, p. 20.

[2] Hobbes, *Leviathan*, xiii (ed. Oxford, 1909).

of Hobbes not only from the traditional conceptions of the jurists, the Fathers, and the medieval writers, but also from Bodin. Bodin was clear that the sovereign *Majestas* was above the positive law, but was subject to the natural and divine laws. The sovereign of Hobbes was subject to no law.

Hobbes, however, while clearly repudiating the moral philosophy of his predecessors, took over from them some of their most important quasi-historical conceptions; he took over from them at least formally the conception of a primitive world in which men lived without an ordered society, and the conception that in this world all men were equal. He argued that they were substantially equal in force of body, and that there was no reason to think that they differed greatly in the 'faculties of mind'.[1]

This primitive world Hobbes maintains was a world of perpetual war of man against man. This again was not a new conception, for the post-Aristotelian thinkers, and the Christian Fathers had conceived indeed of a primitive world in which men were innocent and harmless, a golden age of mutual affection and peace; but this had been destroyed by the appearance of vice or sin, and the actual world of human experience was one of discord and strife; and men were driven to set up some system of common authority and conventional institutions, which should at least mitigate these evils.

The most important difference between Hobbes and the older writers was, that while they thought of men as fallen from their primitive innocence, they also thought of them as retaining some sense of moral principles and obligations. The 'natural law' which they had obeyed in the state of innocence was still in some measure known to them, and it was the main function of the common coercive authority which they set up to enforce this. The foundation of positive law was justice. Hobbes, on the other hand, as we have seen, repudiated the doctrine that right and wrong, justice and injustice, had any meaning apart from a common and coercive authority. As we shall see presently, this determined his whole conception of the nature of the common authority and its laws.

[1] Ibid.

The truth is that while Hobbes uses the term *jus naturale*, what he meant by it was not some system of moral ideas or principles, but 'the liberty each man hath to use his own power as he will himself, for the preservation of his own nature; that is to say, of his own life; and consequently, of doing anything, which in his own judgment and reason he shall conceive to be the aptest means thereto'.[1] It is from this he derived the origin and character of political society.

From this right of self-preservation, the reason of man derives three important principles, as well as some lesser ones, and it is these which Hobbes terms 'Laws of Nature' (*leges naturales*). By these he means not moral laws, but 'precepts . . . found out by reason', by which a man is forbidden to do that 'which is destructive of his life, or taketh away the means of preserving the same, and to omit that, by which he thinketh that it may be best preserved.'

The first of these is that man should seek for peace, and to escape from the state of nature and perpetual war. The second is, that in order to attain peace he should be willing to surrender the equal right to possess all things, which men had in the state of nature, provided that all men were willing to do the same. The third is that men should keep their promises to do this, and this he calls a contract. In this third law of nature lies the fountain and original of 'justice'.[2]

This has a very moral sound, but Hobbes continues in the same chapter:

'But because covenants of mutual trust, when there is a fear of not performance on either part... are invalid; though the original of justice be the making of covenants, yet injustice actually there can be none, till the cause of such fear be taken away; which while men are in the natural condition of war, cannot be done. Therefore, before the names of just and unjust can have place, there must be some coercive power, to compel men equally to the performance of their covenants, by the terror of some punishment, greater than the benefits they expect by the breach of their covenant. . . . So that the nature of justice consisteth in keeping valid covenants: but the validity of covenants begins not but with the constitution of a civil power, sufficient to compel men to keep them; and then it is also that propriety begins.'[3]

[1] Hobbes, *Leviathan*, xiv.   [2] Ibid. xiv and xv.   [3] Ibid. xvi.

It was therefore necessary to create some coercive authority which should enforce the three laws of nature which have just been mentioned, and especially that law of nature which bids men keep their contracts. How then was the coercive authority to be erected?

'The only way', says Hobbes, 'to erect such a common power . . . is, to confer all their power and strength upon one man or one assembly of men, that may reduce all their wills, by plurality of voices into one will: which is as much as to say to appoint one man or one assembly of men to bear their person; and everyone to own, and acknowledge himself to be author of whatsoever he that so beareth their person, shall act or cause to be acted in those things which concern the common peace and safety; and therein to submit their wills, everyone to his will, and their judgment to his judgment. . . . This done the multitude so united in one person is called a commonwealth, in Latin "civitas". This is the generation of that great "leviathan", or rather, to speak more reverently, of that "mortal God", to which we owe, under the "immortal God", our peace and defence. . . . And he that carrieth this power is called "sovereign", and said to have "sovereign power", and every one besides, his "subject".'[1]

This is the conception of a 'Social Contract' among men to form an authoritative government; this also was not a new conception. It is practically the same as that of Hooker, 'To take away all such mutual grievances, injuries, and wrongs there was no way but only by growing unto composition and agreement amongst themselves, by ordaining some kind of government public, and by yielding themselves subject therunto; that unto whom they granted authority to rule and govern, by them the peace, tranquillity and happy estate of the rest might be procured.'[2] The same conception is clearly asserted by Althusius in his *Politica Methodice Digesta*,[3] and in an undeveloped form it may be traced much further back. The conception that political society was created by an agreement among those who founded it was not new. The novelty of Hobbes's conception of the State lay in his contention that the State thus formed possessed an absolute and arbitrary authority. Hobbes developed this conception in detail in the eighteenth chapter of the *Levia-*

---

[1] Ibid. xvii.   [2] Hooker, *Ecclesiastical Polity*, i. 10. 4.
[3] Althusius, *Politica Methodice Digesta*.

than. The most important part of his argument is that in which he maintains that there neither is nor can be any covenant or contract between the sovereign and the newly-created commonwealth. This is a direct contradiction of the traditional medieval conception that the ruler was subject to the law, and that he held his authority in virtue of and subject to the condition that he should obey the law. Hobbes's attempt to prove his view is not very happy; he argues that

'Because the right of bearing the person of them all is given to him they made sovereign by covenant only of one to another, and not of him to any of them; there can happen no breach of covenant on the part of the Sovereign, and consequently, none of his subjects, by any pretence of forfeiture, can be freed from his subjection. That he which is made sovereign maketh no covenant with his subjects beforehand is manifest; because either he must make it with the whole multitude as one party to the covenant, or he must make a several covenant with every man. With the whole as one party, it is impossible; because as yet they are not one person; and if he makes so many several covenants, as there be men, these covenants after he hath the sovereignty are void; because what act soever can be pretended by any one of them for breach thereof, is the act both of himself and of all the rest, because done in the person and by the right of every one of them in particular.'[1]

Hobbes's argument is merely verbal, and has no substance.

The rest of the chapter consists in the main of statements or rather examples of the powers which are included in the sovereign authority. The sovereign is absolute judge of what opinions and doctrines he will allow. It is the sovereign who makes the laws of property, the sovereign has the right of choosing his counsellors and magistrates, the right also of rewarding or punishing according to the law he has made, or if there be no law, according to his discretion. It is only in the last paragraph of this chapter that we come to a real, and not merely verbal argument for the absolute power of the sovereign.

'But a man may here object, that the condition of subjects is very miserable; as being obnoxious to the lusts and other irregular passions of him or them which have so unlimited a power in their hands . . . not

[1] Hobbes, *Leviathan*, xviii.

considering that the state of man can never be without some incom-
modity or other; and that the greatest, that in any form of government
can possibly happen to the people in general, is scarce sensible, in
respect of the miseries and horrible calamities, that accompany a civil
war, or that dissolute condition of masterless men, without subjection
to laws, and a coercive power to tie their hands from rapine and
revenge.'[1]

Here at last is an argument very natural, especially to
timid and short-sighted men; for Europe had in recent years
seen one dreadful civil war in France, and was only emerging
slowly from a more dreadful civil war in Germany. We must
not therefore be surprised that Hobbes should have fallen
into a somewhat gloomy view of all revolts against an established government, as merely leading to the horrors of
anarchy.

But even this argument is merely sophistical, for there is
no reason in the nature of things why men, when they put an
end to one form of government, should not replace it by
another, as was done in England in 1688. There was some
excuse for Hobbes, but an excuse is not a justification. The
fear of anarchy is natural and intelligible, but does not
provide a justification for panic and ingenious sophistries.

Fortunately Hobbes's defence of absolutism was in no
sense characteristic of the political thought of the seventeenth
century; it was as repulsive to such men as formed the
Restoration Parliament in England as to those who sat in
the Long Parliament.

We have in this chapter endeavoured to set out some
examples of the conception of absolutism, and especially of
the absolute monarchy, as it took shape in the political theory
of the sixteenth and seventeenth centuries. We are not here
concerned directly with the development of this in fact, for
this is not a Constitutional History. We have indicated
some of the antecedents of this development, but only as
the background to the theory, the actual development was
very complex, and indeed, varied in different countries. We
have also seen in a previous chapter, that the conception of
absolute monarchy had no relation to the proper character

[1] Ibid.

of medieval thought but was a revolutionary innovation. As we shall see presently this was very clearly recognized and asserted by the defenders of liberty in the seventeenth and eighteenth centuries. The absolute monarchy was to them a new and monstrous thing. And it is very noteworthy that even Bodin recognized very clearly, as we have pointed out, that except in France the absolute monarchy did not exist in the sixteenth century.

THE POLITICAL THEORY OF HOOKER AND ALTHUSIUS

THERE are two great political thinkers of the last years of the sixteenth century, and the first years of the seventeenth, in whom we can find the proper tradition of the Middle Ages, and also its relation to the modern forms of the conception of political liberty; these are Richard Hooker in England and Johannes Althusius in Germany. I do not mean that these were isolated in their time, on the contrary they represent the normal principles of the sixteenth century; they were not isolated or eccentric, but they summed up these principles in larger and more profound terms than any others. They also expressed their judgement in calm and measured terms, rather than in the accents of violent controversy; and they both speak not merely in the terms of abstract political thought, but with a continual reference to the actual traditions and institutions of their countries, England, or the German Empire, as they understood them.

The origins of political society Hooker found partly in the terms of Aristotle, when he says that men were driven to political society, in order to find 'a life fit for the dignity of man . . . to supply the defects and imperfections which are in us, living singly and solely by ourselves'; and partly under those of Seneca and the Christian Fathers, that men had lost their original innocence, and that their vices and follies needed to be restrained by some coercive authority; a conception narrower than that of Aristotle, but not contradictory to it.[1] Althusius set out the same Aristotelian conception, that the solitary man is not capable of a self-sufficing life.[2]

Man is then driven to form a political society, and Hooker and Althusius are again agreed as to the method and authority by which this was created. It was, in the words of Hooker, created by a 'composition or agreement among themselves, by ordaining some kind of Government public,

---

[1] Hooker, *The Laws of Ecclesiastical Polity*, i. 10. 1, 3.
[2] Althusius, *Politica Methodice Digesta*, i. 3, 4, 7, 19, 30.

and by yielding themselves subject thereunto'.[1] This is the theory of the 'social contract' as the foundation of an ordered and authoritative political society; and this is again set out by Althusius in more complete terms.[2]

This unhistorical conception of the origin of political society must not be confused with the historical and immensely important conception of a contract or agreement between the community and the ruler which was one of the most important and practical elements in the political theory of the Middle Ages.

To Hooker and Althusius, however, the theory was little more than the form of their judgement that a political society was founded upon the consent of its members. As Hooker says:

> To fathers within their private families nature had given a supreme power . . . howbeit over a whole grand multitude having no such dependence upon anyone . . . impossible it is that any should have complete lawful power, but by consent of men, or immediate appointment of God; because not having the natural superiority of fathers, their power must needs be either usurped, and thus unlawful; or, if lawful, then either granted or consented unto by those over whom they exercise the same, or else given extraordinarily from God, unto whom all the world is subject.'[3]

It is important to notice that Hooker was here setting aside a notion which Aristotle could think of as theoretically though not practically reasonable, that some men in virtue of their intrinsic superiority might justifiably and reasonably claim and exercise authority over others. Aristotle's conception is intelligible in view of the great importance he attached to the natural inequality of human nature, and the consequent exclusion of the slave and the 'mechanical' person from any share in political authority; while it had become unintelligible to those who accepted the Stoic and Legal and Patristic principles of the equality of men as being all possessed of reason. This has not prevented its lingering on among unintelligent persons.

---

[1] Hooker, *Eccl. Pol.* i. 10. 4.
[2] Althusius, *Politica*.
[3] Hooker, *Eccl. Pol.* i. 10. 4.

Hooker temperately but firmly repudiates this theory of government.

'Without which consent there were no reason that one man should take upon him to be lord or judge over another, because, although there be according to the opinion of some very great and judicious men, a kind of natural right in the noble, wise and virtuous, to govern them which are of servile disposition; nevertheless, for manifestation of this their right, and men's more peaceable contentment on both sides, the assent of those who are governed seemeth necessary.'[1]

To Hooker and Althusius then it is the community itself which is the source of authority in a political society. This coercive authority, Hooker thinks, was at first entrusted to one man, but they soon began to feel 'that to live by one man's will, becomes the cause of all men's misery. This constrained them to come unto laws, wherein all men might see their duties beforehand, and know the penalties of transgressing them.'[2]

We come thus to that fundamental principle of medieval civilization, that the supreme authority in political society was not that of the ruler, but that of the law; that all are subject to it, the king or prince as much as the private man. 'Rex non debet esse sub homine, sed sub deo et sub lege', and 'Attribuat igitur rex legi, quod lex attribuit ei, potestatem et dominium' (The king should not be under any man, but under God and the law, for the law makes the king. The king should recognize in the law, what the law recognizes in him, that is power and lordship.)[3] Again in another place Hooker makes it plain that in England the king was indeed under the law, and his authority was limited by the law.

'In which respect I cannot but commend highly their wisdom by whom the foundations of this Commonwealth, have been laid; wherein though no manner person or cause can be unsubject to the King's power, yet so is the power of the King over all and in all limited, that unto all his proceedings the Law itself is a rule. The axioms of our royal government are these. "Lex facit regem", the King's grant of any favour made contrary to the Law is void: "Rex nihil potest, nisi quod iure potest." '[4]

---

[1] Ibid. i. 10. 4.   [2] Ibid. i. 10. 5.
[3] Ibid. viii. 2. 3.   [4] Ibid. viii. 2. 13.

Althusius in different terms set out very emphatically the same principle. The administration and government of the commonwealth, he said, is nothing else than the execution of the law, and he cites Aristotle as saying that there is no commonwealth when the laws are not supreme, the supremacy of the law is the supremacy of God, while the supremacy of a man is that of a beast, the law should rule, not only over other citizens, but even over kings.[1]

If then we ask whence does the law (that is the positive law) derive its authority, the answer of Hooker and Althusius is plain, the law is made by the community. Hooker makes indeed an important distinction between those men by whom the law should be 'devised', and the authority which gives them their coercive power.

'Most requisite therefore it is that to devise laws which all men shall be forced to obey none but wise men be admitted. . . . Howbeit laws do not take their constraining force from the quality of such as devise them, but from that power which doth give them the strength of laws . . . by the natural law, whereunto he (God) hath made all subject, the lawful power of making laws to command whole politic societies of men belongeth so properly unto the same entire societies, that for any prince or potentate of what kind soever upon earth to exercise the same of himself, and not either by express commission immediately and personally received from God, or else by authority derived at the first from their consent upon whose persons they impose laws, it is no better than mere tyranny. Laws they are not therefore which public approbation hath not made so.'[2]

This principle is embodied by Althusius in his dogmatic judgement that the *Maiestas*, that supreme or sovereign power which recognizes no superior or equal, resides in the community.[3] It was the general councils which represented this in the German Empire and they had power to deal with the fundamental laws of the commonwealth, and other matters which require the calm deliberation and consent of the whole commonwealth.'[4]

The first and fundamental principle of a civilized political order was in the judgement of Hooker and Althusius, the

[1] Althusius, *Politica*, xxi. 16, 17.
[2] Hooker, *Eccl. Pol.* i. 10. 7, 8.
[3] Althusius, *Politica*, ix. 15, 19, 20, 22.
[4] Ibid. xvii. 56, 57.

supremacy of the law, the law which was derived from the community. Hardly less important, however, was the principle of a Contract between the community and the ruler. No doubt this conception has in its formal terms ceased to correspond with the complexity of modern political institutions, but actually it lies behind the structure of all civilized governments. We have no doubt ceased to think, in the terms of the Declaration of the English Convention of 1688, 1689, of an 'Original Contract' between king and people, nor do we conceive of this as men did in the Middle Ages as embodied in the mutual oaths of the Coronation ceremony. We have substituted for this the principle that the political authority is responsible to the community, and that if its action fails to correspond with the will of the community, it must be replaced by another. The form of the conception is different, the substance is the same. In the politically civilized countries we have substituted a change of ministers for a revolution.

Althusius describes the Contract as being embodied in the oaths by which the people and the supreme magistrate bound themselves to certain laws and conditions which determined the nature of their subjection and of his authority;[1] and he says dogmatically that no kingdom or commonwealth was ever created without a mutual contract between the subjects and their future prince, which was equally binding upon both.[2] In another place he maintains that a contract of this kind was a part of the constitution of almost all the kingdoms of his time, whether hereditary or elective; it was to be found in England, in France, Spain, Sweden, and the German Empire, and he relates it to the form of oath taken by the prince at his accession.[3]

Hooker, while maintaining this principle of a 'compact' between king and people, gave it a more significant form, when he said:

'Touching Kings which were first instituted by agreement and composition made with those over whom they reign, how far this power may lawfully extend, the articles of compact between them

---

[1] Althusius, *Politica*, xix. 6.

[2] Ibid. xix. 15.

[3] Ibid. xix. 38, 42.

must show, not the articles only of compact at the first beginning, which for the most part are either clean worn out of knowledge, or else known unto very few, but whatsoever hath been in free and voluntary manner condescended unto, whether by express consent, whereof positive laws are witnesses or else by silent allowance famously notified through custom reaching beyond the memory of man.'[1]

Hooker clearly conceives of the contract, not so much as an original agreement between king and people, as under the terms of the authority of the law, which binds king and people in one commonwealth.

Hooker and Althusius also set out in large and dogmatic terms their judgement that this authority of the commonwealth was embodied in that representative system which had taken form in central and western Europe in the centuries from the twelfth to the sixteenth.

'The Parliament of England', says Hooker, 'together with the Convocation annexed thereunto, is that whereupon the very essence of all government within this kingdom doth depend; it is even the body of the whole realm; it consisteth of the King and of all that within the realm are subject to him, for they are all there present, either in person, or by such as they voluntarily have devised their very personal right unto.'[2]

Althusius not only gives an account of the 'Oecumenical Councils' (i.e. the Diets of the German Empire) and of their function, which was to deliberate and determine upon all the most important affairs of the State, such as the fundamental laws, taxation, &c., but he also sets out some of the most important principles on which this representative system was founded. 'What concerns all', he says, 'should be determined by all, for the many are wiser than the few, and it is by such a form of government that the liberty of the people is protected, for they compel the officers of the government to render an account of their administration, and to recognize that the people is their Lord.[3] And Althusius is also clear that these representative institutions were to be found in almost all the countries of western and central Europe.[4]

---

[1] Hooker, *Eccl. Pol.* viii. 2. 11.
[2] Ibid. viii. 6. 11.
[3] Althusius, *Politica*, xvii. 56, 60.
[4] Ibid. xxxiii.

We have endeavoured to set out some of the most important political principles of these two great political thinkers, as summing up a great deal at least of the development of political civilization during the Middle Ages; and we have done this in order that we may better understand the continuity of these conceptions, as we shall see them in the literature of the seventeenth and eighteenth centuries.

III

THE CONTINUITY OF THE CONCEPTION OF POLITICAL LIBERTY IN THE SEVENTEENTH CENTURY

FRANCE

WE may begin by taking note of the fact that the memory of the older constitutional traditions survived in some important French jurists of the seventeenth century; in some of them, at least, the remembrance of the great French writers on constitutional law and practice like Commines and De Seyssel was still alive. The claims of the Parliament of Paris during the Fronde were indeed exaggerated and impossible, but that does not mean that they had no significance.[1]

We find a good example of these constitutional traditions in a jurist Guy Coquille, whose early work takes us back to the atmosphere of the States General of Blois in 1588. It was on this occasion that he wrote the work entitled *Discours des Estats de France*. He begins indeed by asserting that the government of France was a true monarchy, which did not partake of the nature of an aristocracy or a democracy; but he goes on to say that in certain cases the princes and peers and the Estates have great importance in giving counsel to the king, and he cites the tradition that it was the States General which gave judgement on the competing claims of

---

[1] I must express my great obligation for much in this chapter to the excellent work of M. Henri Sée, *Les Idées Politiques en France au xviime siècle*. He has in this work given an account of the most important political writers in France in that century, and brief but illuminating critical expositions of the opinions expressed in their works. Without this I should have had great difficulty in finding my way to this literature, and especially to the jurists. This is also true though perhaps in a lesser degree, of his earlier work, *Les Idées Politiques en France au xviiime siècle*. I must explain that in this work I make no pretence to deal exhaustively with the whole political literature of Europe in the seventeenth and eighteenth centuries; I have only attempted to set out some illustrations of what seem to me the most important elements in that literature.

Philip of Valois and Edward III of England to the French crown.[1]

He also says dogmatically that it was the Estates of France who declared Charles of Austrasia, the brother of the last king of the line of Charlemagne, unworthy of the crown, and elected Hugh Capet.[2] He adds that during the reign of Hugh Capet and his successors the honourable and ancient liberty of the people, that the king should not impose aids, talliages, or subsidies without their consent, was maintained, and that it was for this purpose, among others, that the kings were wont to call together the Estates.[3] He refers to the institution of the 'Gendarmerie' by Charles VII (1439), as being the first occasion of the ordinary (continuous) levy of the *tailles* without this. He adds that the ancient manner of granting the *tailles* was retained by the Provinces *ayont droit d'Estat*, and mentions Burgundy as an example of this.[4]

It was not, however, he says, only for the purpose of taxation that the Provincial Estates met, but for the establishment of the customs of the several provinces. (Coquille deals with the legislative powers of the States General in a later work, with which we shall deal farther on.) This reference to the Provincial Estates and the customary law is of great importance as bringing out an important aspect of Coquille's conception of the nature of law. It has been pointed out in an earlier chapter that in the normal judgement of the Middle Ages law was primarily the custom of the community, and it is therefore important to notice what Coquille thinks of this. These customs, he says, form the true civil law of each Province, the first movement, the birth and life of the Civil Law was to be found in the will of the three Orders and Estates of each Province, expressed by a "tacite Commandement". This Law was not at first written, but the knowledge of it was handed down from generation to generation. It was only by an "Ordonnance" of Charles VII that these customs were put into writing, and this only after the Estates of each Province, assembled by the royal authority, had recognized which were their customs, and had

[1] Guy Coquille, *Discours des Estats de France*, *Oeuvres*, ed. Paris, 1665, vol. i, p. 323.   [2] Ibid., p. 324.
[3] Ibid., p. 325.   [4] Ibid., p. 326.

added to and corrected them. The Kings of the line of Hugh Capet had found it good that their people should make and establish the laws by which they should be governed, when the King had given the sanction to them.'[1]

It is clear that to Coquille the ancient constitution of France had been one in which the wellbeing of the people was protected by the restraints imposed upon the kings by the States General and the Provincial Estates. It was by Louis XI that the power of the king had been enlarged to the injury both of the seigneurs and the people, and the royal authority had become more absolute. Experience had shown that many serious evils had followed, the people had been miserably overpressed and ruined by excessive taxation, and by the monstrous increase in the number of the officials, and by the licence of the soldiers.[2]

Coquille was also much concerned with the interference of the 'Privy Council' in the administration of justice. In a work on the *Ordonnances* issued by Henry III at the Estates of Blois, Coquille cites the terms of Art. 91 of the *Ordonnances*, in which the king ordered that for the future the Council was not to interfere with cases which belonged to the 'Ordinary Judges', and Coquille in his *Annotations* says that the Deputies of Paris had complained that the 'Privy Council' had frequently called before it cases which belonged to the jurisdiction of the 'Parlement'. He argues in energetic terms, that the 'Privy Council' had been established to deal with 'General affairs' (public business), not with the cases of private people, and he adds, a little contemptuously, that it was composed of princes and other lords who were untrained in matters of law, custom, and judicial business.[3] This concern about the interference of the Royal Council with the regular courts of justice is parallel to the similar question in England, and was obviously of great importance with regard to the security of legal rights and the independence of the administration of law. We shall presently see that this matter was of importance in the disputes between

---

[1] Coquille, *Discours*, Ibid., p. 327.　　　　[2] Ibid., p. 326.
[3] Ibid. *Oeuvres*, ed. 1665, vol. i. 'Ordonnances du Roy Henri III, . . . avec les Annotations de Maitre Coquille,' p. 38 (included in vol. i, but paged separately).

the Parliament of Paris and the Government in the period
of the Fronde.

Such was the treatment of the French constitution by
Coquille in 1588, and it is important to observe that twenty
years later he restated the same principles in his treatise
Institution du Droit des Français. The king, he says, has
authority to make laws and ordinances; but he goes on to
qualify this general statement. In the first place they must
be 'registered' and 'verified' in the *Parlement*, or other
'Sovereign Court', otherwise the subjects are not bound by
them; and, when the 'Court' in publishing them adds that
this had been done by the express command of the king, it
means that this 'Court' had not considered the Edict reasonable (*raisonnable*). Further, Coquille adds, when the king
wished to make perpetual and important laws, the custom
was that he should call together the three Orders or Estates
of the People, that is the clergy, the nobility, and the
bourgeoisie, or Third Estate. When the States General meet
the king sets before them the causes for which they have
been summoned, and commands them to draw up their
'Cahiers'. When he has received these the king ordains
laws, which are entitled, 'Laws made by the King holding
his Estates', and these laws are stable and permanent, they
are irremovable, and can only be changed in a similarly summoned meeting of the Estates. Coquille adds indeed that
several kings had dispensed with this custom.[1]

It is clear that Coquille still thought of the legislative
authority of the king, in important matters, as being exercised properly only in the States General.

Coquille also says that another important right of the
king was that of imposing taxes of various kinds on his
subjects, but he adds that in former times (*d'ancienneté*)
these were not imposed without the consent of the people
assembled in the form of the States General, to whom the
king set out the needs of the kingdom. He adds that the
Burgundians had wisely retained this liberty, and that
the *tailles* were only paid when they had been granted by
the Estates of Burgundy, which met every three years. The
French people as a whole had submitted obediently to the

[1] Ibid., 'Institution du Droit des Français', *Oeuvres*, vol. ii, p. 2.

kings who had imposed and increased subsidies at their will, until the people were unable to pay them.[1]

The position of Coquille is clearly very important as illustrating the fact that the constitutional traditions of medieval France were still remembered in the early years of the seventeenth century.

We find another example of this in the treatises of another eminent jurist Charles Loyseau, whose writings date from about the same time as Coquille's later work.

In his *Traité des Seigneuries* produced in 1608, he repudiated emphatically the doctrine of some writers that the description of the royal tyranny in 1 Samuel viii, was a description of the rights of the king, while it was nothing more than a warning of the arbitrary conduct that might be expected of him.[2] He goes on to enumerate the rights of the sovereign, they are: (1) to make laws; (2) to appoint officials; (3) to make war and peace; (4) 'avoir le dernier ressort de la justice' (i.e. to be the final appeal in matters of justice); (5) to coin money; and (6) as some said, to levy taxes on the people.[3]

These powers seem very comprehensive and complete, but we must examine Loyseau's treatment of them somewhat further. And first as to the legislative authority of the king. He begins by saying that in pure monarchies, and especially in France, which was the most pure and perfect in the world, it is the king only who can make laws; but he goes on to admit that, in the *provinces coutumières*, the king of his goodness permits the people of the province to choose the customs according to which they are to live. It would seem that Loyseau was, like Coquille, aware that the laws of a great part of France had been customary and unwritten, representing rather the habits of life of the community than a conscious legislative process. He is indeed careful to add that these customs had to be *arrestées* (established) by the command of the king in the presence of his commissioners, and to be approved and verified by the *Parlement*.[4] This is

---

[1] Coquille, 'Institution . . .', *Oeuvres*, ed. 1665, vol. ii, p. 9.
[2] Charles Loyseau, *Des Seigneuries*, ed. 1608, chap. iii. 1, 2.
[3] Ibid., chap. iii. 4, 6.   [4] Ibid., chap. iii. 6.

not quite the same as Coquille's treatment of the nature of customary law, but Loyseau had evidently not completely forgotten the people as the source from which laws had arisen.

More important than this, however, is his discussion of the right to levy taxes. 'Les plus retenus Politiques', he says, had held that the king had not the right to levy taxes without the consent of the people. This, Loyseau says, was the contention of that wise statesman-politician Commines, at the States General of Tours (1484); and it is certain that in former times (*anciennement*) *tailles* and other subsidies were not, as they are at present, ordinary and perpetual, but were only levied with the consent of the people when they were necessary; the principal reason for the meetings of the Estates was indeed to obtain their consent to a new levy of taxes. This was still, he says, the rule in England and Poland where the king cannot levy money without this consent.[1]

Loyseau's position is certainly very interesting to us. He seems to hold that the king of France possessed an absolute power of imposing taxation, but he is well aware that this was a new thing, and that great political authorities like Commines had held the opposite. The older constitutional principle was not forgotten.

There is yet another point of great importance in Loyseau's treatment of constitutional principles. This is set out in the work entitled *Du Droit des Offices*, published in 1610. It is the principle that even the king cannot be judge in his own case, but submits himself to receive justice from his subjects and officers, who are in this respect the deputies of God.[2] In the same work Loyseau seems clearly to maintain that the royal judges were irremovable except for misconduct, and refers to Bodin, *De Republica*, iv. 4, and to an *Ordonnance* of Louis XI.[2] It is of great importance to observe that these judgements represent the normal principles of feudal law, of Gerson and De Seyssel, that the king was under the law.

It would seem correct to say that while Loyseau goes

[1] Ibid., chap. iii. 42–7.
[2] Ibid. 'Du Droit des Offices', v, chap. iii, 52–72.

further than Coquille in the assertion of the royal authority, he was well aware that in some important respects this development was a modern innovation.

I have spoken of the Fronde as being the most absurd of all attempts at Revolution, but this applies primarily to the French princes and nobles; the conceptions of the jurists were no doubt in many respects impossible, and show a singular lack of political sense, but they represent at any rate some survival of the political principles of medieval France. The Parliament of Paris at any rate recognized that in a civilized government it was necessary that there should be some power in the country which could restrain the caprices, or the incompetence, of the Crown or its Ministers; and as the States General had not met since 1614 it conceived of itself as being the one body in the country which could do this.

It is not possible here to attempt to deal with the development of the system under which the royal Edicts were laid before the *Parlement* for 'registration' and 'verification' before being put into execution. It was recognized that this was a necessary part of the process of legislation, but it was maintained on the part of the Crown that, if the *Parlement* refused to verify and to register, its opposition could be overpowered in a meeting of the *Parlement* presided over by the king in person, to which the name of a *lit de justice* was given.

We can find a good illustration of the attitude of the *Parlement* in a speech made by Omer Talon, the *Avocat du Roi*, at a *lit de justice* held by the young King Louis XIV, while still a minor, on 15 January 1648. The *lits de justice* were not, Talon said, formerly regarded as expressing the sovereign power of the king, but rather as assemblies for deliberation or counsel; the presence of the king did not close the mouths of the members of the *Parlement*, for the king (and he refers to Francis I) knew that 'verification' implied *la liberté des suffrages*; and that the royal Edicts could not be put into execution until they had been deliberated on by the *Compagnies Souveraines* (i.e. the courts which formed the whole body of the *Parlement*). And, he continues, the authority of the king was indeed from God, and he gives

no account of his actions except to God and his own conscience, but it is the glory of the king that his subjects should
be free men and not slaves.[1]

The words may be rhetorical, but the temper behind them
is plain enough, and the constitutional claims of the *Parlement* found a very important expression in some of the
clauses of a Declaration issued by a meeting of all the *Cours
Souveraines* which took place on 30 June and the following
days of 1648.

The Third Clause laid down dogmatically that no 'im-
positions' or taxes should be levied except under Edicts
vérifiés by the *Cours Souveraines*. This was an attempt to
assert a constitutional control over the finances of the government, which had once belonged to the Provincial Estates and
the States General, and it is intelligible, in view of the fact
that the States General had not met since 1614.

The provisions of the Sixth Clause were equally important
and were more in accord with the traditional relations of the
courts of law to the monarchy. In this clause it was laid
down that no subject of the king of France, of whatever
condition or quality, should be detained in prison for more
than twenty-four hours without being interrogated and
brought before his *juge naturel*.[2] The importance of this
clause requires no explanation to those who remember the
famous Clause 39 of Magna Carta and the continually
repeated demands of the Cortes of Castile in the fourteenth
and fifteenth centuries.[3] The government accepted the first of
these without qualification, and the second in a slightly
modified form.[4]

It must also be noticed that the tradition of the representation of the nation in the States General had not been wholly
forgotten even by the Crown. In January 1649 a summons
was issued in the name of the king calling a meeting of the
States General for 15 March 1649. The king spoke of the

[1] Omer Talon, *Mémoires*, ed. 1732, vol. iv, p. 183.
[2] *Recueil des Anciennes Lois Françaises*, ed. Jourdain, &c., vol. xvii, no. 99,
Clauses 3 and 6.
[3] Cf. our *History of Mediaeval Political Theory*, vol. vi, part i, chap. 4; part
ii, chap. i; part v, chap. i, &c.
[4] *Recueil des Anciennes Lois Françaises*, vol. xvii, no. 109.

wars with Spain and the Empire, the troubles in Paris and some of the Provinces, and declared that the best remedy would be found in a meeting of the States General of the three orders of the kingdom. He therefore gave instructions for the meetings of the electors in each district, who were to deliberate on the reforms which they might desire, and to elect a representative of each order, with ample instructions and powers.[1] This meeting of the Estates was postponed from time to time and never actually took place; but the preparations for it went so far that we have the *Procès verbal* of the election of representatives for the Prévôté of Paris, which took place on 4 September 1651.[2]

There is one French jurist of the time whose work deserves a more detailed examination. This is Claude Joly, who in 1653 brought out a work entitled *Recueil des Maximes véritables et importantes pour l'institution du Roy, Contre la fausse et pernicieuse politique du Cardinal Mazarin, prétendu surintendant de l'éducation de Sa Majesté.* This is a work of real importance in its general political judgements, but perhaps even more as representing the continuing influence of the medieval principles of political liberty; as we shall see, it is in large measure founded upon Joly's acquaintance with the works of Commines and De Seyssel.

The general thesis of Joly may, I think, be best stated in his own words. His conclusion is that 'the power of the King is not absolute, without bounds or limits', and it is noticeable that he goes on to point out that when St. Paul enjoined on Christian men to obey the king, he did this because kings are set by God for the punishment of evil doers and the protection of the good. These are the principal elements of justice, and kings should understand that they must not use their power at their arbitrary discretion against the innocent or the guilty; that is, Joly gives to St. Paul's words their rational interpretation. He follows this up by pointing out that the description by Samuel of the tyranny of the king was not intended to sanction it, but only to show the probable consequences of their demand for a

[1] *Recueil des Anciennes Lois,* vol. xvii, no. 137.
[2] Ibid., vol. xvii, no. 219.

king; and he contrasts the tyrannical king with the good one as described in Deuteronomy xvii, and cites the story of Ahab and Naboth as showing that the kings of Israel were compelled to act at least with a pretence of law.[1]

The first and fundamental principle, then, which is set out by Joly is that the authority of the king is not absolute, but limited, its function is to maintain justice, and therefore law. For, as he says, that which is not conformable to the approved and received laws cannot be just.[2] Here is a good example of the tenacity with which he holds to the political tradition of the Middle Ages, and he justifies this by a variety of arguments drawn from the Middle Ages, and the Roman law. He cites the Golden Bull of the Emperor Charles IV as laying down that the claims of the emperor himself must be decided by the Diets of the Empire, and points out that in France cases between the king and private persons were decided by the *Parlemens*. Plato had said that it was mere tyranny that the prince should not be subject to the law; and Joly cites the well-known doctrine of Theodosius and Valentinian that rescripts which were contrary to the law (*jus*) had no authority.[3] He compares this with what he calls *nos Ordonnances* which forbade the judges to pay any attention to *Lettres de Cachet*, and to (Royal) *Lettres*, which are contrary to the established laws.[4] It is perhaps especially interesting to notice that while he refers to the words 'Licet legibus soluti sumus, attamen legibus vivimus', he only does this to compare them contemptuously with the words of *Cod.* i. 14. 21, which say that it is worthy of the majesty of the ruler that the prince should acknowledge that he is bound by the laws.[5]

It is also very important to notice the important references of Joly to the constitutional tradition of France, as represented in the sixteenth century by De Seyssel and Du Haillan. He cites De Seyssel as having said that the royal authority was in France regulated and restrained principally by three things, religion, justice, and *la Police*, that is by

[1] Claude Joly, *Recueil des Maximes*, &c., ed. 1653, chap. ii, pp. 18, 19, 20, 26, 32.
[2] Ibid., chap. v, p. 149.   [3] *Cod.* i. 18. 7.
[4] Joly, chap. v, pp. 150–3.   [5] Ibid., p. 154.

the *Ordonnances* made by the kings and approved by the people. When the prince oversteps these limits and wishes to exercise an unrestrained will, he is held to be an evil and intolerable tyrant, and earns the hatred of God and his subjects. He also refers to the Coronation Oath which, as he understood De Seyssel, bound the kings of France to keep the laws.[1]

Joly also cites du Haillan, an important political writer of the late sixteenth century, who, as Joly thinks, may have been influenced by De Seyssel. He described the government of France as having three elements, the monarchy, the aristocracy, and the democracy or *Gouvernement Populaire*. The French monarchy had a great authority and liberty, but this liberty was regulated, limited, and bridled by good laws and ordinances. The monarch was not permitted to do anything, but only what was just and reasonable, and prescribed by the *Ordonnances*, and by the advice of his Council.

And thus, as the powers of the French kings were limited, they were much more loved, honoured, and feared than the rulers whose authority was immoderate and unrestrained.[2]

Joly was also acquainted with Machiavelli's praise of the French Constitution under which the king was bound by the laws,[3] and he cites the words of a French jurist, Pybrac, 'Je hay ces mots, De puissance absolue; De plein pouvoir; De propre mouvement'.[4] (Pybrac was only repeating the protests of the Cortes of Valladolid in 1442 and of Zasius of Freiburg in the early sixteenth century.)

The truth is that Joly was clear that the authority of kings was derived from the people, and that this was given them in order to secure the administration of justice; and he very wisely brings the authority of the Roman law to prove this. He cites the famous passage from the *Digest*, 'Quod Principi placuit legis habet vigorem, utpote quum lege Regia, quae de eius Imperio lata est, populus ei et in eum omne imperium suum et potestatem concessit',[5] and he

---

[1] Joly, *Recueil des Maximes*, &c., pp. 164–7.
[2] Ibid., p. 167.
[3] *Discorsi* on Livy i. 16.
[4] Joly, pp. 16–19, 170.   [5] *Dig.* i. 4. 1.

refers to the tablet in the Lateran, which Cardinal Zabarella had seen in the fifteenth century, which described the powers given by the Roman Senate and people to the Emperor Vespasian,[1] and contends that this implied that the legitimate authority of princes was derived from the people.[2]

The authority of the king was derived from the people, and was given to him on the condition that he should govern in accordance with the laws. No people had ever the intention to submit without reservation to the absolute discretion of a king, but only on the condition that he should govern subject to the provisions of the law; and Joly describes this as a *Contrat Synallagmatique*. It follows from this that the king is not master of the law, and cannot amend it at his pleasure, for by this contract the people submit to him only on the condition that he maintains the laws.[3]

The first and most essential principles of Joly's political work are thus to be found in his contentions that the authority of the State rests upon justice, justice which is embodied in the law; that the authority of the king is derived from the community, and is given to him for the purpose of the administration of the laws and is limited by the laws. These are the first and most essential principles of liberty, as understood in the Middle Ages.

This is not, however, the whole of Joly's contribution to the political thought of the seventeenth century in France. He seems clearly to have thought that an improvement of the political order in France could only be obtained if the king were to call for the co-operation and counsel of the whole community through its representative assemblies, and he does not think that this would be a revolutionary innovation, but only a return to the traditional method of the Middle Ages. In one place he says of the meeting of the States General of Orleans in 1560, that at that time men still had a good judgement of the power of the State and of the ancient liberty of France. He finds that the historian Davila, in his account of that assembly, said that men still thought that the consent of the people was necessary to validate the

[1] Cardinal Zabarella, *Comm. on Decretals*, i. vi. 34.
[2] Joly, *Recueil des Maximes*, &c., chap. v, pp. 131–3.
[3] Ibid., chap. v, pp. 157, 158.

wishes of the kings, and that the government could not be held legitimate, or properly royal, without the consultation of the nation by the prince.[1]

It is true that Joly, like some of the political writers of the sixteenth century, had a somewhat fantastic conception that the States General of the Middle Ages were continuous with the National Assemblies of the Gauls before the Roman Conquest, but this does not affect the importance of his discussion of their functions, and their importance as they actually developed. He was familiar with the descriptions of the character and importance of the States General by Commines and l'Hôpital, and he was also acquainted with the details of some of the meetings and proceedings of the States General at different times. He repeats the tradition that it was the Estates of 1328 who decided that the succession to the throne of France belonged to Philip of Valois, and not to Edward III of England. He mentions the declaration of the Estates of 1338 that without the authority of the Estates no *Taille* could be raised, and the important part taken by them in the appointment of the regency in 1380 and 1390.[2]

Joly thus looked upon the States General as representing an essential element in the traditional method of government in France, and he cites the contemptuous words of Commines in his *Mémoires* with regard to those ill-informed and unimportant persons who ventured to maintain that to demand the meeting of the Estates was to diminish the authority of the king; while they were really afraid that the Estates would expose their evil doings.[3]

It is indeed clear that Joly looks upon the authority of the Estates as having been formerly much greater than in later times. He does not enumerate what were in his judgement the precise constitutional powers of the States General; but that he thought of them in large terms is apparent from his references to the desirability of the king consulting the Estates of the kingdom before entering upon a war, and he refers to an interesting passage in Commines in which he

[1] Joly, *Recueil des Maximes*, &c., chap. viii, p. 342.
[2] Ibid., chap. viii, pp. 291, 318, 320.
[3] Ibid., chap. viii, p. 266. (Cf. Commines's *Mémoires*, v. 19.)

speaks with admiration of the king of England who would
not enter upon a war without consulting his Parliament—
Commines knew that the English Parliament was equivalent
to the States Generals in France.[1]

Joly very clearly and emphatically asserts the principle
that the king of France had no right to levy any *Taille*
without the consent of the States General. As we have
already said, he cites the declaration of the Estates of 1338,
made, as he says, in the presence of the king, that no *Taille*
could be imposed in France on the people without the consent of the Estates.[2] He also cites the declaration of the
States General of Tours of 1484, who in making a large
grant of money to the king intimated that they did not
contemplate that for the future any mo·ey should be levied
without their voice and consent.[3]

It is, however, again in Commines that he found the most
important statement of the principle that the prince's power
to lay taxes upon his people depends upon the Estates. Is
there any king on earth, Commines had said, who has the
right to lay *un denier* on his subjects without their authority
and consent, except by tyranny and violence. What makes
the opinion of Commines so remarkable is that he was
speaking of a time when the king (of France), Charles VII,
had, as he says, already begun to impose the *Tailles* without
the consent of the Estates, and laid a heavy burden on his
own soul and those of his ministers. These evils had become
so insupportable that Joly thinks that they should be dealt
with at that meeting of the States General which was evidently still expected when he wrote.[4]

When we look back over the political conceptions of Joly
we recognize that they represent a very emphatic defence
of a constitutional as opposed to an absolute monarchy, and
that this rested both on the assertion of general principles
of political authority, and upon a clear view of what he conceived to be the historical constitution of France.

The king is not absolute, for his function is to maintain

[1] Ibid., chap. viii, p. 266. (Cf. Commines's *Mémoires*, v. 18.)
[2] Ibid., viii, p. 318.
[3] Ibid., xi, p. 438.
[4] Ibid., viii, pp. 333, 334, 335.

justice, and this in practice means that he must govern according to the laws of his country. This, however, is not all, for he is equally clear in asserting the importance of the Estates as representing the historical liberties of the French people, and their traditional authority, not only in questions of taxation, but in other matters of national concern.

It might be thought that however interesting these survivals of the political civilization of the Middle Ages might be, survivals which represented some of the principles of political liberty, the absolutist administration of Louis XIV put an end to them in France. This was not, however, the case, for in the later years of the seventeenth century we find the tradition of liberty represented in France by at least two writers of great importance.

The first of these was an eminent French Protestant theologian, Jurieu, the second a great Catholic, Fénelon, the archbishop of Cambrai. It is indeed an interesting thing to see once again that as in the political controversies of the sixteenth century, the political opinions did not coincide with the theological. If Bossuet represented in an extreme form the doctrine of the absolute king in France, Jurieu the Protestant and Fénelon the Catholic maintained the principles of political liberty, just as in the sixteenth century the political opinions of John Knox and George Buchanan in Scotland were substantially the same as those of the Jesuit Mariana in Spain.

Jurieu had been a professor in one of the Protestant Faculties of Theology in France, and when these were suppressed he took refuge in Holland, and became Professor of Theology in Rotterdam. From 1686 to 1689 he addressed a series of *Lettres Pastorales* to the Protestants in France. In the third series of these letters he had occasion to defend the Protestants against the charge of being the 'natural enemies of sovereigns', with special relation to the revolution of 1688 in England; he prefixed to this a discussion of the general question of the authority of princes.

He begins by affirming that men are naturally free and independent of each other. This was of course not a new doctrine, it was derived from the post-Aristotelian philosophers, the Roman jurists, and the Christian Fathers. From the philosophers and the Fathers Jurieu also derives the doctrine that it was sin which had made the subjection of men to each other necessary, and it was the same cause which had produced private property. Jurieu adds that while the lordship of men over men was not created by the divine or natural Law, it was in accordance with the divine intention and the order of Providence. There was, however, no positive divine law which established the authority of the master over his slave, or of the sovereign over his subject. Men of high intelligence and temper might conceivably live without masters or sovereigns, without offending against the natural or positive law of God. At the same time it was not probable that such a condition of life could have continued after the appearance of sin, for human passions would bring about disorder. Men are therefore free to set rulers over themselves or not; but if they do this, then they are bound by conscience and necessity to obey.[1]

Peoples who are free and have no master have therefore the right to set over themselves whatever form of government they prefer, monarchy, democracy, or aristocracy. Some monarchs are absolute, and the whole sovereign authority is placed in their hands, others share the legislative and executive authority with the people, but none of these forms of government are of divine right.[2] So much then for Jurieu's conception of the origin of political authority; it is practically a necessity imposed on human nature by men's vices and faults, but the form and character of this authority is a matter to be determined by the judgement of the community.

Jurieu then proceeds to discuss the legitimate limits of human authority. It is the people which has set up kings, and has given them their authority, and the cause is greater than the effect. Kings are indeed above the people in one sense, but in another the people are above the king. This, Jurieu remarks, is exactly the doctrine of the Gallican theologians with regard to the Pope, he is the head of the Church,

---

[1] Jurieu, *Lettres Pastorales, Troisième Année*, ed. Rotterdam, 1689, Lettre XVI, i. pp. 361–5.

[2] Ibid. ii. pp. 365–6.

F

and above the Church, and yet the whole Church is above him. It is the people who give the sovereignty, but it is certain that no one can give what he does not possess; the people indeed possess the sovereignty in a more eminent degree than the king, but they cannot give the king an authority which they do not themselves possess. They cannot give him authority over man's conscience, that belongs only to God; they cannot give him authority to destroy the people; they cannot authorize him to violate the fundamental laws of the State.[1] This conception of an 'eminent' sovereignty of the community is probably derived by Jurieu from the political writings of the Huguenots in France in the sixteenth century, but it is also to be found in the Spanish Jesuit, Mariana, and in Althusius; and it is at least implied by Hooker.[2]

This brings Jurieu to the assertion that there is a mutual contract between the people and the sovereign; it is unnatural to think that any people would give itself to any one man unconditionally; no people could be so blind as to do this, and Jurieu holds that, if they were to do it, their action would be null and void; for it would be contrary to the rights of nature. We are not absolute masters of ourselves or our wives and children; our own authority is limited, and we cannot give an unlimited authority to the sovereign. There is nothing surprising therefore in the fact that the recent Convention in England had declared that there was a mutual contract between the king and the nation. It is certain, Jurieu repeats, that there is a mutual contract between the sovereign and the subjects, and when one of the parties violates his obligation the other ceases to be bound.[3]

The authority of the sovereign comes then from the people, and the people give more or less authority. In some countries the monarchy is elective, in some hereditary. In some they grant the whole sovereignty to one man, in others they retain a part of it, and this is the case in most Christian States. In England, for example, they have retained in

[1] Jurieu, *Lettres*, iv, pp. 367–70.
[2] Cf. our *History of Mediaeval Political Theory*, vol. vi, part iv, chap. ii, (2).
[3] Jurieu, *Lettres*, v, pp. 370–2.

their own hands the legislative authority, and that of imposing taxation, while the king has the execution of the laws;
but even in regard to these the English Parliament has the
right, acting with the king, to take legal proceedings against
anyone. (Jurieu is no doubt referring to the parliamentary
right of impeachment.)[1]

Jurieu, however, admits that a people may confer an
absolute power on the king; though he doubts whether any
people has ever been so imprudent as to do this; but in theory
he admits the possibility. This brings him, however, to the
distinction between an 'absolute' power and a power without
limits. By 'absolute' power he means that the whole sovereignty is placed in one man, but there is no sovereignty
without limits. First, they can only give this authority to
secure the preservation of society. Second, men are not the
absolute masters of their lives, nor of their families, nor even
of their own liberty; men cannot give an authority which
they do not possess. God himself cannot govern unjustly.[2]
These are the general principles of Jurieu with regard to
the origin and nature of political authority. He adds in the
seventeenth 'Lettre' a contemptuous discussion of the arguments of those who maintained that the example of the early
Christians showed that it was contrary to the principles of
the Christian religion to resist oppression; and their attempts
to prove the necessity of non-resistance from the Scriptures.
The eighteenth 'Lettre' is occupied with a discussion of the
circumstances, and a defence, of the English Revolution of
1688.

It is evident that Jurieu's treatment of political principles
and his defence of political liberty are very different from
those of most of the jurists whom we have so far discussed in
this chapter, and also, as we shall presently see, from those of
Fénelon and Boulainvilliers. The latter are in the main occupied with the historical and constitutional position of the
French Crown, while Jurieu deals primarily with the general
conceptions of the origin and nature of government. If he
had written a little later we should have been inclined to
think that he had been influenced by Locke, and indeed the

[1] Ibid. vi, p. 373.
[2] Ibid. vii and viii, pp. 373-9.

stress he lays upon the argument that a political society neither possesses nor can give more authority than the individual members of it, is very like the important argument of Locke against any absolute power in the State.

For the rest, however, the sources of his contentions are obvious. The principles of the natural equality and independence of the individual man, of the sins and vices of human nature as the main causes which compelled men to set up a common political authority, are obviously derived from the theories of the Stoics, the Christian Fathers, and the medieval political thinkers, while the conception of the contract between king and people was founded upon the character of medieval society; and the doctrine of the ultimate sovereignty of the people had been drawn out with great force by some of the most important political writers of the sixteenth century.

The other most important Frenchman who represented the tradition of political liberty at the end of the seventeenth century was Fénelon, the Archbishop of Cambrai. It is indeed with a great sense of relief that we turn from the foolishness of many ecclesiastical writers of the seventeenth century to the manly common sense of Fénelon. Some of us may have been, like myself, brought up as children upon *Télémaque*, but probably, like myself, they did not understand how much of a penetrating criticism of the policy and administration of Louis XIV is contained in that work.

It was in 1689 that Fénelon was appointed to be the 'Preceptor' of the young Duke of Burgundy, the grandson of Louis XIV, who was the heir presumptive of the French Crown, after his father the Dauphin. *Télémaque* was published in 1699, and it is significant of Fénelon's political instinct that he had seized the opportunity to train his pupil for the great responsibilities which lay before him. Bossuet had occupied the same office with the Dauphin, having been appointed his Preceptor in 1670, and it is indeed interesting to compare the temper in which the two men approached the task of training those who were expected to be the future rulers of France. Bossuet dwells primarily on the absolute authority of the king; Fénelon insists primarily upon his obligations.

We cannot here discuss Fénelon's implicit, but drastic, criticism of Louis XIV's foreign policy, and of his government of France, which is contained in the *Télémaque*, but we should notice some very significant observations on the relation of the king to the law, and on the disastrous future which attends an absolute and oppressive government of the people.

When *Télémaque* asks what it is in which the authority of the king consists, Mentor replies: 'He has all power over the people but the laws have all power over him. He has an absolute power to do good, but his hands are tied when he wishes to do evil.'[1]

In another place Télémaque complains, with a rather childish petulance, that the position of a king is an unhappy pretence, the authority which he seems to have is not really authority at all, for it is nothing but that of the laws. He is little more than a slave who sacrifices his rest and his liberty for the liberty and happiness of the community. Mentor replies with an ironic gravity, which may well have been disconcerting to some of his readers: 'Do you think, my dear Télémaque, that it is an unhappy thing to have to do good to so many people? Is it not enough glory to compel obedience to the laws? To put oneself above the laws is a false glory which inspires nothing but hatred and contempt.'[2]

Such words may seem to the careless and ignorant reader merely commonplaces, but they are not so, they are the echoes of the greatest political tradition of the Middle Ages, the supremacy of the law.

In another passage Mentor warns Idomeneus against the arbitrary and oppressive government of the people. What a detestable judgement, he says, it is which thinks to find safety only in the oppression of the people, to leave them in ignorance, to drive them by terror into desperation, to face them with the frightful alternative between bondage and revolt against your yoke? Is this the way to a peaceful reign, is this the path of glory? You should remember that those

[1] Fénelon, *Les Aventures de Télémaque* (ed. 1773), ii. 74.
[2] Ibid. x. 416.

countries in which the sovereign is most absolute are those
where the sovereign has least real power. Kings may take
everything, but the fields are deserted. A king can only be
great in and through his people, he destroys himself in
destroying his people. Men may flatter him, may pretend to
admire him, but the smallest revolution will overthrow this
monstrous authority, it has no foundation in the hearts of
the people; at the first blow the idol is overthrown, all men's
passions are united against so odious an authority, and the
king who in his prosperity did not find a single man brave
enough to tell him the truth, will not in his misfortune find
a single man to defend him.[1] Mentor repeats his warning,
in a later part of the work, to Télémaque himself.

Remember, Télémaque, says Mentor, that there are two evils
in the government of the people for which there is hardly ever any
remedy. The first is an unjust and too violent authority in the King,
the second is a luxury which corrupts men's moral character. When
Kings recognize no laws but their absolute will, when they put no
restraint on their passions, they seem all powerful, but they undermine
the foundations of their authority. Everyone flatters them, but they
have no longer a People, they have only slaves. Who will tell them
the truth? Men yield to them, but the wise men fly and hide themselves. It is only a sudden and violent revolution which can turn this
exaggerated power into its natural course. Often indeed the force
which might moderate it, overthrows it beyond recovery. There is
nothing which threatens a fatal catastrophe so much as an authority
which is pressed too far, it is like a bow which is overstretched and
suddenly breaks if the strain is not relaxed; but who will dare to relax it![2]

Fénelon had been made Archbishop of Cambrai in 1697,
but he continued to be concerned for the political education
of the young Duke of Burgundy, and produced a remarkable
political work entitled *Examen de Conscience sur les Devoirs
de la Royauté*. The King, Fénelon says, is the highest judge
in the State; it is he who makes the laws, and judges in his
Council according to the laws which he has made or which
were made before him. To judge rightly is to judge according to the laws, and in order to judge according to the laws, one
must know them.[3] Fénelon therefore asks: Have you studied

[1] Fénelon, *Télém.* vi. 222.   [2] Ibid. x. 382.
[3] Fénelon, *Examen de Conscience sur les Devoirs de la Royauté, Œuvres* (ed.
1878, vol. iii), Art. II. 7.

the fundamental laws and the abiding customs which have the force of law for the general government of your nation? Have you endeavoured to know what are the limits of your authority? Do you know what were the forms of government under the various races (dynasties)? Do you know what were the ancient *Parlemens*, and the States General which succeeded them? What was the nature of feudal subjection? Do you know how it is that the present conditions have arisen, and on what this change was founded; do you know what is the meaning of Anarchy, what is Arbitrary Power, and what is a Monarchy controlled by the laws, which is a mean between these two extremes?[1]

In a later passage Fénelon expresses his own judgement directly. You know, he says, that formerly the king could take nothing from his people by his sole authority, it was the *Parlement*, that is the assembly of the nation, which granted him the money required for the extraordinary needs of the State; apart from these he lived on the resources of his own domain: what has changed this system except the absolute authority which the kings have taken to themselves? We have even in our day seen the *Parlemens*, bodies infinitely inferior to the ancient *Parlemens*, or Estates of the nation, remonstrate against the registration of some edicts.[2]

It is certainly interesting and important to observe that Fénelon, like the jurists to whom we have referred, not only upheld the supremacy of the law, but looked upon an absolute monarchy as something new, which was in violent contrast with the older political institutions of France; and that he remembers the importance of the States General.

It is this which gives significance to the plans for the reform of the system of government in France, which seem to have been prepared by Fénelon and the Duc de Chevreuse in 1711 for submission to the Duke of Burgundy, who had, by the death of his father, become the immediate heir to the French Crown.

The most important conception of these plans was the re-establishment of a representative authority for all the provinces, as it still existed in Languedoc and some others, and for the whole country. The Provincial Estates were to

[1] Ibid., Art. II. 8.   [2] Ibid., Art. III. 18.

be composed of the deputies of the three Orders and to have large administrative powers. Above them there was to be the States General of the whole kingdom. Its members were to be the bishop of every diocese, one seigneur of ancient and high nobility, elected by the nobles of the provinces, and one important member of the Third Estate, elected by that Estate. These deputies were to be freely elected without any interference by the king, there were to be no perpetual deputies, but they were to be eligible for re-election, and no deputy could receive any preferment from the king until three years after his term as deputy terminated. These States General were to meet every three years and sit as long as they thought it necessary. They were to be superior to the Provincial Estates, and their authority should extend to all important matters, such as justice and 'Police', finance, war and peace, and alliances. They were also to have control of such social reforms as the reclamation of uncultivated land, and the abuses of the Game Laws.[1]

It may indeed be questioned how far these plans had any real importance. The Duke of Burgundy died before his grandfather, and with the accession of the Duke of Orleans as Regent they fell to the ground. They are, however, very interesting to us as illustrating once again that the memory of an older and more constitutional system of government had not entirely died out in France. It was only a few years later, in 1727, that several important posthumous works by the Count de Boulainvillier were published, and among them is one which is, as far as I know, the first attempt at a history of the States General to the time of the meeting in 1484 at Tours, and a 'Mémoire' addressed to the Regent urging that they should be called again. It is best, however, to leave the consideration of this to the next Part of the work, when we shall consider it in relation to the other political writings of the eighteenth century.

[1] Fénelon (ed. 1878), Œuvres, vol. iii: *Plans de Gouvernement, concertés avec le Duc de Chrevreuse, pour être proposés au Duc de Bourgogne*, 1711, Art. II. 1–3.

IV

THE CONTINUITY OF THE CONCEPTION OF POLITICAL LIBERTY IN THE SEVENTEENTH CENTURY

SPAIN

IN our *History of Mediaeval Political Theory* we have pointed out that in Spain the Representative system was developed earlier than in any other country in Europe, the Cortes were meeting from the fourteenth to the sixteenth centuries more frequently, and were more active than in any other European country except England. Even in the latter part of the sixteenth century the Cortes were meeting every third year, and were very insistent in presenting their grievances to Philip II.

This was accompanied in the sixteenth century by a very important development of political theory, especially in the works of a number of ecclesiastical writers of the Dominican Order, and of the Society of Jesus, Soto, Victoria, Molina, Suarez, Mariana, and others. Their first principle was that political authority was derived, ultimately indeed from God, but immediately from the community itself, and, as Suarez says, subject to such conditions as the community had imposed.[1] Secondly, at least Mariana is clear that the prince is subject to the laws;[2] and thirdly the prince who used his authority unjustly and tyrannically might be resisted, and deposed.[3] One of these writers, Mariana, was indeed in some respects very near to the constitutional conceptions of Hooker, for he had behind his theories the historical principles of the nature and authority of the Cortes in Castile, as Hooker had those of Parliament in England.[4]

We must carry the memory of these conceptions with us,

---

[1] Suarez, *De Legibus*, iii. 4. 3.

[2] Mariana, *De Rege*, i. 1. 2, p. 23; i. 1. 9, p. 79.

[3] Soto, *De Justitia et jure*, iv. 4. 1; Molina, *De Justitia et Jure*, Tract II, Disp. 23. iv; Suarez, *De Legibus*, iii. 4. 6; Mariana, *De Rege*, i. 6.

[4] Mariana, *De Rege*, i. 6. 8.

if we are to understand the character of the political literature of Spain in the following period.[1]

We must begin by noticing the position of an important writer of the late sixteenth century, that is Diego Covarruvias, who was Bishop of Segovia and 'Praefectus Summi Praetorii'. It is clear from his works that he was primarily a jurist, learned in Roman and Canon law, but he was also familiar with some of the historical traditions of the Spanish kingdoms, and with some of the traditional political theories of the Middle Ages. He begins an important work entitled *Practicarum Quaestionum Liber* by laying down dogmatically that all temporal power and civil jurisdiction belong to the commonwealth, and that no ruler could be created, except by the commonwealth, without tyranny. He is not appointed by God; Saul and his successors were indeed appointed by God, but no other kings or princes, and he contrasts this very emphatically with the nature of the ecclesiastical authority which was given by Christ to Peter and the other Apostles, and their successors. It was the Roman people who conferred their authority upon the emperor, and the emperor was still chosen by the electors, who act as representatives of the community. Hereditary succession to the monarchy came in by custom and the tacit consent of the people.[2]

There is, indeed, nothing to surprise us in this dogmatic judgement, for it represents the normal tradition of the Roman jurists and the Middle Ages, but it is important to notice how sharply it contrasts with contemporary theories of the 'Divine Right' which we have considered in previous chapters. Covarruvias is dogmatically repudiating these. So much then for his theory of the source of political authority.

When he comes to discuss the best government, he enumerates the three forms, monarchy, aristocracy, and

[1] I must express my very great obligations to Professor Fernando de los Ríos, of the 'New School for Social Research' in New York, for his kindness in assisting me to find some of the most important Spanish writers of the late sixteenth and the seventeenth century, and the most valuable notes which he gave me on some of them. Our English libraries are unfortunately not very completely supplied with this literature, but I have, I hope, found enough to serve as examples of it.

[2] Covarruvias, *Practicarum Quaestionum Liber, Opera* (ed. 1592), ii. 375–8.

democracy, and he gives his preference to monarchy; but the monarchy which he praises is that in which the king does not act by his free and absolute will, but after consultation with the *Seniores et probatissimi viri*. Otherwise the prince or king may easily fall into tyranny; and an aristocracy founded on good and fixed laws would be better than an absolute royal authority.[1] The three forms of political authority are all approved by God, and when once established, whether by election, by law, or by custom in hereditary succession, kings must not be deposed, unless they fall into extreme tyranny.[2] The exception is obviously very important.

He goes on to say that the Visigothic monarchs in Spain had been elected by the magnates and the people; but after the Moorish invasion, by the tacit consent of the people, the kingdom became hereditary. And thus the whole power and jurisdiction in Castile is in the hands of the king, and it is he who grants authority to nobles or towns.[3]

So far Covarruvias's principles are clear, but when we come to the nature and extent of the authority of the prince their interpretation is more difficult. In another work he contemptuously repudiated the doctrine which he attributes to Paulus de Castro, an eminent Italian civilian of the fifteenth century, that there was a distinction between the ordinary and the absolute power of the prince.[4] Whatever authority the prince may have of dispensing (*derogandi*) with the laws, belongs to his ordinary power; for no absolute power is given even to the prince, and what the prince cannot do by human, divine, or natural law, belongs not to an authority derived from law (*jus*), but to tyranny. We, he says, who are treating of law (*jus*) cannot attribute to the prince an authority which expresses only his desires and free will, and is not limited by right reason.[5] A little farther on Covarruvias speaks with equal contempt of the contention that the prince

[1] Ibid., p. 378.
[2] Ibid., pp. 378, 379.
[3] Ibid., p. 379.
[4] This distinction had been made in the fourteenth century by Baldus, *Comm. on Code*, i. 14. 4.
[5] Covarruvias, *Variarum Resolutiones*, iii, *Opera*, ii. 234.

could make his dispensation (*derogatio*) effective by insert-
ing a clause which intimated that he was acting *ex certa
sententia*.[1]

This sounds very clear, but Covarruvias had said also,
that while the prince does evil and sins in dispensing with
human constitutions without just cause, the action which
arises from this was valid (*actus tamen ex eis secutus validus
est*).[2] He is answerable, however, to God.

In another place he says that it is lawful for a man to
resist unjust princes or judges, when he cannot otherwise
escape from death,[3] and in yet another passage while he
maintains that a man is in conscience bound to pay a just
tribute to the prince, he limits this to the case that the
tribute is not so excessive as to amount to tyranny.[4]

To sum up, Covarruvias is clear that all political authority,
while it comes ultimately from God, comes immediately
from the community. He distinctly and dogmatically repudiated the 'Divine Right'. He does not indeed, as far as
I have seen, refer explicitly to the Cortes, but he prefers a
monarchy which acts in consultation with *Seniores et probatissimi viri*. This is better than an absolute monarchy,
which easily degenerates into a tyranny; and he seems to
mean that as the private man may resist tyranny, the community may resist the tyrant. It is not, however, very easy
to make out what he means about the normal relation of the
prince to the positive law, but he probably means no more
than that the prince has a certain dispensing power.

Covarruvias has not the clearly defined constitutionalism
of Mariana, but he has a good deal of the medieval tradition.

Pedro Ribadeneyra of the Society of Jesus, in his work
entitled *Tratado de la Religion y Virtudes que deve tener el
Principe Christiano*, published in 1597, was especially urgent
in maintaining that justice was the most important of the
virtues of the prince, after piety. This might be taken as a
mere abstract generalization, but he gives it a very important
practical and constitutional meaning.

He illustrates what he meant by justice by some examples.

---

[1] Covarruvias, *Variarum Resolutiones*, iii, *Opera*, ii. 235.   [2] Ibid., p. 234.
[3] Ibid., p. 16.   [4] Ibid., i. 526.

First by the well-known story about Trajan, of whom it was related that, when investing the Praetor with a sword as a symbol of his authority, he said that the Praetor should use this for him when he commanded what was just, and against him when his commands were unjust; secondly by referring to a tradition that the kings of Egypt, and Philip the Fair of France, caused their magistrates to swear that they would not obey unjust royal commands; and thirdly, that Antigonus the Third commanded the *Presidentes* and Ministers of Justice that they were not to carry out his orders even if they were signed by his own hand, if they were contrary to justice and the customs or laws of the kingdom.[1]

In another place he speaks of those wicked men who sought to flatter the prince, to destroy the proper order of government, and to pervert the divine and human law by teaching that he could dispose of the property of his subjects at his pleasure. They would change a just prince into a cruel and detestable tyrant. He illustrates this again by a story about Antigonus who, when a flatterer said to him that all actions were just and honourable in kings, replied that this might be so among barbarians, but not 'among ourselves' where honourable things were honourable, and just things just. And Ribadeneyra adds that the true king is subject to the laws of God and of Nature; the true king maintains piety, justice, and faith, while the tyrant takes no account of them.[2] In another place Ribadeneyra maintains that when Samuel (1 Sam. viii.) describes the actions of the king, he is not describing the true law of the kingdom, but only the actions of a king who was controlled by passion rather than by reason.[3]

It may be thought that these contentions are still rather abstract and general; but Ribadeneyra was evidently specially concerned about the question of the interference of the unjust prince with the property of his subjects, and this is developed in an important statement of a constitutional principle.

The prince, he says, should above all understand that he

[1] P. Ribadeneyra, *Tratado de la Religion*, &c., ii. 5, p. 243 (ed. 1597).
[2] Ibid. ii. 9, p. 260.
[3] Ibid. ii. 9, p. 263.

is not absolute master of the properties of his subjects. (I take the word *haziendas* to mean not only landed estates, but property in general; this is evidently the meaning from the later words of the passage.) If, he says, the dominion and property of his subjects belonged to the king, and only the use and possession to his subjects, there would be no reason for the meetings of the Cortes of the kingdom to deal with the needs of the kings, nor would the grants of money which they made be called services, subsidies, or donatives, or by any other name which showed that they were voluntary and not obligatory.[1]

We have in this passage not merely a statement of the general principles of justice, but a reference to the Cortes as an important part of the constitutional government of Spain. We have in another work dealt with the history and importance of the Cortes of Castile,[2] in the later Middle Ages in Spain, but it is important to observe this at the very end of the sixteenth century.

These two writers, Covarruvias and Ribadeneyra, while they do not represent the traditional principles of Spanish liberty with the same fullness and precision as their contemporary Mariana, indicate clearly enough that the principles of political liberty were not yet forgotten. We find, however, a much more complete and explicit statement of these, some forty years later, in a work entitled *Idea de un Principe Politico Christiano*, written by Diego Saavedra Fajardo, and published in 1640. Saavedra was a member of the Supreme Council for the Indies, and at one time Ambassador Extraordinary in Mantua and at another *Esquizano i Residente* in Germany. He was therefore a man of some public position and experience.

This work of Saavedra is very important, for it does not merely deal with some particulars in the theory and practice of politics, but does, up to a certain point at least, present a systematic conception of the origin and nature of civil government.

---

[1] P. Ribadeneyra, *Tratado de la Religion*, &c., ii. 9, p. 260.

[2] Cf. *History of Mediaeval Political Theory*, vol. v, part i, chap. 9; vol. vi, part i, chap. 6; part ii, chap. 6; part iv, chaps. 2, 4, and 5.

We may notice first an important passage in which he says that all princes destroy themselves (*que se pierden*) when they persuade themselves that the kingdom is an inheritance and property of which they can dispose at their pleasure; that their greatness, that is their absolute power, is not subject to the laws, but only to their own will; and that without this liberty the princely authority would be merely a hard servitude. The prince should understand the nature of his authority, that it is not supreme; the people had reserved from the first its authority to take action against a notoriously unjust and tyrannical prince. Good princes are pleased that their subjects should enjoy some liberty, while tyrants assume an absolute domination.[1] This is, as we shall see, an excellent introduction to the political principles which Saavedra maintained, and he goes on to a summary exposition of the origin and nature of political society.

In the primitive ages there was, he says, no need of punishment, for men loved the good for its own sake; but, as time passed, the wickedness of the world developed, and men's ambition and violence created *las dominaciones* (lordships), and these compelled men to form *la compania civil* (i.e. political society). It is interesting to notice that Saavedra's conception of the origin of the political community was still the Senecan and Patristic view that political society had its origin in the need of an authority to control men's vices and sins.

This political society was founded upon the common consent, and the function of the community, as illuminated by the light of Nature, was to maintain justice and peace, and to restrain men's vices. Inasmuch as it was impossible that this authority should be diffused in the whole body of the people, it was placed in one person, or in few, or in many, that is in a monarchy, or in an aristocracy, or in a democracy.[2]

The first form of government was a monarchy, which was invested with the sceptre and crown as an emblem of majesty and the supreme power. This authority consisted principally in the maintenance of justice and peace for the people. If it failed in this, the order of the commonwealth and the

[1] Saavedra, *Idea de un Principe Politico Cristiano* (ed. 1640), pp. 120–3.
[2] Ibid., pp. 124, 5.

authority of the king broke down. This had happened in Castile, when two kings, Don Ordeno and Don Fruela, were excluded from the government on account of their unjust actions, and it was entrusted to two judges.[1]

So far then for the form of government, and Saavedra goes on to discuss the nature of law and its relation to political authority. The administration of justice, as has just been said, was the primary function of political authority, but the law of nature is not adequate to the variety of cases which may have to be determined, and it was necessary that the commonwealth should provide itself with laws (*leges*, i.e. positive laws), some penal and some distributive.[2] It is in this foundation of law, not of mere will, that true political authority (*la vera politica*) is founded. The administration of justice cannot be entrusted to the inconstancy of a will subject to emotions and passions; it must be controlled by firm and immutable decrees, which proceed from reason and prudence, and are equal for all citizens, without hatred or reference to private interests. Such are the laws which are taught men by the experience of the past. Tyranny is nothing but the ignoring of the law.[3]

Saavedra had spoken of laws as written, but he modifies this a little later, and recognizes that customs are laws, written not on paper, but in the souls and memories of men; and they are the more loved inasmuch as they are not mere commands. And, he says of them, in a very noteworthy phrase, that they are a form of liberty, and that the same common consent which first established them retains them tenaciously.[4]

All this meant that in Spain the kings were subject to the positive laws, and he illustrates this by pointing out that even in cases concerning the royal patrimony, the Fisc (i.e. the Royal Treasury) is subject to the same judgement as any vassal; and judgement may be given against it; and he cites the authority of commands of Philip II and of Philip IV. A glorious kingdom indeed, he exclaims, when the cause of the prince is of less authority (than the law).[5] It need hardly

---

[1] Saavedra, *Idea de un Principe Politico Cristiano* (ed. 1640), pp. 125, 6.
[2] Ibid., p. 126.   [3] Ibid., p. 128.
[4] Ibid., p. 132.   [5] Ibid., p. 134.

be pointed out that Saavedra's contention is of high importance as signifying that, at least in certain cases, the kings of
Spain were subject not only to the laws, but to the courts of
justice, as in England and France. This does not mean that
Saavedra had not a high conception of the source and nature
of the royal authority. He is the vicar of God; but he is
also the vicar of his people, by whose consent he holds the
authority of justice.[1]

This, however, is not yet a complete account of Saavedra's
conception of the proper nature of a reasonable monarchy.
He is clear and emphatic in asserting, in one place, that no
monarchy could endure unless it was 'mixed', and included
the elements of aristocracy and democracy.[2]

We may take as a particular example of what he meant by
this, that he says in another place that the kingdom of Castile
had been established on the condition that no taxes should
be levied without the consent of the community. This was
ratified by a decree of the Cortes of Madrid in the time of
Alfonso XI and by immemorial prescription, and meant that
no taxes could be levied without the consent of the Cortes.[3]
It is interesting to notice that Saavedra points out the
dangerous consequences to France, when Charles VII determined to impose a tax arbitrarily.

It will be evident from all this that Saavedra's work
expresses an incisive criticism of absolute monarchy, not
merely in some particular details, but in the discussion of
the fundamental principles of political authority. He criti-
cizes not only particular abuses of absolutism, but sets out
the traditional medieval doctrine, that political authority in
all its forms found its origin in the consent of the community,
and was controlled by the positive laws of the community.
The monarchy if it was to be effective and enduring must
be a mixed government, and must include the elements of
aristocracy and democracy. Absolute monarchy is merely
tyranny, and the king who obtains it achieves his own ruin.

It is evident that the tradition of political liberty still survived in Spain in the middle of the seventeenth century, and

[1] Ibid., pp. 135, 138.   [2] Ibid., p. 262.
[3] Ibid., p. 355. Cf. *Cortes of Castile and Leon*, ed. Royal Academy of
Madrid, i. 47, 68, and our *History of Med. Pol. Theory*, vi. 92.

it is worth while to notice that Saavedra's work corresponds in many important elements with the political conceptions set out in France by Joly in a work written only a few years later.[1] It is true that in France the States General had already ceased to meet—their last meeting was that of 1614—and in Castile the financial authority of the Cortes was transferred to the local authorities in 1665, and they ceased to meet until 1810.

I have not been able to find evidence that there was a development in Spanish political literature analogous to that of France in the eighteenth century. In the absence of this it is very important to consider the characteristic features of the demand for the restoration of political liberty as it took shape in the first decade of the nineteenth century; and we have an excellent illustration of this in the works of Francesco Martinez Marina, a Canon of San Isidro in Madrid. He published in 1808 the work entitled *Ensayo historico-critico sobre la antiqua legislacion de Leon y Castiella*, and in 1813 that entitled *Teoria de las Cortes*. The most important aspect of these works is, from our present point of view, that they present the demands for the establishment of a limited and constitutional government, not as a thing new and revolutionary, but as founded both on what seemed to the author to be the sound principles of a political order, and upon a proper appreciation and interpretation of the historical character of the government of Castile and Leon in the Middle Ages and down to the seventeenth century.

This will be evident from a brief examination of the character of the second work mentioned above, the *Teoria de las Cortes*. This work consists of a lengthy Prologue, which deals with the general principles of political society, and especially with a summary view of the history of political freedom in Europe and in Spain. The main body of the work is occupied with a more detailed account of the history of the Cortes of Castile and Leon, and with a discussion of some amendments which Marina thought to be of importance for them as revived in 1810.

It is clear that Marina represents the tradition of the

[1] Cf. p. 66 & ff.

Middle Ages, and of some of the great political writers of the sixteenth and seventeenth centuries. He cites St. Thomas Aquinas, but he also refers to Hooker, and cites Sidney and Locke, as having maintained that the people is the source of political authority, and that this was founded upon the common consent. In primitive conditions men knew and obeyed the law of nature, but they were driven out of this innocent state of nature by their own vices, and political society was created for mutual assistance and protection under the laws of the State. Marina contrasts this with Filmer's attempt to defend the absolutism of the prince, as being of divine right.

Governments were created for the good of the subjects, and their authority was founded upon a contract, and Marina cites St. Thomas Aquinas as maintaining that if the appointment of the prince belonged to the community, it could restrain, and even depose, him if he were to act tyrannically.[1]

It was natural that in the first ages men should have given their authority to one man, but the primitive monarchy had only a limited power. This was followed by a period of tyranny, owing to the foolishness and lack of energy of the people, but Greece and Rome maintained their liberty for a long time. In Spain, Marina says, the love of liberty continued until they were conquered by Carthage and Rome.[2] Rome fell, and the Visigoths established a 'tempered monarchy', mixed with aristocracy and democracy; the king had the executive power, but legislation belonged to *las grandes juntas populares*, composed of representatives of the most illustrious members of the nation. Marina also says that the Visigothic kings had on their accession to swear to observe the constitutional and fundamental laws of the kingdom, and that the authority of the *juntas* extended to all the political affairs of the kingdom.[3]

The invasion and conquest of Spain by the Arabs interrupted this, and it was only slowly that the Spaniards

---

[1] Marina, *Teoria de las Cortes* (ed. 1813), Prologue, pp. 13–26.
[2] Ibid., pp. 36, 41.
[3] Ibid., pp. 46–9. (This is probably a reminiscence of the Ecclesiastical Councils of Toledo.)

reconquered their liberty, and resumed their native political development. In the twelfth century the representatives of the people were summoned to the Cortes. It was the princes of the House of Hapsburg who established a despotic monarchy. The Emperor Charles V and King Philip II did not indeed venture to abolish the Cortes, but succeeded in reducing their power. Marina cites the work of Saavedra, which we have already discussed, in praise of the Cortes.[1]

As we have already seen, the financial authority of the Cortes had been in 1665 transferred to the municipal and provincial assemblies, and the Crown had ceased to summon the Cortes.

In the treatise itself which follows this Prologue, Marina gives an account of the history and functions of the Cortes in detail, but we are not here concerned with this. We must, however, cite a passage in which he sums up what he conceived to have been their powers and importance. These, whether Councils, Diets, Estates, Parliaments, or Cortes, were august assemblies in which the whole people exercised the legislative power, and developed their sovereign authority. In these they elected and deposed princes, in them the general will dictated the laws and decided the most important affairs of the State. It was these which secured the liberties of the political societies of Europe.[2]

A proper treatment of the importance of Marina's work would require a discussion of the whole constitutional movement in Spain in the first twenty years of the nineteenth century; but for our purpose it will be sufficient to point out that his work serves admirably to show that in Spain, as in the other European countries, the conception of political liberty was not a mere revolutionary modernism, but represented the survival of the memories of a political system in which the constitutional principles of the Middle Ages had found their expression and form.

It is indeed interesting to notice that Marina seems to be careful not to refer much to the French Revolution, perhaps because he felt that this might give the impression that he was advocating a revolutionary innovation, and he was

[1] Marina, *Teoria de las Cortes* (ed. 1813), Prologue, pp. 56–64.
[2] Ibid., *Teoria de las Cortes*, i. 1. 8, p. 5.

anxious to show that this was not so, but that he was asserting traditional principles, and defending traditional forms in which the principles of political liberty had found their appropriate embodiment.

Marina's conceptions of the primitive state of man, and of the origin of civil government, were founded on Seneca, the Roman lawyer, and Patristic traditions, while his conceptions of the community as the source of law and political authority were derived from the Roman jurists and medieval writers, and the principle that the law was supreme over the prince was founded on medieval principles and practice. While he restated these conceptions he was much concerned to show that the demand for a representative system and a limited or constitutional monarchy was not the expression of a revolutionary temper, nor even an appeal to the example of other countries, but an invocation of the historical principles and forms of Spain itself.

If we now try to sum up the principles of the nature of political liberty as represented in the Spanish literature which we have been considering in this chapter, we find that in various terms these writers express the same general principles, and that these were the principles of the medieval tradition.

All political authority is derived from the community and there is no such thing as the divine right of an absolute king. This contrasts very sharply with the conceptions expressed by some of the English and French defenders of the absolute monarchy. Absolute authority is the characteristic of the tyrant, not of the king, and the community is entitled to resist the tyrant. One of these writers, that is Saavedra, also sets out very carefully the relation of the king to the positive laws which, whether written or unwritten, are derived from the community, and to which the king himself is subject; and they embody the liberty of the community. It may indeed be said that the treatment of this by Covarruvias is somewhat ambiguous, but he may only mean that the king had a certain power of dispensing with the laws, and he does not hesitate to express his distrust and dislike of the absolute king or tyrant.

Ribadeneyra and Saavedra are very emphatic in asserting the authority of the Cortes in matters of taxation and private property, and even Covarruvias, though he does not actually mention the Cortes, is clear in preferring the monarchy which acts in consultation with *Seniores et probatissimi viri*, and Saavedra says emphatically that no monarchy can endure which is not mixed, and includes the elements of aristocracy and democracy.

We have concluded our observations on the theory of liberty in the seventeenth century in Spain by pointing out that when the demand for liberty revived in the nineteenth century, Marina finds the justification of the demands for constitutional liberty, not only in general principles, but in the recollection of what seemed to him the characteristics of the political order of medieval Spain.

V

THE CONTINUITY OF THE CONCEPTION OF POLITICAL LIBERTY IN THE SEVENTEENTH CENTURY

HOLLAND

IT is at first sight a strange thing that it should be difficult to determine precisely the actual principles of political liberty, and their relation to absolutism, as set out by Grotius. It is strange to find that the greatest jurist of the great Republic which, after the struggle of a generation, had triumphantly vindicated its independence against the king of Spain, speaks in an apparently uncertain tone of the principles of liberty, and should be best known, as far as he deals with political theory, by his suggestion that a people, just as much as an individual person, might submit itself to the authority of one man, and retain no part of its lawful authority over itself.

It is certainly strange, but we may find some partial explanations. In the first place Grotius was a learned Roman lawyer, and could not therefore deny that the great Roman community had transferred its authority to the emperor. In the second place, when Grotius wrote his great work *De Jure Belli ac Pacis*, he was a fugitive in France from the intolerance of the extreme Calvinistic party in Holland, and the work was dedicated in 1625 to Louis XIII, the head of a monarchy powerful, if not yet absolute, and we can understand Grotius's repudiation of the doctrine that always and everywhere the supreme political authority belonged to the people in such a sense that they could coerce and punish kings who abused their authority.

In order to form a judgement upon the question of Grotius's conception of political authority and liberty we shall do well to begin by considering his general political principles. In some most important matters Grotius followed the tradition of Cicero and the Stoics, of the Christian Fathers and the Middle Ages. He repudiated emphatically the doctrine of Carneades as represented by Cicero, that justice and law were merely the expression of what men find to be useful or convenient.[1] He defines the natural law as being *dictatum rectae rationis*; it declares what is forbidden or commanded by God, who is the Creator of Nature.[2] A little later he adds that the natural law is immutable and cannot be changed even by God himself.[3]

Civil law he defines as that which proceeds from the civil authority, that is from the authority which is over the *Civitas*; and he defines the *Civitas* in terms which are closely related to Cicero's definition of the commonwealth. 'Est autem civitas coetus perfectus liberorum hominum iuris fruendi et communis utilitatis causa sociatus.'[4] In the 'Prolegomena' to this work, he had already said that it is according to the law of nature that men should keep their contracts, and that it was from this source that civil laws proceed; for those who have joined any society of men have expressly or tacitly promised to obey that which the majority, or those to whom authority has been given, have established.[5] These are important statements, but they are not new. Grotius was so far repeating substantially the political principles of the Middle Ages.

It is a different matter when we turn to the detailed discussion of political authority; he appears not to be developing one consistent view, but to be balancing between different principles. He begins by repudiating the doctrine that everywhere and without exception the supreme authority belongs to the people in such a sense that they may coerce and punish kings who abuse their authority;[6] and he defends his view by two important arguments.

His first argument is famous (or infamous): that, as any individual man could by Hebrew and Roman law make himself the slave of another, so any people might submit itself to some one man or men, and retain no part of its lawful authority over itself. He admits indeed that this might have inconvenient consequences, but all forms of

---

[1] Grotius, *De Jure Belli ac Pacis*, 'Prolegomena', i. 5, &c.
[2] Ibid. i. 1. 10. 1.   [3] Ibid. i. 1. 10. 5.
[4] Ibid. i. 1. 14. 1. 1. Cf. Cicero, *De Republica*, i. 25, 39.
[5] Ibid., 'Prolegomena', 15.   [6] Ibid. i. 3. 8. 1.

government have inconveniences.[1] Another important argument which he brings forward is that, as Aristotle had pointed out, there are men who are naturally slaves, men and peoples who are more fit to be ruled than to rule; and again, the circumstances of a State may be such that it can only be in safety under the rule of one man; and many wise men have thought that this was the condition of Rome in the time of Augustus.[2]

This will be sufficient to illustrate what Grotius meant when he refused to admit that the authority of the people was always and everywhere greater than that of the prince.

In the next chapter of Book I, Grotius begins by setting out the general principle that obedience to the ruling authority in the State is a necessary condition of 'civil society', and is commanded by God;[3] and he repudiates specifically, with reference no doubt to Calvin and other sixteenth-century writers, the conception that there might be 'inferior Magistrates' whose right and duty it was to resist the superior authority, if it behaved unjustly.[4] So far then Grotius repudiated the conception that the community was necessarily superior, and asserts that in some cases an absolute monarchy might be useful and desirable. This was not, however, the whole of his theory of political authority.

It is, he says, a very grave question whether the law of non-resistance is always binding upon men. There have been cases when even the laws of God admitted exceptions, and human laws are and must be subject to the fact of human infirmity. If it is contended that it is the law of God which compels men to obey their superior, it must be remembered that political society is a human institution, created not by God's command but voluntarily. St. Peter calls it a human *ordinatio* (1 Peter ii. 13), even though he also calls it a divine *ordinatio*, for God approved it as *salubre institutum*. God approves human law, *humano modo*.[5]

Grotius then appeals to Barclay, whom he terms the most

---

[1] Ibid. i. 3. 8. 1.
[2] Ibid. i. 3. 8. 4 and 5.
[3] Ibid. i. 4. 1.
[4] Ibid. i. 4. 6. 1. (Cf. Calvin, *Institutio*, ed. 1559, iv. 20. 51.)
[5] Ibid. i. 4. 7. 1–3.

vigorous defender of monarchical rule, as having admitted
that there might be circumstances in which it would be right
that the community should protect itself against intolerable
cruelty on the part of its ruler.[1] A little later he enumerates
seven cases in which it was lawful in his judgement to resist
the king. First, if under the constitution of the commonwealth the prince is subject to the people, he may be punished,
even by death, if he transgresses against the laws and the
commonwealth; second, if the king abdicates, or deserts his
kingdom; third, if he alienates or transfers his kingdom to
another; fourth, if he attacks not merely individuals, but
the whole community; fifth, if the king violates his allegiance
to his feudal superior; sixth, if the king has only a part of the
supreme authority, and the Senate or people another part,
and the king endeavours to seize that authority which does
not belong to him; seventh, if when his authority was given
to the prince, it had been laid down that in a certain case he
might be resisted. (Grotius in a note refers among other
examples of this to Brabant and Flanders, that is to the revolt
of the Netherlands against Philip of Spain.[2])

These are very important exceptions to the principles of
a necessary obedience to the king, and go far beyond Barclay,
who had only admitted the third and fourth exceptions.

It is therefore difficult to determine precisely the place of
Grotius among the political thinkers of the seventeenth
century. He does indeed repudiate the position of those who
maintained that the supreme authority in the commonwealth
everywhere and without exception remains with the people,
that is he rejects that doctrine of the continual sovereignty
of the people which had been set out in some of the most
important tracts of the sixteenth century in France, and by
Althusius in Germany in the sixteenth and early seventeenth
centuries, and was virtually implied in the works of Mariana
in Spain, and of Hooker in England.

On the other hand, he does not think of the transference
of all their authority by the Roman people as a normal form

---

[1] Grotius, *De Jure Belli ac Pacis*, 'Prolegomena', i. 4. 7. 4.
[2] Ibid. i. 4. 8–14, and Grotius' note, n. to 14. (Cf. William of Orange,
Apologie, ed. 1858, pp. 46, 47, and Ste. Aldegonde, *Œuvres*, ed. 1859, vii.
134.)

of government; he does not agree with the appeal to religion as forbidding all resistance to misgovernment like the supporters of the 'Divine Right'; and he does not, like Bodin, denounce the governments which were controlled by the community as being perverse and incompetent.

It is very interesting and important to notice that the eminent Dutch writer, Gronovius, who belongs to the second half of the seventeenth century, criticized the work of Grotius, so far as it dealt with the nature and conditions of political authority, with great severity in his notes to Grotius' *De Jure Belli ac Pacis*.

The first criticism which we should notice is that Grotius had put the question of the nature of the supreme authority in a political society *invidiose*. He had emphatically repudiated the doctrine that everywhere and always the supreme authority belonged to the people. This, Gronovius says, is not the real question, which is properly, whether a people which has a legitimate government, whether that of a king, a senate, or a republic (he means by this a community ruled by the assembly of the different orders), can change its government, if the larger and better part judge that it is mischievous; that is if the king had degenerated into a tyrant, or the senate into an oligarchy, or the assembly into a confused mass of seditious persons.[1]

To the contention of Grotius that, as the individual could surrender himself to slavery, a people could do the same, Gronovius replies in the first place by the contemptuous question—Where are we to find such a people? Not the Germans, for to this day they elect the emperor, and the princes hold their fiefs from the emperor, not as a master of slaves, but as representing the whole German people; not the French, for they had created their kings by free election in their assemblies; not the Spaniards, for they accepted the House of Austria by marriages and agreements. Indeed there are no such peoples in Europe, except those who are oppressed by the Russian, Turkish, or Tartar tyrannies.

But, he continues, even if the contention of Grotius were true, and a people could give itself into slavery, slaves, by

[1] Gronovius, Note 68 to Grotius, *De Jure Belli ac Pacis*, i. 3. 8. 1, ed. 1712.

the laws both of Athens and Rome, had the right to the protection of the law against the master who treated them with
cruelty. And in the last resort they could take refuge in
flight, or resist force with force.[1]

In another note Gronovius urges that there is an ambiguity about the meaning of the word *dominium* as though
it implied the right, not merely to use, but to abuse authority
without interference. This is false, according to the *Jus
Gentium*, as well as the civil law. For there is a *societas* even
of masters and slaves; slaves were made in war, not to be
killed but to be preserved alive; and this is also true of
peoples who are conquered in war; even those who have
submitted unconditionally have done so on the tacit under-
standing that their lives should be spared.[2]

These are interesting observations on slavery, but Gronovius returns to the more strictly political question, and sets
out his judgement on more general principles. Neither the
words of Holy Scripture, nor of the Greek and Latin writers
annul the *jus populi*. The people cannot give more authority
than it possesses, it has no authority to destroy itself, or to
treat itself unjustly, and therefore it cannot give such an
authority to the king. To argue that because the king is
supra populum he can do what he pleases is a mere absurdity
(*ludificatio*). The consuls were *supra populum* in Rome, and
the archons in Athens, but they could not do whatever they
pleased.[3] It is true that the Roman people conferred their
authority on the emperor, but this was the authority which
they themselves possessed, not a tyrannical one. It is true
that the people gave it, but it was a just authority. This
could not be recalled in ordinary circumstances, but if one
man gives another a sword, and he uses it for the destruction
of the giver, the giver may and should reclaim it.[4]

Gronovius refers to Plutarch as saying that kings had
authority not only to rule according to the laws, but also
authority over the laws; but Gronovius explains this as
meaning that kings have authority to make laws which are

[1] Gronovius, Note 70 to Grotius, *De Jure Belli*, &c., i. 3. 8. 1.
[2] Ibid., Note 81 to Grotius, *De Jure Belli*, &c., i. 3. 8. 6.
[3] Ibid., Note 85 to Grotius, *De Jure Belli*, &c., i. 3. 8. 7.
[4] Ibid., Note 90 to Grotius, *De Jure Belli*, &c., i. 3. 8. 9.

useful, and to abrogate those which by process of time have ceased to be useful, but this does not mean that they have authority to overthrow all laws. A free people has the same power with regard to the laws, and yet in a free commonwealth the authority of the laws is far above that of the people.[1]

It is true, he says again, that kings do not render an account of their actions, for there is no ordinary magistrate before whom they can be summoned; but this does not mean that they have licence to overthrow all things, and that there is no one who can punish them if they violate the laws in the highest degree; and he points out that in Carthage, though the *imperatores* did not render an account of their actions, if they attacked the commonwealth they were crucified.[2] In another note he points out that the Roman Senate condemned Nero to death when he abused his authority.[3]

Again, Gronovius says, a little contemptuously, that there is a perpetual play on the word 'superior'. The prince and his magistrates are indeed 'superior' to the people, but only as the head is superior to the members; he is a moral and artificial head, and can be removed without endangering the safety of the body. He who appointed another over himself and gave him all his authority, under a contract that he should rule according to the laws, and should defend and preserve the well-being of all, has power to remove and punish the ruler if he becomes an enemy. If it is true that the government of States is established for the sake of the people, and it appears that the well-being of the ruler cannot be reconciled with that of the people, by the detestable fault of the ruler, it is better that the tyrant should be removed than that the people should be destroyed by the tyrant.[4]

In another note again Gronovius explains what he meant by the words tyrant and people. By the word tyrant he meant either the ruler who usurped an authority to which he had no lawful right, or the ruler who had obtained power by lawful means, but whose vices tend to dissolve the commonwealth, to destroy the safety of the people, and the

---

[1] Ibid., Note 92 to Grotius, *De Jure Belli*, &c., i. 3. 8. 9.
[2] Ibid., Note 94 to Grotius, *De Jure Belli*, &c., i. 3. 8. 9.
[3] Ibid., Note 96 to Grotius, *De Jure Belli*, &c., i. 3. 8. 10.
[4] Ibid., Note 98 to Grotius, *De Jure Belli*, &c., i. 3. 8. 10.

laws of the kingdom. By the word people he meant, not the dregs of the 'Plebs', but the good men who form the largest part of all the 'Orders'; the chief men of the 'Optimates' and of the 'Plebs', who have an interest in the safety of the commonwealth.[1]

In another place he indignantly repudiated the contention that the Divine Authority forbade Christian men to resist the ruler who endeavoured to suppress their religion, and urged that this would imply a condemnation of those heroic men to whom they owed in Belgium, in Germany, and in France their liberty of conscience.[2]

It is certainly interesting and important to find an eminent Dutch jurist criticizing with this freedom and force the political opinions of so great a man as Grotius, on the ground that they were not compatible with the principles of political liberty. It is perhaps even more interesting to find that Gronovius, while admitting that the Romans had indeed transferred their authority to the emperor by the *Lex Regia*, looks upon this, not as an example to be imitated, but as a lamentable result of political degeneration. This contention is expressed in an Oration which Gronovius delivered in 1671. This is a discussion of the *Lex Regia*, as Gronovius thought it, which was recorded on what he calls the *Aes Capitolinum* (presumably the same tablet as Cardinal Zabarella had seen in the Lateran in the fifteenth century,[3] which described the powers which the Roman people had bestowed upon Vespasian).

The most important matter in Gronovius' Oration is, from our present point of view, the indignant contempt with which he treats it. He appears to think that the surrender of its liberty by the Roman people had been already accomplished in fact, but this had been a *secretum horribile*, which was now openly acknowledged. The Roman people had now lost even the memory of and desire for liberty, and it was no longer a subject of grief and indignation that the prince could do all, and the people nothing.[4]

---

[1] Gronovius, Note 14 to Grotius, *De Jure Belli*, &c., i. 3. 8. 15.
[2] Ibid., Note 76 to Grotius, *De Jure Belli*, &c., i. 4. 7. 8.
[3] Cardinal Zabarella, *Comm. on Decretals*, i. 6. 34.
[4] Gronovius, *De Lege Regia*, ed. Lugd. Batav., 1678, p. 80.

I have not observed that any civilian before Gronovius had expressed this hearty and dogmatic contempt for the action of the Roman people in transferring their authority to the emperor. Some of the civilians like Azo and Hugolinus in the thirteenth century had indeed contended that the Roman people had reserved the right to reclaim their authority,[1] and others, especially Cujas and Zazius of Freiburg, had in the sixteenth century maintained that the imperial authority was limited by law;[2] but, as far as I know, such a criticism of the action of the Roman people as that of Gronovius was new and significant.

[1] Azo, *Summa Codicis*, 1. 14. 8; Hugolini, *Distinctiones*, Dist. 148. 34.
[2] Cf. *History of Mediaeval Political Theory*, vol. vi, part iii, chap. v.

VI

THE CONTINUITY OF THE CONCEPTION OF POLITICAL LIBERTY IN THE SEVENTEENTH CENTURY

GERMANY

WE turn to some examples of conceptions of a Constitutional Order in German writers of the seventeenth century; two from the earlier part, and two from the later. The first is Adam Contzen, a Jesuit and Professor in the 'Academia' of the Archbishop of Maintz; the second is Arumaeus, an eminent Professor of Law in the University of Jena; the third Puffendorf, perhaps the best-known European jurist of the later part of the seventeenth century; the fourth is the great Leibniz.

Adam Contzen's work *Politicorum Libri Decem* was published in 1620, and represents a moderate and cautious, but firm, constitutionalism. He is clear that the best form of government is a monarchy tempered by aristocracy, and by what he calls *Politia*. A despotic government, that is one where the prince is absolute, is *iniqua* and of little continuance. Such was the empire of Turkey, where the inhabitants called themselves the slaves of the emperor. There is no need, he says, to prove that this is an evil government, for there is no man who does not abhor slavery and desire freedom.[1]

A 'tempered' monarchy is one in which the 'Optimates' have authority, while the cities and other orders have some power, and in which the prince judges justly and according to the laws.[2] Again, he expresses his detestation of tyranny and the παμβασιλεια, and his approval of a monarchy tempered by laws and bound by custom, which rests upon the authority of the 'Optimates' and the just desires of a good people, and is bound by mutual oaths to the people. He approves of a commonwealth in which the prince can do the largest amount of good, and the least possible evil. It is

[1] Adam Contzen, *Politicorum Libri Decem*, i. 21. 2. 4, ed. Maintz, 1621.
[2] Ibid. i. 21. 9.

very interesting to see that, like Machiavelli, he praises the
French monarchy as an example of a kingdom in which the
prince, if a dispute arises between him and his subjects about
property, submits, like his subjects, to the judgement of
the law.[1]

In another chapter he deals with some of the most important restraints on the authority of the prince. The first is that
he must not impose any new taxes without consulting the
commonwealth; this, he says, is the rule in Germany, in
Spain, and other kingdoms, and is a wholesome bridle on
the licence of the prince and the avarice of his ministers. A
second is that the authority to establish laws belongs to the
whole commonwealth, not only to the prince, or the Senate,
composed of the 'Optimates'. A third is that the prince
should not have the power of appointing his successor. A
fourth, that the commonwealth and not the prince should
have the power of making war and peace. It is well that the
power of the prince should be so limited by the laws that he
may not easily become a tyrant, while they leave him free
to restrain the wicked, to protect the good, and to be a terror
to the enemies of the commonwealth.[2]

It is interesting to observe that Contzen's political theory
has a good deal of the tradition of the great Spanish Jesuits
of the sixteenth and early seventeenth centuries, of their conception of political liberty as protected by constitution and
law, his principles also coincide in a considerable measure
with those of Althusius; but, what is more important, he
represents the normal tradition of the Middle Ages, that
the prince should be under the control of the law, the law
which is the embodiment of the will not only of the prince
but of the whole commonwealth.

The second German work which we may consider is that
of Arumaeus and his pupils. He was, as I have said, a
professor in the University of Jena. In a work entitled *De
Jure Publico*, published in 1621, the nature of the government of the German Empire is discussed, and Bodin is
quoted as saying that in Germany the *iura Maiestatis* belong

[1] Ibid. i. 22. 1.
[2] Ibid. i. 24. 4, 5, 6, 7.

to the Diet, and not to the emperor, and that the Empire is
properly an aristocracy rather than a monarchy. Arumaeus
can only answer by saying that the same limitation extended
to other monarchies.[1]

In another passage of the same work the question is
discussed whether, and in what sense, the emperor may be
said to be *legibus solutus*. The Golden Bull of Charles IV,
he says, repeated the declaration of the 'Sachsenspiegel'
that legal cases against the emperor should be brought before
the Elector Palatine, and he was therefore in some sense
under the law; this was illustrated by the depositions of the
Emperors Adolf and Wenceslas. The emperor, he contends, is not free from the divine law, or from the law of
nature and of nations, or from the fundamental civil laws;
he is free from the *leges mere civiles*, but Arumaeus does not
actually define these. The relations of the king of France
to the *Parlement* of Paris are cited as being parallel.[2]

Another 'Discursus' again in the same work deals with
the importance and nature of the national assemblies in
various countries, and it is said dogmatically that these had
always existed, in different forms, in all kingdoms and
empires—in former times in Greece and Rome, to-day in
Spain, France, England, Poland, and other countries; and
the Diet in Germany is described as a 'Convention' of all the
Estates (Orders) of the Empire, summoned by the emperor,
with the consent of the electors, to deliberate in the presence
of the emperor or his commissioner, and to make decrees on
matters concerning the dignity, well-being, and tranquillity
of the commonwealth. It is added that there were also
special councils, which are attended only by the electors, to
consider such matters as the deposition of an emperor. The
other princes are not present at these, it was the electors
who deposed Adolf and Wenceslas.[3]

This is an interesting and important statement of constitutional principles, and it should be compared with the
closely parallel theory of the General Councils of the Empire
in Althusius. They are treated as normal institutions of

---

[1] Arumaeus, *De Jure Publico*, ed. 1621, Discursus I, pp. 6, 7.
[2] Ibid., Discursus VII, pp. 29–33.
[3] Ibid., Discursus IX, pp. 7–11.

political society, and as found in almost all European countries, and as dealing with all the more important concerns of public life.[1]

Our third illustration is drawn from a work of Puffendorf, which belongs to the second part of the seventeenth century. The original cause of the formation of political societies was, he thinks, the fear of the evils which men might inflict upon each other, a judgement which is similar to the Senecan and Patristic view that the coercive State was made necessary by man's sinful disposition, and corresponds with that of Hobbes. He differs, however, radically from Hobbes by asserting the existence and authority of the natural law, even in that state of nature which preceded organized society.[2]

Men found it necessary to create a society and a political authority, and in order to do this they found that not one but two contracts were necessary. The first contract was that by which individual men formed themselves into a society, and pledged themselves to obey the authority which the society should recognize. This is the same as that of Hobbes and Locke.[3] The second contract was that whose possibility Hobbes had so dogmatically denied, a contract with the person or persons to whom the government of the community was to be entrusted. By this contract the ruler is bound to take care of the common security and well-being, and the subjects should promise obedience to him. Puffendorf thinks indeed that in the case of democratic governments, this formal pledge and declaration may not seem so necessary, but when the government is aristocratic or monarchical, it is evidently necessary that the king or the nobles should be bound by the contract, as well as the subjects.[4]

Puffendorf then discusses the question why it was that Hobbes had denied the possibility of any contract between the prince and the citizens, and he thinks that Hobbes had been moved to do this by the recollection of the recent English revolt against the king, and the attempt to subject him to his people, and that Hobbes had therefore maintained

[1] Cf. Althusius, *Politica*, xvii, xxxiii, xxxviii.

[2] Puffendorf, *De Jure Naturali Gentium*, ed. 1704, vii. 1. 7, 8. (The first edition of the work was published in London, 1672.)

[3] Ibid. vii. 2. 7.   [4] Ibid. vii. 2. 8.

that the royal authority was absolute and unlimited. Puffen-dorf rejects this and expresses his own view by saying that when a man submits to a prince, he promises obedience, but reserves the right to defend himself.[1]

This is apparently quite plain, but in the next section Puffendorf guards this by saying that while the superior has the general right of enforcing the mutual contract, the subjects can only do this in three cases; that is, if the prince abdicates the care of the commonwealth; if he behaves with hostility to all his subjects; or if he is guilty of a manifest departure from the rules of government. (These exceptions are obviously analogous to those made by Barclay and Grotius.[2])

It would seem to be right to conclude that Puffendorf's position was clearly that the monarchy possessed a great and far-reaching authority, but also that he conceived of it as being limited by the nature of the contract upon which the relations of prince and subjects are founded.

When we turn to Leibniz we find him repudiating the principles of an absolute monarchy, and the contentions of Hobbes, even more emphatically. The arguments which he brings against Hobbes are at least as much founded on an appeal to the actual conditions of European society as on general or abstract considerations. No people in Europe, he says, was governed as Hobbes suggested. Hobbes indeed maintained that men had by nature the right to do anything which they conceived to be useful to them, that from this right there arose internecine wars, and that this made it necessary for men to make peace, and to give up the right of all men to all things. This, he had said, compelled men to surrender all their rights to a commonwealth, that is either to a monarchy, an aristocracy, or a republic. The civil power of the commonwealth represented all the individuals who formed it, and was one and single, and its authority could not be divided between different persons or groups. If, for example, one body possessed the power of legislature, another the power of raising taxes, the commonwealth would be dissolved.

---

[1] Puffendorf, *De Jure Naturali Gentium*, ed. 1704, vii. 2. 9.
[2] Ibid. vii. 2. 10.

Leibniz's comment on this is an appeal to common sense. The contention of Hobbes is, he says, extravagant, for he argued that nothing which may cause inconvenience is endurable, but that is wholly incompatible with the nature of human conditions.

Leibniz admits indeed that there are inconveniences in a division of the supreme power, and points to examples of this in the Polish and Dutch constitutions, but yet by the prudence and good sense of those who hold the superior authority the government is able to deal with public affairs satisfactorily. In the German Diet not all things are determined by the majority of votes, some decisions require unanimity. All this appeared to Hobbes and some others as mere anarchy, but these persons should observe that the same conditions held in England, Spain, and France.

It is particularly important to notice that Leibniz specially appeals to the older constitutional system of France, when, as he says, the Estates discussed in public assemblies the fundamental laws of the kingdom, and the limitations of the royal authority; and he points out that in half the Provinces of France, which are termed *Pays d'Estats*, such as Brittany and Burgundy, the king could not impose even now taxation till he had consulted the Estates, like the king in England. He points out that even in Turkey, where the sultan was held to be above all laws, the Sultan Ibrahim had been called to answer by the Chief Mullah before a sacred court, and when he refused, his subjects were released from their oath of fidelity.

Leibniz therefore considers that the system of authority defended by Hobbes existed nowhere, either among the more civilized people or among the barbarians, and would be neither possible nor desirable unless those who had the supreme authority were endued with angelic virtue. Men will normally judge it to be well to retain their own authority, and to provide for their own well-being as they think best. The political system of Hobbes would hold only in that commonwealth of which God is the king, for to him alone can we safely trust all things.[1]

[1] Leibniz, *Works*, ed. 1678, iv. 360.

VII

THE CONTINUITY OF THE CONCEPTION OF POLITICAL LIBERTY IN THE SEVENTEENTH CENTURY

ENGLAND

WE have so far been considering the history of political liberty in the seventeenth century in the literature of some of the countries of the European continent, and it will be evident that in spite of the progress of absolutism, the medieval conceptions of the supremacy of law and of the authority of the community had not been forgotten, even in France and Spain.

It is, however, true that it was only in England and Holland that the progress of absolute monarchy was arrested, and that a more normal development of the constitutional authority of the medieval monarchy took place; but this was not done without a conflict which resounded throughout Europe. It was therefore natural that it was in England that the political thought of the time found a larger and more important expression than elsewhere.

We must be careful to observe that the literature in which this was expressed had a twofold character, that the questions at issue were discussed sometimes under the terms of an appeal to history, sometimes under those of an appeal to general principles, which were thought of as necessarily underlying the whole system of rational political thinking. It is something of a misfortune that the two English works which are most familiar to those interested in political thought, that is Hobbes's *Leviathan* and Locke's *Second Treatise on Civil Government*, should be in the main concerned rather with the principles than with the historical traditions, for this has in some measure tended to mislead men as to the real character of the great debate.

We begin by taking note of some of the principles set out by Sir Edward Coke in his *Institutes of the Law of England*, published in 1628. We must bear in mind that when this work was published the great dispute upon the authority of the Crown and the liberties of Englishmen was in the main concerned with the question of the right of the Crown to imprison men indefinitely without trial, and the right to levy taxation, in some form, without the authority of Parliament.

With regard to the first question, Coke appealed directly to the famous 41st clause of Magna Carta, as reissued by Henry III in 1225,[1] and stated it in the following terms: 'No man shall be taken (that is restrained of liberty) by petition or suggestion to the King, or to his Council, unless it be by indictment or presentation of good and lawful men.'[2]

It is hardly necessary to insist upon the importance of this principle. As we have seen in a previous chapter, even in France men had not forgotten it in the seventeenth century, and in England and Spain it was the most important practical form of the supremacy of law over the merely arbitrary will of the prince.

This was the first form of political liberty which was asserted by Coke, but the second was not less important. Again Coke appealed to history, to the Great Charter and to the 'Confirmatio Chartarum' of 1297. 'And herewith agreeeth the Act of Parliament commonly called "Confirmatio Chartarum", (which is but an expansion of the heads of Magna Carta) where it is enacted that for no occasion any aids, tailes, or takings shall be taken by the King or his heirs, but by the common consent of the Realms, saving the ancient aids and takings due and accustomed.'[3] And in commenting on the 'Confirmatio Chartarum' he says, 'thereby it is enacted that every aid and taile and other taking must have two special properties, the one in the creation, that it must be given by the common consent of the whole Realm in Parliament, the other in its execution, viz: that it be given and impledged for the common benefit of the whole Realm, and not for private or other respects'.[4]

We should also take notice of Coke's statement of the

---

[1] Clause 39 in 1215.
[2] Edward Coke, *Institutes*, &c., ed. 1671, Part II, Magna Carta, 29.
[3] Ibid., 30.   [4] Ibid., Part II, 'Confirmatio Chartarum', 6.

independence and supreme authority of Parliament, even as related to the Courts of Law.

'It is', he says, ' "lex et consuetudo Parliamenti", that all weighty matters in any Parliament, moved among Peers of the Realm, or Commons in Parliament assembled, ought to be determined, adjusted and decided by the course of Parliament and not by the Civil Laws, nor yet by the Common Laws of the Realm used in more inferior Courts; which was so declared to be "Secundum legem et consuetudinem Parliamenti", concerning the Peers of the Realm, by the King and all the Lords Spiritual and Temporal; and the like "pari ratione" is for the Commons for anything made or done in the House of Commons; and the rather for that by another law and custom of Parliament, the King cannot take notice of any thing moved or done in the House of Commons, but by report of the House of Commons: and every member of Parliament hath a judicial place, and can be no witnesse. And this is the reason that Judges ought not to give any opinion of a matter of Parliament, because it is not to be decided by the Common Laws, but "secundum legem et consuetudinem Parliamenti".'[1]

A little later Coke adds: 'Of the power and jurisdiction of the Parliament, for making of laws proceeding by Bill, it is so transcendent and absolute, as it cannot be confined either for causes or persons within any bounds.'[2] Coke adds indeed that he considered the process of attainder of a man unheard by Parliament to be evil, but it could not be questioned in law. These assertions of the freedom and supreme authority of Parliament are specially important as coming from a great jurist.

It may be thought that there is a great gulf between the work of Coke and that of William Prynne, whose treatise, *The Sovereign Power of Parliament and Kingdom*, was published in 1643; and indeed much had happened in the years between 1628 and 1643, and there is a great difference between the precise and careful arguments of Coke and the large and sweeping statements of Prynne. It is, however, important to observe that Prynne was developing, if somewhat recklessly, the same appeal to historical tradition as Coke, and he was a man of considerable, if somewhat

[1] Edward Coke, *Institutes*, &c., ed. 1671, Part IV, cap. 1, p. 15.
[2] Ibid., 36.

indiscriminate, learning, not only in English history but in that of Europe.

Prynne begins by asserting the principle that Parliament had possessed, even in 'Popish' times, an authority greater in some respects than that of the king, and he cites the words of the interpolater of Bracton, and of *Fleta*, that the king had three superiors, God, the Law, and his Court (*Curia*), that is the counts and barons, who were to restrain the king's power by the bridle of the law.[1] He seems to have been acquainted not only with Bracton and *Fleta*, but also with the *Mirror of Justices* and the *Modus Tenendi Parliamentum*, with Fortescue and Sir Thomas Smith.[2] He points out the coercion of English kings like John and Henry III by force, and the depositions of Edward II and Richard II, and of many Saxon kings,[3] and draws attention to the fact that strict hereditary succession by primogeniture was not recognized under the Norman and early Plantagenet kings.[4] He brings forward examples of meetings of Parliament summoned by the counts and barons without the king, and cites parallels from Aragon and the German Empire, and the analogous meetings of Church Councils without the Pope.[5] Parliament, he maintains, is the 'highest Sovereign power over all other, even above the King himself, for the King is only a part of Parliament, and the least, because but one person'.[6] Parliament is supreme, it is above the law, for it can abrogate and alter the law, while the king is under the law.[7]

In the second part of the work Prynne is concerned to establish the right of Parliament to demand the removal and punishment of the king's officers. The third part sets out a justification of the war against Charles, as being defensive, and a somewhat long-winded refutation of the arguments for the 'Divine Right'.

In an appendix Prynne brought together a collection of passages from various historical and other writers to show that in ancient and modern times the supreme power resided

[1] W. Prynne, *The Sovereign Power of Parliament and Kingdom*, ed. 1643, i. 5. Cf. Bracton, *De Legibus*, ii. 16. 3; *Fleta*, i. 17. 9.

[2] Prynne, *The Sovereign Power*, &c., vi. 36–9.

[3] Ibid. v. 19–31; ii. 7.   [4] Ibid. II. 9.

[5] Ibid. iii. 9–15.   [6] Ibid. vi. 33, 41–4.

[7] Ibid. vi. 45–50.

and still resides, not in kings, but in senates, parliaments, and people. He refers to Rome, Greece, the Empire, ancient and medieval, France, Spain, Portugal, Hungary, Bohemia, Poland, Denmark, Sweden, and Scotland. And he sums up, as the conclusions from this: (1) All royal authority is derived from the people. (2) The assemblies of the various nations are superior to their kings. (3) Kings are subject to the laws of the kingdoms. (4) Kings cannot make laws, or impose taxes without the consent of the people and the Parliament. (5) Kings are bound by their Coronation oaths. And, very felicitously, he concludes by referring to the doctrine of St. Thomas Aquinas that resistance to an unjust authority is not sedition.[1]

Prynne's statements and arguments are large and sweeping, and their historical accuracy may in some cases be reasonably criticized, but it must, I think, be clear to any serious student of medieval political institutions and theory that his general contentions are much nearer the truth than those of the defenders of absolute monarchy. Perhaps the best confirmation of this may be found in the reluctant admission by Bodin in the sixteenth century that it was difficult to find an absolute monarchy in Europe, except, as he contended, in France.[2]

At any rate, it is very important to make clear to ourselves that those writers who in the seventeenth century defended political liberty, did this, not only on general and abstract principles, but by the appeal to history.

We come to a great and majestic figure among the defenders of political liberty, that is to Milton. He turned aside for many years from the great 'task' of his life to another which some foolish people have thought unworthy of his high power. It was not indeed thus that Milton thought of his services to the cause of what seemed to him the freedom of his country. To apply his own words: 'I cannot praise a fugitive and cloistered virtue unexercised and unbreathed, that never sallies out and sees his adversaries, but slinks out of the race where that immortal Garland is

[1] St. Thomas Aquinas, *Summa Theologica*, 2. 2. 42. 2.
[2] Cf. p. 29.

to be run for, not without dust and heat.'[1] He could not stand by indifferent and inactive when he saw 'a noble and puissant nation rousing herself like a strong man after sleep, and shaking her invincible locks; methinks I see her as an eagle shewing her mighty youth, and kindling her undazzled eyes at the full midday beam'.[2]

We are here concerned especially with the work entitled *The Tenure of Kings and Magistrates*, which was published in February 1649, and was related to the trial of Charles I which was then impending. This work seems to me indeed that which most completely represents Milton's political principles, and expresses them most profoundly.

In this treatise the question of political freedom is dealt with primarily, not on the grounds of historical precedent, but on the general principles of human nature and society. Milton begins with a statement of the origin of political society which is clearly related to the tradition of Seneca, the Christian Fathers, and the Roman jurists, rather than to that of Aristotle.

'No man,' he says, 'who knows aught, can be so stupid as to deny, that all men were born free . . . and that they lived so till from the root of Adam's transgression, falling among themselves to do wrong and violence, and foreseeing that such courses must needs tend to the destruction of them all, they agreed by common league to bind each other from mutual injury, and jointly to defend themselves against any that gave disturbance or opposition to such agreement. Hence came cities, towns and commonwealths. And because no faith in all was sufficiently binding, they saw it needful to ordain some authority that might restrain by fear and punishment what was violated against peace and common right.'[3]

To Milton, as to the medieval writers in general, political society represented, not so much, as to Aristotle and St. Thomas Aquinas, the method of perfection of human life, but a necessity imposed upon men by their own vices and crimes. It was from the Stoics, the Roman lawyers, and the Christian Fathers that Milton had learned his contempt for those who did not understand that men were born free, and

[1] Milton, *Areopagitica*, *Prose Works*, ed. Bohn, ii, p. 68.
[2] Ibid., p. 94.
[3] Milton, *Tenure of Kings and Magistrates*, *Works*, ed. Bohn, ii, p. 8.

had not learned to look upon slavery as being contrary to the proper quality of man's nature. Political society could only be conceived of as resting upon the free association of men with each other.

This was to Milton the origin of political society, for political authority was derived from the community. To him, as to George Buchanan and Hooker, it seemed that men might at first have been satisfied to appoint one man, or some men, as rulers, on account of their wisdom and integrity, 'not to be their lords and masters . . . but to be their deputies and commissioners, to execute, by virtue of their entrusted powers, that justice, which else every man by the bond of nature and of covenant must have executed for himself, and for one another.'[1] But again, like Buchanan and Hooker, Milton contends that they soon found this to be intolerable, on account of the failings and vices of their rulers, and were thus driven to 'invent laws, either framed or consented to by all, that should confirm and limit the authority of whom they chose to govern them: that so men, of whose failing they had proof, might no more rule over them, but law and reason, abstracted as much as might be from personal errors and frailties. . . . "While, as the magistrate was set above the people, so the law was set above the magistrate".'[2] Milton was stating no new doctrine, but restating the first principle of medieval society, that it is the law, and not the king, which is supreme.

This is then related by Milton to the principle that the authority of the ruler is determined and limited by a contract between him and the community:

'When this would not serve, but the law was either not exercised, or misapplied, they were constrained from that time, the only remedy left them, to put conditions and take oaths from all kings and magistrates at their first instalment, to do impartial justice by law; who upon those terms and no others, received allegiance from the people, that is to say, bond or covenant to obey them in execution of those laws, which they, the people, had themselves made or consented to. And this oftimes with express warning, that if the king or magistrate proved unfaithful to his trust, the people would be disengaged.'[3]

[1] Milton, *Tenure of Kings and Magistrates*, *Works*, ed. Bohn, ii. 9.
[2] Ibid., *Works*, ii. 10.   [3] Ibid., *Works*, ii. 10, 11.

This conception of a contract between the king and the community was not in any sense new. It can be traced far back in the Middle Ages, it was embodied in the mutual oaths of king and people in the coronation ceremonies, and it had been restated by many of the political writers of the sixteenth century, not least by so careful and moderate a man as Hooker. The contractual principle was indeed the foundation of the whole feudal system.

The principle of the limitation of the authority of the king or prince was indeed the foundation of all the constitutional law of the Middle Ages; and it is interesting to observe that Milton appeals to the authority of Claude de Seyssel's *Grant Monarchie de France*, a very important work of the early sixteenth century. 'Therefore saith Claudius a Sesell, French statesman, "The Parliament was set as a bridle to the King;" which I instance rather, not because in England lawyers have not said the same long before, but because the French Monarch is granted by all to be a far more absolute one than ours.'[1]

The authority of the king is then derived from the community, and is held by him subject to a covenant or contract to obey the laws which the community has made, and Milton does not hesitate to draw the conclusion that this authority may be forfeited for sufficient reason.

'It being thus manifest, that the power of kings and magistrates is nothing but what is only derivative, transferred, and committed to them in trust from the people, to the common good of them all, in whom the power yet remains fundamentally, and cannot be taken from them, without a violation of their natural birthright; and seeing that from hence Aristotle and the best of political writers, have defined a king, "him who governs to the good and profit of his people, and not for his own ends", it follows from necessary causes, that the title of sovereign lord, natural lord, and the like, are either arrogancies or flatteries, not admitted by emperors and kings of the best note, and disliked by the church both of Jews and ancient Christians, as appears by Tertullian and others. . . . Secondly, that to say, as is usual, the king hath as good right to his crown and dignity as any man to his inheritance, is to make the subject no better than the king's slave, his chattel, or his possession that may be bought and sold. . . . But, suppose it to be right hereditary, what can be more just and legal, if a subject

[1] Ibid. ii. 11.

for certain crimes be to forfeit by law from himself and posterity all his inheritance to the king, than that a king for crimes proportional, should forfeit all his title and inheritance to the people. . . . Thirdly, it follows that to say kings are accountable to none but God, is the overturning of all law and government. For, if they may refuse to give account, then all covenants made with them at coronation, all oaths, are in vain and mere mockeries; all laws which they swear to keep, made to no purpose; for, if the king fear not God (as how many of them do not), we hold then our lives and estates by the tenure of his mere grace and mercy, as from a God, not a mortal magistrate; a position that none but court parasites or men besotted would maintain. Aristotle therefore, who we commonly allow for one of the best interpreters of nature and morality, writes in the fourth of his Politics, Chap. X, "that monarchy unaccountable is the worst sort of tyranny, and least of all to be endured by freeborn men".'[1]

A little later Milton turns again to the subject of the supposed Divine and 'unaccountable' authority of the prince;

' "There is no power but of God", saith Paul (Romans xiii. 1), as much as to say, God put it into man's heart to find out this way at first for common peace and preservation, approving the exercise thereof; else it contradicts Peter, who calls the same authority, an ordinance of Man (1 Peter ii. 13). . . . Therefore St. Paul in the forecited chapter tells us, that such magistrates he means, as are not a terror to the good, but to the evil; such as bear not the sword in vain, but to punish offenders, and to encourage the good.'[2]

He concludes the general argument:

'Thus far hath been considered chiefly the power of kings and magistrates, how it was and is originally the people's; and by them conferred in trust only to be employed to the common peace and benefit; with liberty therefore and right remaining in them, to re-assume it to themselves, if by kings and magistrates it be abused; or to dispose of it by any alteration, as they shall judge most conducing to the public good.'[3]

Milton had thus in the first part of the treatise set out his general principles of the origin and nature of political authority, and it is important to notice that these are in the main derived from the tradition of medieval political thinkers. The principle that all political authority is derived

[1] Ibid., *Works*, ed. ii. 11–13.   [2] Ibid., *Works*, ii. 16.
[3] Ibid., *Works*, ii. 17.

from the community itself; the principle that it is the law of the community which is supreme, and not the ruler; the principle that the ruler holds his authority in virtue of the contract to obey the laws, and that if he violated this contract the community might resume the authority which it had entrusted to him; these were not new and revolutionary conceptions, but rather represented the continuity of the normal principles of the political theory of the Middle Ages.

The later part of the Treatise is more directly addressed to the question what it was right and expedient that the English people should do under the circumstances of that time; and he turns, though a little contemptuously, to examine some of the historical precedents and some of the more or less contemporary experience of Europe.

'We may', he says, 'from hence with more ease and force of argument determine what a tyrant is, and what the people may do against him. . . . Against whom what the people lawfully may do, as against a common pest and destroyer of mankind, I suppose no man of clear judgment need go further to be guided than by the very principle of nature in him. But because it is the vulgar folly of men to desert their own reason, and shutting their eyes to think they see best with other men's, I shall show, by such examples as ought to have weight with us, what hath been done in this case heretofore.'[1]

He appeals first to the Greeks and Romans who, 'as their prime authors witness, held it not only lawful, but a glorious and heroic deed, rewarded publicly with statues and garlands, to kill an infamous tyrant at any time, without trial',[2] but he turns from these, lest it should be objected that they were only heathen, to Holy Scripture, and appeals, though rather meagrely, to the Middle Ages; the only important reference being to the trial and deposition of Richard II.[3]

It is different with the treatment of recent events in Europe. 'In the year 1546,' he says, 'the Duke of Saxony, the Landgrave of Hesse, and the whole Protestant League, raised open war against Charles the Fifth, the Emperor, sent him a defiance, renounced all faith and allegiance toward him, and debated long in council whether they should give

[1] Ibid., *Works*, ii. 17, 18.   [2] Ibid., *Works*, ii. 18.
[3] Ibid., *Works*, ii. 18–24.

him so much as the title of Caesar.'[1] His most important examples are, however, taken from Scotland and the Netherlands, the first being specially important to Milton on account of the actual attitude of the Presbyterians, especially in Scotland. He cites the terms of the important debate between John Knox and Maitland of Lethington, in which, as Milton says, Knox had maintained 'that subjects might and ought to execute God's judgment upon their king . . . that kings, if they offend, have no privilege to be exempted from the punishment of law more than any other subject.'[2] And again he cites from George Buchanan the report of a declaration made by the Scottish Commissioners to Elizabeth, justifying the deposition of queen Mary. 'They had used towards her more lenity than she deserved . . . that the Scots were a free nation, made kings whom they freely chose, and with the same freedom unkinged them if they saw cause, by right of ancient laws and ceremonies yet remaining . . . all which, with many other arguments bare witness that royal power was nothing but a mutual stipulation between king and people.'[3]

With regard to the Netherlands Milton says: 'In the year 1581 the States of Holland, in a general assembly at the Hague, abjured all obedience and subjection to Philip king of Spain, and in a declaration justify their so doing; for that by his tyrannical government, against faith so many times given and taken, he had lost the right to all the Belgic provinces; that therefore they deposed him and declared it lawful to choose another in his stead.'[4]

It is not necessary to deal with other parts of this Treatise; they are concerned with particular details of the contemporary controversies, and we may therefore conclude with a passage, which sets out his practical conclusion in terms, drastic indeed, but intelligible and eloquent.

'And surely they that shall boast, as we do, to be a free nation, and not have in themselves the power to remove or to abolish any governor supreme or subordinate, with the government itself upon urgent causes, may please their fancy with a ridiculous and painted freedom, fit to cozen babies; but we are indeed under tyranny and servitude, as

[1] Ibid., *Works*, ed. Bohn, ii. 34.   [2] Ibid., *Works*, ii. 25, 26.
[3] Ibid., *Works*, ii. 26.   [4] Ibid., *Works*, ii. 27.

wanting that power, which is the root and source of all liberty, to dispose and economize in the land which God hath given them as masters of familys in their own house and free inheritance. Without which natural and essential power of a free nation, though bearing high their heads, they can in due esteem be thought no better than slaves and vassals born, in the tenure and occupation of another inheriting lord; whose government, though not illegal, or intolerable, hangs over them as a lordly scourge, not as a free government; and therefore to be abrogated.

How much more justly then may they fling off tyranny, or tyrants; who being once deposed can be no more than private men, as subject to the reach of justice and arraignment as any other transgressors! And certainly if men, not to speak of heathen, but wise and religious, have done open justice upon tyrants what way they could soonest, how much more mild and humane then is it, to give them fair and open trial; to teach lawless kings, and all who so much adore them, that not mortal man or his imperious will, but justice, is the only true sovereign and supreme majesty upon earth! Let men cease therefore out of faction and hypocrisy, to make outcries and hard things of things so just and honourable. Though perhaps till now, no protestant state or kingdom can be alleged to have openly put to death their King, which lately some have written, and imputed to their great glory; much mistaking the matter. It is not, neither ought to be the glory of a protestant state never to have put their king to death; it is the glory of a protestant king never to have deserved death. And if the parliament and military council do what they do without precedent, if it appear their duty, it argues the more wisdom and magnanimity, that they know themselves able to be a precedent to others; who perhaps in future ages, if they prove not too degenerate, will look up with honour, and aspire toward the exemplary and matchless deeds of their ancestors, as to the highest top of their civil glory and emulation; which heretofore, in the pursuance of fame and foreign dominion, spent itself vaingloriously abroad; but henceforth may learn a better fortitude, to dare execute highest justice on them that shall by force of arms endeavour the oppressing and bereaving of religion and their liberty at home. That no unbridled potentate or tyrant, but to his sorrow, for the future may pursue such high and irresponsible license over mankind, to havoc and turn upside down whole kingdoms of men, as though they were no more in respect of his perverse will than a nation of pismires.'[1]

Milton wrote his *Tenure of Kings and Magistrates* at the moment when the revolt against what he conceived to be a tyrannical misgovernment of England had reached its

[1] Ibid., *Works*, ii. 33, 34.

highest point. Algernon Sidney wrote his *Discourse concerning Government* at the time when the reaction against Milton's conceptions was at its highest.

Sidney's work was formally a reply to Filmer's *Patriarcha*, which, though written much earlier in the century, was only published in 1680. Sidney's *Discourse* was written before 1683, when he was executed, but was not published till 1698. The work, however, makes only occasional reference to Filmer's absurd work, and ranges over the whole field of the conflict between the theory of absolute monarchy and that of political liberty.

After some introductory observations, Sidney begins by saying that the common judgement, both among Catholics and Protestants, was 'That man is naturally free, that he cannot be justly deprived of his liberty without cause, and that he doth not resign it, nor any part of it, unless it be in consideration of a greater good which he proposes to himself'.[1] What he meant by this is clear when we observe that a little later he points out that man cannot 'enter into society without resigning it (liberty) for the choice of that society, and the liberty of forming it according to our own wits, for our own good, is all we seek'.[2] And again, in a later passage, 'He is a free man who lives as best pleases himself, under laws made by his own consent.'[3] Sidney frankly recognizes that the relation of men to society necessarily involved a certain restriction of individual liberty.

We should put beside this his treatment of justice and its relation to political order and to law. Filmer, he says, might have urged that, to give power to the community to abrogate the authority which it had created, might cause a disturbance of the public peace, but he ought to have known that: 'There can be no Peace when there is no Justice, nor any Justice if the Government instituted for the good of the nation be turned to its ruin.'[4]

And, in another place:

'[We shall find] that to be Law, which being as I have said "sancta ratio", must be founded upon that eternal principle of Reason and

[1] Algernon Sidney, *Discourse concerning Government*, ed. 1698, chap. i, sect. 2.   [2] Ibid. i. 10.
    [3] Ibid. iii. 21.   [4] Ibid. i. 6.

Truth, from which the rule of Justice which is sacred and pure ought to be deduced, and not from the depraved will of men which fluctuates according to the different Humours and Passions that at several times reign in several nations, one day abrogating what had been enacted the other.'[1]

The law is not that which the arbitrary will of men may command, but it must conform to the 'eternal principles of Reason and Truth'.

It is under the terms of such judgements that we must understand an important passage in the *Discourse*, which, taken by itself, might seem to mean that Sidney thought that the authority of the community was unlimited.

'If it be objected,' he says, 'that I am a defender of arbitrary Power, I confess I cannot comprehend that any Society can be established without this, for the establishment of Government is an arbitrary act, wholly depending upon the will of men. . . . The authority that judges of the circumstances is arbitrary, and the Legislators show themselves to be more or less wise and good, as they do rightly or not consider this power. The difference between ill and good government is not, that those of one sort have an arbitrary Power which the others have not, for they all have it, but that those which are well constituted, place the Power so as it may be beneficial to the people, and set such rulers as are hardly to be transgressors; whilst those of the other sort fail in one or both of these points. . . . But I think that I may justly say that an Arbitrary Power was never well placed in any men or their successors who were not obliged to obey the Laws they should make.'[2]

If law is then founded upon reason and truth, it has authority over all men and all rulers, and Sidney is naturally indignant at the audacity of Filmer in citing Bracton for the authority of the king, while he omits Bracton's famous words that the king is under God and the law.[3] Sidney also cites the passage of Sir John Fortescue in the *De Laudibus Legum Angliae*, in which he says that the judges in England swore that they would administer justice indifferently to all men, even if the king by his letters should command the contrary.'[4]

Sidney's conception of the source of political authority is

[1] Ibid. iii. 11.   [2] Ibid. iii. 45.
[3] Ibid. iii. 9. (Cf. Bracton, *De Legibus*, i. 8. 5.)
[4] Ibid. iii. 14. (Cf. Fortescue, *De Laudibus Legum Angliae*, 51.)

well illustrated in two other important passages. In one place he says: "Tis hard to comprehend how one man came to be a master of men, unless it be by Consent, or by Fear. If by consent, we are at the end of our controversy. Governments and the Magistrates who execute them are created by men.[1]' In another place he appeals to Hooker, who had said that fathers have indeed a supreme authority over their families: 'Howbeit over a whole grand multitude having no such dependence upon anyone . . . impossible is it that any one should have complete lawful power, but by consent of men, or immediate appointment of God.'[2]

Governments then are created by the community, and Sidney follows Hooker in thinking that men had been content at first to put this authority in the hands of one man, but, finding that this led to grave mischief, they turned to laws, 'to live by one man's will became all men's misery, this constrained them to come unto laws, wherein all men might see their duties beforehand, and know the penalties of transgressing them. . . . Laws therefore they are not which public approbation hath not made so'.[3] The law then derives its authority from the community, and Sidney in another place declared that, 'To this end a Law is set as a rule to him (the monarch), and the best men, that is such as are most like to himself, made to be his assistants; because say they: "Lex est mens sine affectu et quasi Deus", whereas the best of men have their affections and passions, and are subject to be misled by them.'[4]

Again, he points out that Aristotle's conception of an unrestricted monarchy as a good government was only intended by him to apply to cases where some one man was incomparably wiser and better than the other members of the community; but he himself thinks that normally the best government would be 'mixed', that is composed of monarchy, aristocracy, and democracy, and he appeals to the history of Greece, Rome, Germany, and all the northern countries; and, like St. Thomas Aquinas, he thinks that it

[1] Ibid. i. 11.
[2] Ibid. ii. 6. (Cf. Hooker, *Eccl. Polity*, i. 10. 4.)
[3] Ibid. ii. 6. (Cf. Hooker, *Eccl. Polity*, i. 10. 5 and 8.)
[4] Ibid. ii. 30.

was a government of this kind which was given to the Israelites by Moses.[1]

Sidney, it should be observed, was not friendly to democracy in the strict sense.

'As to popular government in the strictest sense (that is pure Democracy, when the People in themselves, and by themselves, perform all that belongs to Government), I know no such thing, and, if it be in the world, have nothing to say for it. . . . If it be said that those Governments in which the Democratical part govern most, do most frequently err in the choice of men, in the means of preserving that purity of manners which is required for the wellbeing of a People, than that wherein Aristocracy prevails, I confess it, and that in Rome and Greece the best and wisest men did for the most part incline to Aristocracy.'[2]

To return to the condition on which a tolerable monarchy can exist; its authority proceeds from the community, and is limited by the law of the community; and Sidney, like Milton, conceives of the relation between the community and the ruler as finding its form in a contract:

'If any doubt do therefore arise, I hope to remove this, premising in the first place that several nations have plainly and explicitly made contracts with the Magistrate. 2. That they are implicit and to be understood, when they are not plainly expressed. 3. That they are not dreams but real things and perpetual obligations. 4. That Judges are in many places appointed to decide the contest arising from the breach of the contract.'

(Sidney refers to Roman history and the Old Testament, but the chapter is unfinished, and I should conjecture that he may have had some knowledge of the position of the Count Palatine in the medieval empire, and of the Justiza in Aragon.)[3]

In another place Sidney appeals to the history of Europe as confirming his judgement that:

'The practise of most nations has been as directly contrary to the absolute power of one man over their Constitutions. . . . Aristotle seems to think that the first monarchs, having been chosen for their virtue, were little restrained in the exercise of their power, but that they or their children, falling into Corruption and Pride, grew odious; and that

[1] Ibid. ii. 16 and 9.   [2] Ibid. ii. 19.
[3] Ibid. ii. 32.

Nations did on that account either abolish their authority or create
Senators and other Magistrates, who having part of their power might
keep them in order (He refers to the Spartan Ephors). . . . The Germans who pretended to be derived from the Spartans, had the like
Government. Their Princes, according to their merit, had the power
of persuading, not the power of commanding. . . . Whoever under-
stands the affairs of Germany knows that the present Emperors, notwithstanding their lawful title, have a power limited as in the days of
Tacitus. If they are good and wise, they may persuade, but they can
command no further than the Law allows. . . . All the kingdoms
peopled from the North observe the same rule. In all of these the
powers were divided between the Kings, the Nobility, Clergy and
Commons; and by the decrees of Councils, Diets, Parliaments, Cortes
and Assemblies of Estates, Authority and Liberty were so balanced, that
such Princes as assumed to themselves more than the Law did permit
were severely punished.'[1]

Sidney was indeed aware that, at least in France, things
had somewhat changed, and attributes the change to Louis
XI, like those French writers who have been cited in earlier
chapters, but he maintains that even in France the change
was not complete, and refers to the meetings of the States
General in the latter part of the sixteenth century; and he
cites a Treatise published, as he thinks, with the authority
of the king of France in 1667, in which it was said that kings
are under the happy inability to do anything against the
laws of their country.[2]

With regard to England he is clear and dogmatic: 'As
soon as the Saxons came into this country they had their
Micklegemots, which are general assemblies of the Nobles
and Freemen',[3] and 'The coercive power of the Law proceeds from the authority of Parliament', and he contradicts
the statement of James I in his *True Law of Free Monarchies*.[4]

We may conclude with some passages in which Sidney
defends the right of resistance to misgovernment:

'If the Laws of God and of men are therefore of no effect, when the
Magistracy is left at liberty to break them, and if the hosts of those who
are too strong for the tribunals of Justice cannot be otherwise restrained than by Sedition, Tumults, and War, then Sedition, Tumults
and Wars are justified by the Laws of God and of Man. . . . When he

[1] Ibid. 11. 30.   [2] Ibid. ii. 30.
[3] Ibid. iii. 28.   [4] Ibid. iii. 46. Cf. p. 32.

or they, which are rightly called, do assume a power . . . that the Law does not give, or greater than that which the Law does give, to an end different and contrary to that which is intended by it. . . . The same course is justly used against a legal magistrate who takes upon him . . . to exercise a power that the Law does not give. . . .

'Those who delight in cavils may ask, who shall be the Judge of the occasion? And, whether I intend to give the People the decision of their own case? To which I answer that when the Contract is between the Magistrate and the People, the party to which the determination is referred must be the Judge of his own case, and the question is only, whether the Magistrate should depend upon the judgment of the People, or the People on that of the Magistrate. . . . They must either be suffered to continue in the free exercise of their rage, that is, to do all the mischief they design, or must be restrained by a legal, judicial, or extrajudicial way, and they who disallow the extrajudicial, do as little like the judicial. They will not hear of bringing a supreme Magistrate before a Tribunal, when it may be done. They will, says our author (Filmer), depose the King. Why should they not be deposed, if they become enemies to the People, and set up an interest in their own persons inconsistent with the publick good, for the preservation of which they were created? . . . There must therefore be a right of proceeding judicially or extrajudicially against all persons who transgress the Law.'[1]

A little farther on Sidney illustrates the view that civil wars and tumults are not the greatest evil that can befall a nation, from the history of Greece and Italy.[2] And, in another place, he says: 'The whole body of a nation cannot be tied to any other obedience than is consistent with the Common Good, according to their judgment,' and again: 'The Rights therefore of kings are not grounded upon conquest; the Liberties of Nations do not arise from grants of their Princes, the Oath of Allegiance binds no private man to more than the Law directs, and has no influence upon the whole body of every nation.'[3]

It may be complained that I have imposed upon Sidney's work a more systematic development of his argument for political liberty than belongs to it, but I do not think that there is much importance in such a criticism. If the actual order of presentation of his subject is not always very clear, it must be remembered that the work, as we have it, is

[1] Ibid. ii. 24.   [2] Ibid. ii. 26.   [3] Ibid. iii. 36.

obviously, in some places at least, unfinished. The substance
of the work is clear and coherent; and represents not merely
a passionate indignation, but the tradition of medieval
Europe.

The original or natural liberty of man was the doctrine
of the Stoics, the jurists, and the Christian Fathers. The
principle that political authority is derived from the community came down from the Roman law, the tradition of
the Middle Ages, from St. Thomas Aquinas, and from
Hooker.

The theory that a mixed government is better than the
simple forms of monarchy, aristocracy, or democracy had a
respectable descent from Aristotle and St. Thomas Aquinas.
The conception of a contract between the community and
the prince was related to the mutual oaths of the Coronation
Ceremony of medieval kingdoms, and had the sanction of
the great authority of Hooker. And it is to the actual historical tradition of medieval Europe that Sidney appeals
when he says, 'The practise of most nations . . . has been
directly contrary to the absolute authority of one man in
their constitutions', and says that in all these states 'political
authority was divided between the King, the Nobility,
Clergy, and Commons'.

There is a great contrast between the political writings of
Milton and Sidney, and those of Lord Halifax, who wrote
his famous work, *The Character of a Trimmer*, probably in
1684–5, though it was only published in 1695. The temper
of Halifax was indeed as different from that of Milton or
Sidney as his style; he had nothing of the indignant and
majestic eloquence of Milton, nor the elaborate theory and
argument of Sidney; his style and manner were comparatively cool and restrained. And yet, perhaps just for that
reason, he may be thought to represent more nearly that
normal temper of the average Englishman which found its
expression in the Revolution of 1688, and the expulsion of
the Stuarts from the English throne.

It is, perhaps, a dangerous thing to suggest that Halifax's
political thought can be reduced to a systematic form, but,
whether he would have approved or not, it will be convenient

for us if we consider his political conceptions under five terms: the supremacy of law, the love of liberty, the excellence of the English constitution, the value of a representative element in that constitution, and his dislike and contempt for such an absolute monarchy as that of France.

It is indeed very significant that Halifax should begin his most important work, *The Character of a Trimmer*, by affirming his profound veneration for the laws, and his conviction that the laws are ultimately derived not from the caprice of men, but from Nature itself:

'He' (that is a Trimmer) 'looketh upon them (the Laws) as the chains that tye up our unruly passions, which else, like wild beasts let loose, would reduce the world into its first state of barbarism and hostility; the good things we enjoy, we owe to them; and all the ill things we are freed from is by their protection. . . . All Laws flow from that of Nature, and where this is not the foundation, they may be legally imposed, but they will be lamely obeyed.'[1]

Whether Halifax was aware that he was following the tradition of the Middle Ages when he thus found in the law that power which had brought man into the civilized life, and when he thus dogmatically laid down that all these laws are derived from Nature, I do not know, but this was obviously the real origin of his conceptions.

Again, a few years later, in his *Maxims of State*, he dealt with the relation of the ruler to the laws, and says 'That a Prince who falleth out with laws, breaketh with his best friends' and 'That the exalting of his own authority above his laws is like letting in an enemy to surprise his guards; the laws are the only guards he can be sure will never run away from him'; and again, 'A Prince that will say, he can do no good, except he may do everything, teacheth his people to say they are slaves, if they do not do whatsoever they have a mind to.'[2] Halifax was repeating in his own terms the medieval principle that the law is the supreme authority in political society and is above the prince himself.

We must not, however, misunderstand Halifax, for, while he had a great veneration for the law, he had also, in his own phrase, 'a passion for liberty'. 'Our Trimmer owneth a

[1] Halifax, *The Character of a Trimmer*, *Works*, ed. 1912, p. 50.
[2] Ibid., *Maxims of State*, *Works*, p. 180.

passion for liberty, yet so restrained that it doth not in the least impair or taint his allegiance; he thinketh it hard for a soul that doth not love liberty ever to raise itself toward another world; he taketh it to be the foundation of all vertue, and the only seasoning that giveth a relish to life.'[1] And again, 'Our Trimmer admireth our blessed constitution, in which dominion and liberty are so well blended . . . the Crown hath power sufficient to protect our liberties, the People hath so much liberty as is necessary to make them useful to the Crown'.[2] And in the *Maxims of State* he says, 'That power and liberty are like heat and moisture, where they are well mixed, everything prospers, where they are single, they are destructive.'[3]

It was in the Constitution of England that Halifax found the best form of government, at least for the English people. Dealing with the dispute about the respective merits of monarchy and commonwealth he says:

'We in England, by a happy use of this controversy, conclude them both in the wrong, and reject them from being our pattern, not taking the words in the utmost extent, which is Monarchy, a thing which leaveth men no liberty, and a Commonwealth, such as alloweth them no quiet. We think that a wise mean between these barbarous extremes is that which self preservation ought to dictate to our wishes; and, we may say we have attained to this mean in a greater measure than any nation now in being, or perhaps any we have read of, though never so celebrated for the wisdom or felicity of their constitutions. We take from one the too great power of doing hurt, and yet leave enough to govern and protect us; we take from the other the confusion, the parity, the animosities and the licence, and yet reserve a due care of such a liberty as may consent with men's allegiance; but, it being hard, if not impossible, to be exactly even, our government hath now the strongest biass towards monarchy.'[4]

Halifax not only approved of the limitation of authority by laws, he maintained that no constitution could be satisfactory unless it embodied the consent and authority of the whole community.

'Our Trimmer is a friend to Parliaments, notwithstanding all their faults and excesses, which of late have given such matter of objection to

[1] Halifax, *The Character of a Trimmer, Works,* ed. 1912, p. 61.
[2] Id., *Trimmer, Works,* p. 62. [3] Id., *Maxims of State, Works,* p. 180.
[4] Id., *Trimmer, Works,* p. 53.

them. He thinketh that though they may at some times be trouble-some to authority, yet they add the greatest strength to it under a wise administration; he believeth no government is perfect except a kind of omnipotence reside in it, to exercise upon great occasions. Now this cannot be obtained by force alone upon people, let it be never so great, there must be their consent too, or else a nation moves only by being driven, a sluggish and constrained motion, void of that life and vigour which is necessary to produce great things, whereas the virtual consent of the whole being included in their representatives, and the King giving his sanction to the united sense of the people, every act done by such an authority, seemeth to be an effect of their choice, as well as a part of their duty. . . . And by the means of this political omnipotence, whatever sap or juice there is in a nation, may be to the last drop pro-duced, whilst it rises naturally from the root, whereas all power exercised without consent is like the giving of wounds and gashes, and tapping of a tree at unseasonable times, for the present occasion, which in a very little time must needs destroy it.'[1]

It should be observed that Halifax clearly thought that a government controlled by the consent of the community, as expressed through its representatives, is much more power-ful than one which embodied merely the will of the ruler; that it is only such a government which can possess an absolute authority. Indeed he is clear that it is only such a government which possesses that omnipotence which a political society requires. In a work, only published in 1750, he had restated this conception very emphatically.

'I lay down then as a fundamental, first that in every constitution there is some power which neither will nor ought to be bounded. . . . The laws under the protection of the King govern in the ordinary administration; the extraordinary power is in Acts of Parliament, from whence there can be no appeal but to the same power at another time. To say a power is supream and not arbitrary is not sense. . . . There is then no other fundamental but that every supream power must be arbitrary.'[2]

Halifax was restating the doctrine of Coke:

'Of the power and jurisdiction of the Parliament, for making of laws proceeding by Bill, it is so transcendent and absolute, as it cannot be confined either to courts or persons within any bounds.'[3]

[1] Id., *Trimmer, Works,* p. 621.
[2] Id., *Political and Miscellaneous Thoughts and Reflections, Works,* pp. 211, 213, 214.   [3] Cf. p. 112.

In a work published in 1694, entitled *A Rough Draft of a New Model at Sea*, he declared that:

'The forms of Government to which England must be subjected are, either Absolute Monarchy, a Commonwealth, or a mixed Monarchy as it is now; with those natural alterations that the exigency of affairs may from time to time suggest.

'As to absolute Monarchy I will not allow myself to be transported into such invectives as are generally made against it; neither am I ready to enter into the aggravated style of calling everything slavery that restraineth men in any part of their freedom ... (and he seems to think that an absolute monarchy makes a government in some sense more effective) I see and admire this; yet I consider at the same time that all things of this kind are comparative: that, as on one side, without Government men cannot enjoy what belongeth to them in particular, nor can a nation be secure or preserve itself in general: so, on the other side, the end of Government being that mankind should live in some competent state of freedom, it is very unnatural to have the end destroyed by the means that were originally made use of to attain it. . . . And, if it should be so that it is not possible for a State to be great and glorious except the subjects are wretchedly miserable, I am not ashamed to own my low-spirited frailty, in preferring such a model of Government as may agree with the reasonable enjoyment of a free people, before such a one by which empire is to be extended, at such an unnatural price. . . . If we would be measured by our acres, we are poor, inconsiderable people; we are exalted above our natural bounds by our good laws and our excellent constitution. . . . In my judgment therefore, there is such a short decision to be made upon this subject that, in relation to England, an Absolute Monarchy is as unreasonable a thing to be wished, as I hope it will be impossible to be attained.'[1]

We may conclude by observing that Halifax expressed in *The Character of a Trimmer* a supreme contempt for the absolute monarchy and its ruler, and he is clearly referring to France and Louis XIV.

'Whatever faults our Government may have . . . let any other be set against it, and then it showeth its comparative beauty. Let us look upon the most glittering outside of unbounded authority, and upon a nearer inquiry we shall find nothing but poor and miserable deformity within. Let us imagine a Prince living in his Kingdom as if in a great gally, his subjects tugging at the oar, laden with chains, and reduced to real rags, that they may gain him imaginary laurels. . . . A mistaken creature swelled with panegyrics and flattered out of his senses, and

[1] Halifax, *A Rough Draft of a New Model at Sea, Works*, pp. 171–3.

not only an incumbrance, but a nuisance to mankind. . . ., This picture laid in right colours would not incite men to wish for such a government, but rather to acknowledge the happiness of our own.'[1]

We have come to the period of the English Revolution, and to the well-known 'Second Treatise' of Locke on *Civil Government*, which to many people is the principal, if not the only vindication of that great event. It is unfortunate that many intelligent persons should regard it as an isolated and revolutionary work, and fail to understand that Locke's treatise is in the first place a restatement of the fundamental traditions of the political civilization of the Middle Ages. It has, indeed, long been noticed that Locke from time to time appeals to the authority of Hooker; and, indeed, he does so, and for good reasons; for the defence of the absolute monarchy was largely founded in theory upon the appeal to the doctrine of the Divine Right, and it was therefore especially, for that moment, and in England, important to show that Hooker's conception of political authority was very different. It is, however, rather lamentable that it should not be always clearly understood that Hooker was not stating a theory of political authority which was merely his own, but that he was in masterly fashion restating the great traditions of medieval political civilization; and that therefore Locke in appealing to Hooker was asserting the continuity of modern political civilization with the medieval. That is not to say that Locke's political theory coincides in all points with the medieval or the modern one. It would, indeed, be true to say that in some important points Locke represented that unhistorical mode of thought which in the Middle Ages was derived from the post-Aristotelian philosophers, through the Roman law and the Christian Fathers, and which only disappeared in the course of the eighteenth and nineteenth centuries under the influence of the historical movement. It is true that under the influence of Aristotle St. Thomas Aquinas had to some extent passed beyond the post-Aristotelian tradition, but in spite of his immense influence he had only superficially affected the thinkers of the later Middle Ages, and those of the sixteenth and seventeenth centuries.

[1] Id., *Trimmer, Works*, pp. 63, 64.

Locke still, formally at least, held to the tradition of a primitive State of Nature, which preceded the condition of the world as we know it.[1] Indeed Locke developed this theory in a different and more extreme form than his predecessors. 'But I', he says, 'affirm that all men are naturally in that state, and remain so, till, by their own consent, they make themselves the members of some political society.'[2] This is obviously an expression of that extravagant individualism which we find in some of the Stoics, and contradicts the rational and historical conception of Aristotle that men are by nature not only social but political beings; or, as we might say to-day, members of a political society of some form or another. This is what Aristotle meant when he said that political society exists 'by nature'; it is only in society, and even in a society which claims and exercises a coercive authority, that we grow towards that perfection which is true 'nature'. For in Aristotle the 'nature' of a thing is neither that which it was, nor that which it is, but that which it tends to become, that is its perfection. We shall return to this when we deal with Rousseau's *Contrat Social*.

So far Locke was restating a conception of a primitive State of Nature, as we have already seen it in Hobbes, and this goes back, not only to Hooker and Althusius, but to Seneca and the Fathers. Locke has to explain why men ever left this state of nature; for that they have left it, or do leave it, is plain. The primary reason for this was to Locke, as it was to the Stoics and Fathers, the actually vicious impulses and desires of men.[3] The doctrine that it is men's faults and vices which compel them to establish societies with a coercive power over their members was not, as some, or most, persons imagine, only a theological but a philosophical theory,[4] and though we may not accept the theory of a fall from a primitive state of innocence and happiness, we recognize that there are important elements of truth in this conception.

---

[1] Locke, *Second Treatise on Civil Government*, chap. ii (ed. H. Morley, 1884).

[2] Ibid., chap. ii, section 15.

[3] Ibid., chaps. ii and iii.

[4] Cf. Seneca, *Epistles*, xiv. 2.

It is the foundation of what has been called the police theory of the State, and though we must feel that this is a singularly meagre and inadequate theory of the function of the State, it does represent one part of our conception.

Locke then so far agrees with Hobbes, but we must also observe that, following Seneca and the Fathers, he differs from him radically in regard to another aspect of the State of Nature. To Hobbes the condition of perpetual war which belonged to the State of Nature was the inevitable result of two things, the one, the absence of any common authority to restrain men's natural passions of greed and ambition, and their consequent mutual distrust; the second, and perhaps the more fundamental, that in the State of Nature men had no moral sense or principles. 'The notion of right and wrong, justice and injustice, have there no place.'[1]

This is not the place to deal with the whole philosophical conceptions of Hobbes, but it is necessary to understand that Locke, following the Stoics, the Roman jurists, the Fathers, and the medieval thinkers, maintains a conception which is directly contradictory to Hobbes. 'The State of Nature has a law of Nature to govern it, which obliges every one, and reason, which is that law, teaches all mankind who will but consult it that being all equal and independent, no one ought to harm another in his life, health, liberty or possessions.'[2] Locke was restating in his own terms the tradition of the Stoics, the Roman law, the Fathers, and the Middle Ages, that there is a law which was antecedent to and independent of all political systems, which man recognizes by his reason as binding upon him. That is, he conceives of man as a being who recognizes that behind the positive law of any community there are principles of a moral order apprehended by man's reason which are of greater authority than any positive laws. As we shall see presently, this has a very important relation to his theory of political authority, for it means that to Locke there neither is nor can be any absolute authority in the State.

We can now therefore consider what is the origin and

---

[1] Hobbes, *Leviathan*, chap. xiii.
[2] Locke, *Second Treatise on Civil Government*, ii. 6.

nature of that political authority to which man or men are driven by the inconveniences of the State of Nature. And first its origin.

'Men', says Locke, 'being by nature all free, equal, and independent, no one can be put out of this estate and subjected to the political power of another without his own consent, which is done by agreeing with other men, to join and unite into a community for their comfortable, safe, and peaceable living, one amongst others, in a secure enjoyment of their properties, and a greater security against any that are not of it. This any number of men may do, because it injures not the freedom of the rest; they are left, as they were, in the liberty of the State of Nature. When any number of men have so consented to make one community or government, they are presently incorporated and make one body politic, wherein the majority have a right to act and conclude the rest.'[1]

This conception of the origin of a political community by an agreement or contract between certain men to form themselves into a society which shall have authority over all its members is the same as that which we have seen in Hooker,[2] and Althusius,[3] in Milton,[4] and Hobbes.[5]

The supreme political authority which is thus created is that of the community, or rather more precisely the majority, as having the power of the whole community. The history of this conception is long and complicated, and we cannot here enter upon a discussion of it.[6] Locke's treatment of it is naïve, and certainly infelicitous:

'For,' he says, 'when any number of men have, by the consent of every individual made a community, they have thereby made that community one body, with a power to act as one body, which is only by the will and determination of the majority. For that which acts any community, being only the consent of the individuals of it, and it being one body must move one way, it is necessary the body should move that way whither the greater force carries it, which is the consent of the majority, or else it is impossible it should act or continue one body, one community, which the consent of every individual that united into it

---

[1] Locke, *Second Treatise on Civil Government*, viii. 95.
[2] *Ecclesiastical Polity*, i. 10. 4.   [3] *Politica*, i. 1.
[4] *Tenure of Kings*, &c., *Works*, ii. 8.   [5] *Leviathan*, chap. 17.
[6] This subject of the majority was dealt with in an important paper read to the Historical Congress in 1913 by Von Gierke, and since then in a series of valuable monographs by Dr. Ruffini Avondo. Cf. *Il Principio Maggioritario*, &c.

agreed that it should; and so everyone is bound by that consent to be concluded by the majority. And therefore we see that in assemblies empowered to act by positive laws, where no number is set by that positive law which empowers them, the act of the majority passes for the act of the whole, and of course determines as having by the law of Nature and reason the power of the whole.'[1]

Locke's conception that it is a law of nature that the majority should control the minority is only less unfortunately expressed than his suggestion that it is because the majority has a greater force than the minority.

It is, however, true that Locke's treatment of this matter has not the significance it might seem to have, for Locke does not allow his political society to have any absolute authority. This is, indeed, one of the most important elements in his political theory.

This is most clearly expressed in a passage on the 'Legislative Power':

'Though the legislative, whether placed in one or more, whether it be always in being or only by intervals, though it be the supreme power in every commonwealth; yet, first, it is not, nor can possibly be absolutely arbitrary over the lives and fortunes of the people. For it being but the joint power of every member of the society given up to that person or assembly which is legislator, it can be no more than those persons had in a state of Nature, before they entered into society and gave it up to the community. For nobody can transfer to another more power than he has in himself, and nobody has an absolute arbitrary power over himself, or over any other, to destroy his own life, or take away the life or property of another. A man, as has been proved, cannot subject himself to the arbitrary power of another; and having in the state of Nature, no arbitrary power over the life, liberty, or possession of another, but only so much as the law of nature gave him for the preservation of himself and the rest of mankind, this is all he doth or can give up to the commonwealth, and by it to the legislative power, so that the legislative can have no more than this.'[2]

Here is a direct contradiction of Hobbes, and it is important to observe that it is a direct contradiction, not only of the absolute sovereignty of the king, but also of the State. We do not, indeed, use those terms under which Locke expresses this judgement, we do not speak of a state of Nature, or a law of Nature as antecedent in time to the being

[1] Locke, *Second Treatise on Civil Government*, viii (96).   [2] Ibid. xi (135).

of society, but unless we sophisticate ourselves we do not believe that a political society possesses an unlimited authority over the individual. No doubt it is difficult to find exact terms for our conception of the relation of individual liberty to the authority of society, but no reasonable person really believes that this society can do what it pleases. The conception of an absolute sovereignty in the State is merely an illusion. It is important to observe that here again Locke is not setting out any new doctrine, but is only restating the most fundamental doctrine of the Middle Ages, that all laws, secular or ecclesiastical, which are contrary to the natural law are, *ipso facto*, null and void; Locke illustrates, and in its most important character, the continuity of the political principles of the Middle Ages, with regard to the nature of liberty.

Whatever the form of government, it is the legislative authority which is supreme, but it is not absolute or arbitrary, as we have seen in the passage just quoted. Locke is careful to add that the legislative authority always remains under the final control of the community.

'Though in a constituted community standing upon its own basis and acting according to its own nature—that is, acting for the preservation of the community—there can be but one supreme power, which is the legislative, to which all the rest are and must be subordinate, yet the legislative being only a fiduciary power, to act for certain ends, there remains still in the people a supreme power to remove or alter the legislative, when they find the legislative act contrary to the trust reposed in them. . . . And thus the community perpetually retains a supreme power of saving themselves from the attempts and designs of any body, even of their legislators, whenever they shall be so foolish or so wicked as to lay and carry on designs against the liberties and properties of the subject. . . . And thus the community may be said in this respect to be always the supreme power, but not as considered under any form of government, because the power of the people can never take place till the government be dissolved.'[1]

The authority of the community is limited by the natural law, and the authority of the legislature is also limited by the authority of the community; but the authority of the legislature is also limited by the principle that it 'cannot assume

[1] Locke, *Second Treatise on Civil Government*, xiii (149).

to itself a power to rule by extemporary arbitrary decrees, but is bound to dispense justice and decide the rights of the subject by promulgated standing laws, and known authorized judges. . . . Absolute arbitrary power, or governing without settled standing laws can neither of them consist with the ends of society and government.'[1]

It is clear what is the source of this doctrine, it is the normal tradition of the Middle Ages, that the positive law is supreme over the ruler.

Locke not only restates the principle of the supremacy of law, but in a later chapter he treats the contempt for, and disregard of, law as being the proper essence of tyranny. 'As usurpation is the exercise of power which another has the right to, so tyranny is the exercise of power beyond right, which nobody can have a right to.' And he ingeniously confirms this judgement with some sentences from speeches of James I to Parliament in 1603 and 1609 (I cite the latter).

'The King binds himself, by a double oath, to the observation of the fundamental laws of his Kingdom—tacitly, as by being a King, and so bound to protect, as well the people as the laws of his Kingdom; and expressly by his oath at his coronation; so as every just king, in a settled kingdom is bound to observe that paction made to his people, by his laws, in framing his government agreeable thereunto. . . . And therefore a King, governing in a settled kingdom, leaves to be a king and degenerates into a tyrant, as soon as he leaves off to rule according to his laws.'[2]

Locke sums up his own principles in a later sentence:

'Wherever law ends, tyranny begins, if the law be transgressed to another's harm; and whosoever in authority exercises the power given him by the law, and makes use of the force he has under his command to compass that upon the subject which the law allows not, ceases in that to be a magistrate, and acting without authority may be opposed, as any other man who by force invades the right of another. This is acknowledged in subordinate magistrates. . . .And why this should not hold in the highest as well as in the most inferior magistrate, I would gladly be informed.'[3]

I have endeavoured to set out some of the main principles

[1] Ibid. xi (136, 137).   [2] Ibid. xviii (200).
[3] Ibid. xviii (202).

of the political theory of Locke, for as it appears to me we find in his work the continuity of the modern with the medieval conceptions, and some of the most important principles of a rational and intelligible system of political liberty.

It is, of course, quite true that he still sometimes thought in terms which are to us unhistorical. He thought, or at least he has presented his thoughts, under the terms of the Senecan and Patristic conception of a primitive state of Nature, in which men once lived without organized society; and like Seneca and the Christian Fathers he thought that it was men's vices which compelled them to form political societies with a coercive authority. And he has, at least in theory, a very inadequate grasp on the profound Aristotelian conception of political society as the method and form of that great co-operative system through which men live, and have achieved such progress as they have achieved.

He thought of men as being governed in the state of Nature by the law of Nature; we do not use the term, but it is reasonable to say that the real meaning of the conception is not strange to us; for, if we take the trouble to get behind the form of the conception, we find that it really means that men are directed, and properly controlled, by moral principles which we do not make but discover, and that therefore it is necessarily true that the political society has no more of an arbitrary and absolute authority than the individual.

We do not think of the individual and independent men as having come together to form political societies, for we know nothing of a world without them, but rather we recognize that men have always been members of some society or group, in and through which they live; and that the conception of a primitive isolated man is a mere and unreal abstraction. Indeed we rather see the individual as slowly emerging through the long process of the ages, and as slowly growing into a fuller consciousness of his individual personality. This is true, and so far Locke was thinking, or at any rate speaking, in the traditional terms, which we have left behind us.

On the other hand, we also find that Locke had inherited, and was developing with intelligence and force, the principles of political liberty which he had drawn, partly at least with Hooker, from the medieval world.

To him as to them the supreme principle of human society is the pursuit of a rational moral order which controls the positive law, and the conduct of political society, and this is what the medieval thinkers meant by justice. To him, as to them, it was the community which was the source of all positive law, of all political order; and all political authority, whether legislative or executive, is derived from, or delegated by, the community.

To him as to them this authority must be embodied in positive laws; to use his own words: 'There wants an established, settled, known law, received and allowed by common consent to be the standard of right and wrong, and the common measure to decide all controversies between them.'[1]

And finally, like the normal political thinkers of the Middle Ages, he not only thinks that the ruler should be subject to the law, but that if he were to attempt to go beyond his proper authority, he should be resisted.

The truth is that while Locke no doubt sets out the principles of government as they were to be developed in the eighteenth century in England and the United States and France, and in the more civilized countries of Europe in the nineteenth century, it is also true that he retained the general principles of the great political thinkers of the Middle Ages such as John of Salisbury, and Bracton, and St. Thomas Aquinas, and Marsilius of Padua, as well as those of George Buchanan and Mariana, and Hooker and Althusius in the sixteenth century. Locke may not be a very profound or subtle political thinker, but he represents the continuity of an intelligible and rational conception of political liberty.

If we look back over these political writers of the seventeenth century we shall see that behind the variety of the expression there is a real unity of thought, and that this is due to the fact that they represent, in different terms no doubt, the continuity of the political principles of the Middle Ages. It is not true that in these writers we find new and revolutionary innovations, but rather it is in those writers

[1] Locke, *Second Treatise on Civil Government*, ix. 124.

who defended the principles of absolutism, whether in theological or legal terms.

It was not these writers any more than the thinkers of the French Revolution of the eighteenth century who invented the doctrine of the 'natural' equality and freedom of men, or the principle that all political authority was derived from the community. The first had come down to them from the Stoics, from the great Roman jurists, and from the Christian Fathers. The second they had learned from the Roman jurists, and from the medieval conception that the positive law was either the immemorial custom of the community or represented the will of the community.

It was again from the Roman jurists, the Christian Fathers, the canon law, and the medieval writers that they derived the principle that the positive law itself had and could have no authority except so far as it expressed the principles of justice and the natural law.

It was from the whole tradition of the Middle Ages that they had learned that it was the law, and not the prince, which was supreme; that the authority of the prince was limited by a contract to obey the law, and that the prince who violated the contract should be deposed.

And it is important to notice that these principles rested not only on theory, but on the historical tradition of the forms and methods of medieval government. The political authority of medieval society, as the medieval men saw it, had been a limited one, and the form of its government had been a mixed one.

PART III

THE DEVELOPMENT OF THE CONCEPTION OF POLITICAL LIBERTY IN THE EIGHTEENTH CENTURY

I

THE CONSTITUTIONAL CONCEPTION OF POLITICAL LIBERTY AS EMBODIED IN THE REPRESENTATIVE SYSTEM

ENOUGH has been said to make it clear that the memory of the constitutional principles of modern Europe had not died out in Europe in the seventeenth century, not even in France. From the beginning of the century to the end of it, the principles of the supremacy of law over the arbitrary will of the prince, and of the place of the community in controlling its concerns had not been wholly forgotten. We have seen this in Coquille, and Joly, and Fénelon. It is true that in France an almost absolute monarchical authority had in fact been established, and that in some other European countries one can see a development similar, or at least in the same direction; and that some writers, from Bodin in the sixteenth to Bossuet in the later seventeenth century, had defended this, but it can hardly be said that the arguments of these writers had any great weight. Bodin's doctrine that there must be in all states some authority supreme even over the positive law was indeed important, even if it was little more than the recognition of the fact that the conception of the law as the custom of the community had to be modified by the conception of law as expressing the deliberate will of the political authority. But even Bodin is compelled to say that this authority was limited by the more majestic principles of the supremacy of the natural and of the divine law. His assertion that this supreme authority was in France placed in the monarch was, however, simply an arbitrary statement supported by no serious argument. Bodin himself could find no parallel to it in the other civilized countries of central and western Europe. Bossuet's assertion

of the absolute divine authority of the monarch was not
indeed so absurd as the arguments of the English writers
like Filmer, but had no real foundation either in reason or
in history.

We may therefore begin by noticing that the development of the conception of political liberty in France from
the beginning of the eighteenth century to the French
Revolution was in large measure based upon the principle
of the re-establishment of the authority of the community.
As we shall see this was reinforced by the resounding victory
of constitutional principles in England, and no doubt also
by the fact that in the long-drawn-out struggles of the later
seventeenth and early eighteenth centuries it was the constitutional monarchy of England and the republic of Holland
which had triumphed over the centralized and absolute
monarchy of France.

It is, indeed, one of the curious absurdities of which many
intelligent people are guilty, to assert that it is the absolute
and irresponsible governments which are normally stronger
than the democratic and constitutional states, while it really
requires only a little knowledge and reflection to see that it
is in the long run the temper or mood of a community
conscious of itself and of its own mind and resolution which
normally triumphs over the merely docile and obedient.
This had been well seen in the struggles of Holland, first
against Spain, and then against France.

It is thus significant that it is in the early years of the
eighteenth century that we have in the work of the Comte
de Boulainvilliers not merely general statements about the
political liberties of France and other medieval states, but
also what is, as far as I know, the first serious attempt at a
history of the States General in France down to the reign
of Louis XI.

In the work entitled 'Mémoires Historiques', which deals
with the history of France to the accession of Hugh Capet,
referring to the Merovingian kingdom, he makes the statement that, of all the customs of that time, that which contributed most to the maintenance of public liberties was that
of the General Assemblies of the nation.[1] In a work on the

[1] Boulainvilliers, *État de la France*, vol. i: 'Mémoires Historiques', p. 25.

history of the States General he says that it was not Charlemagne who first created those General Assemblies which
were known as Estates; for all the world knows that the
French were originally a free people who elected chiefs
under the name of kings to carry out the laws which the
people had established; or to lead them in war. They did
not consider their kings to be arbitrary legislators, the
Ordonnances of those early times were only made with the
consent of the General Assemblies of the *Champs du Mai*,
and it was only in these Assemblies that war could be
declared.[1]

In another of these 'Lettres', Boulainvilliers puts these
principles into terms which apply to all the kingdoms formed
out of the ruins of the Roman Empire. If, he says, we consider what still obtains in England, in Germany, in Poland,
and what had been till lately the rule in Denmark, Sweden,
and France, we shall recognize that the governments of these
kingdoms were very careful not to surrender themselves to
the power of the king in such sort that it was not tempered
by the co-operation of various *Tribunaux*. We find the same
institutions everywhere, though under different names;
Diets in Germany and Poland, Parliaments in England,
Estates in France, Sweden, and Denmark, Cortes in Spain
and Portugal, and even in Castile.

'The peoples who created these kingdoms were no doubt barbarians,
who had no knowledge of Letters and Philosophy, and even less of the
elaborate political systems of the legislators who had prepared the laws
of the cities and republics of Greece, in the time of their liberty; but
they followed their good common sense, and knew that, while a Monarchical government was necessary and even indispensable to a people
of conquerors, the disadvantages of an unlimited power in their kings
were such that they restrained it by the establishment of these Assemblies. There is no one who does not recognize the unhappy consequences of a despotic authority, by his own reason, or in the examples
of the Oriental Monarchies, or even in that of the Roman Empire.'

And Boulainvilliers breaks out into that indignant denun-
ciation of Bossuet which we have cited.

'Je pense que tout homme non intéressé, et d'ailleurs suffisamment

[1] Ibid., vol. iii: 'Lettres sur les Anciens Parlements que l'on nomme États
Généraux', Lettre II, p. 12.

éclairé, regardera le Système Politique de l'illustre Bossuet, Évêque de Meaux comme un des plus hauts témoignages de l'indignité de notre siècle et de la corruption des cœurs, contre lesquels l'érudition et les lumières de l'esprit ne donnent point de secours, que l'artifice ne peut détourner et employer contre la vérité même. Il n'y a rien en effet de si mauvaise foi que l'abus perpétuel, qu'il a fait des textes de la Sainte Écriture, pour forger de nouvelles chaînes à la liberté naturelle des hommes et pour augmenter le faste et la dureté des Rois.'

We must, he goes on to say, praise the foresight of our fathers, and think with them that the wisest government is that where the supreme authority is tempered by a wise and impartial Council, such as that to which the great Charlemagne gave his confidence.[1]

It is, no doubt, easy to criticize the details of the historical references of Boulainvilliers, but the broad contrast which he was making between the medieval forms of government and that of the seventeenth century in France is just and reasonable.

This is followed by a summary account of the system of Feudalism, and of the Assemblies of Nobles and Bishops in which *Ordonnances* or *Constitutions* were made. This takes him to the first meeting of the Three Estates under Philip the Fair in 1302,[2] and to an account of the meetings of the States General in the first half of the fourteenth century.[3] It is very significant that he gives a more detailed account of the meeting of the States General under King John in 1355, and asserts that it was the States General who granted taxes to the king.[4]

Boulainvilliers saw very clearly the importance of this, for in Lettre XII he gives an account of the creation of a permanent *Taille* at the States General of Orleans in 1440, to pay for the *Gensdarmerie*, and in the *Francs Archers* in 1448, and says that though this may have been necessary for the safety of the kingdom

'(ils) peuvent néanmoins être regardés comme le principe effectif de la corruption de tout le gouvernement François, non seulement parcequ'ils ont été donnés sans précautions contre les abus qui en pouvaient

---

[1] Boulainvilliers, Ibid., 'Lettres sur les Anciens Parlements', Lettre III, pp. 20 and 21.
[2] Ibid., Lettres IV–VII. [3] Ibid., Lettre VIII. [4] Ibid., Lettre IX.

naître, soit en favorisant le Despotisme et l'Autorité arbitraire, soit en livrant les biens de tous les particuliers à la discrétion des Rois, et au Caprice de leurs Ministres, mais particulairement en ce qu'ils ont servi à confondre, presque sans ressources tous les ordres du Royaume.'[1]

He goes on to point out in the next 'Lettre' that it was Louis XI whose political system showed in principle and practice the methods on which the despotic authority of the seventeenth and eighteenth centuries was founded.[2]

He considered that there could be no security for the peoples except in those political systems which overthrew the Roman Empire; these survived only in England, or at least in those countries where the power of the princes and nobles might serve, in some measure, as a protection against an unlimited authority.[3]

As I have already said, we may feel that Boulainvilliers's treatment of the political structure of Merovingian and Carolingian times may not be very accurate, but the importance of his contentions lies in the fact that he recognized the general limitations of the authority of medieval monarchy, in France as in western Europe in general, and that it was to him clear that the representative councils of the later Middle Ages were the normal development of the limited monarchy, while the absolutist tendencies of the fifteenth and sixteenth centuries, and still more the absolute monarchy of Louis XIV, represented a revolutionary and disastrous innovation and revolution. It is evident that Boulainvilliers was not a belated exponent of a worn-out system, but represented one element of that political movement which culminated in the Great Revolution.

We turn to Montesquieu, whose famous work *De l'Esprit des Lois* was published in 1748, and we shall do well to begin by noticing that this work is of great importance from two points of view. In the first place Montesquieu's object was to show that human laws and institutions in general are not only the expression of the deliberate reason and will of men in society, but are, in at least a large measure, determined by the varying conditions and circumstances of human life.

---

[1] Ibid., Lettre XII, p. 158.   [2] Ibid., Lettre XIII.
[3] Ibid., Lettre XIV, p. 176.

This may be exaggerated into the assertion that they have nothing to do with human reason and human will, as embodied in communities or individuals. That is from the point of view of a serious historian a mere absurdity; human reason and conscious purpose, the personality of the individual and the temper of the community are the finally determining forces which produce the infinite variety of the life of the individual or the community. Human reason recognizes partly at least the conditions of life, but the individual personality and will inspire and direct the action and movement of society rightly, or haply wrongly. I do not mean that the living movement and growth of human institutions had never been apprehended before by ancient or medieval thinkers, but it was the great merit of Montesquieu that, while he is often absurd enough in the illustrations or applications of this general principle, he should have seen its importance.

This is not, however, the aspect of his work with which we are here specially concerned, and we must turn to the second, and from our present point of view the more important, of his contributions to political thought. This lies in his restatement of some of the most important principles of the medieval political thinkers, and in his apprehension of the fact that in England these principles had found an adequate, even if imperfect, form. We shall have to deal with this particular aspect of his work in a separate chapter.

His political principles are well illustrated in a passage in which he sets out three forms of government, the Republic, the Monarchy, and the Despotism: the Republic, in which the people have the sovereign power; the Monarchy, where one man governs, but according to established and fixed laws; the Despotism, where one man governs but without laws, or fixed rules, and controls all things by his will and his caprice;[1] and again in a passage in a later part of his book where he says that liberty consists principally in that a man cannot be compelled to do anything that the law does not command; we are therefore free when we live under the control of the civil laws.[2] To Montesquieu as to the Middle Ages, liberty meant the supremacy of law, not of the king.

[1] Montesquieu, *De l'Esprit des Lois*, ii. 1.   [2] Ibid. xxvi. 20.

Montesquieu does not consider in detail the constitutional systems of Europe or of France in the Middle Ages, like Boulainvilliers, but in one important passage he sums up the characteristics and development of what he calls the Gothic system of government, in terms which we may certainly find a little extravagant, but which at any rate served to express the contrast which he felt between them and the government of France in the seventeenth and eighteenth centuries. The German nations, he says, which conquered the Roman Empire were as we know very free; while they were in Germany the whole nation could assemble; when they were dispersed in the course of their conquests they could no longer do this, but it was still necessary that the whole nation should deliberate on its affairs, as it had done before, and it provided for this by the method of Representation. This was the method of the Gothic government; it had, however, one great defect; the lower classes of the people were slaves. The custom of enfranchisement, however, grew up, and soon the civil liberty of the people, the prerogatives of the nobles and clergy, and the authority of the king were in such measure united that Montesquieu doubts whether any government in the world was ever better tempered than that of Europe while this political system lasted.[1] In an earlier passage he had said that when we read the admirable work of Tacitus on the Germans we see that it was from them that the English had derived the principles of their political order. It was in the forests of Germany that this admirable system of government was first formed.[2]

This is not a history of the Revolution but only pretends to illustrate some of the traditional conceptions of liberty which lay behind it, and it will therefore be sufficient to point out that the tradition of Fénelon, of Boulainvilliers, and of Montesquieu continued to influence the minds of Frenchmen throughout the eighteenth century, and that it was not only on theoretical and abstract grounds, but on the traditions and precedents of medieval France that they founded their claim to the recovery of their political liberties.

[1] Ibid. xi. 8.   [2] Ibid. xi. 6.

II

THE INFLUENCE OF ENGLAND IN THE DEVELOPMENT OF THE CONCEPTION OF POLITICAL LIBERTY IN THE EIGHTEENTH CENTURY

VOLTAIRE AND MONTESQUIEU

WE have in the last chapter considered the continuity of the medieval principles of political liberty in the eighteenth century in France. We must now observe the beginnings of the influence of the political system of England, as it had developed in the seventeenth century, on Europe, and in particular on France.

It is indeed a remarkable thing that from the beginning of the eighteenth century down to our own day, the English conception of the nature and forms of political liberty should have exercised this immense influence on the political civilization of Europe. This was no doubt due to many causes, but we can distinguish three as probably the most important. First, we can see from various references in French literature that from the sixteenth century many French political writers recognized in the English constitutional system characteristics which had once belonged to their own political order. Second, the success of the English resistance to the attempts of the Stuarts to develop the power of the monarchy towards absolutism. The Civil War, and the execution of Charles I may have shocked Europe, but the comparatively tranquil revolution of 1688 impressed and reassured them. The third was no doubt the overwhelming defeat which England and Holland with the Grand Alliance had inflicted on France. The French monarchy under Louis XIV had seemed overwhelmingly powerful, and England under Charles II and James II unimportant and incapable; while now under the constitutional government of William III and Queen Anne it had proved itself resolute, competent, and effective. The power of the French monarchy had been broken not only by the military genius of

Marlborough but by the resolute determination of the
English people.

The first great French writer who held up the English
political history and institutions to the admiration of Frenchmen was Voltaire. It was in 1726 that he went to England,
and he remained there till 1729, but it was not till after his
return to France that he brought out the *Lettres Philosophiques*, in 1733 in England, and in 1734 in France. These
Lettres range over the religious conditions, the science, the
literature, and the political characteristics of England as
Voltaire saw them. We are here only concerned with his
treatment of politics, and it is in the eighth and ninth letters
that Voltaire discusses the nature and history of English
political institutions.

Voltaire was indeed under no illusions about English
history, in which he found the record of the same barbarity,
stupidity, and religious ferocity as in other countries, but he
found in English history the record of a successful vindication of political and religious liberty.

There was, he says, one essential difference between
Rome and England; the result of the civil wars of the
Romans was their enslavement, the result of the conflicts
in England had been the achievement of liberty. The
English nation was the only one which had succeeded in
controlling its kings by resisting them; and it had succeeded
in establishing a wise government in which the prince was
all powerful to do good, but his hands were tied when he
endeavoured to do evil. In England the lords are great,
without vassals and without insolence, and the people have
their part in the government, without causing confusion.

Voltaire was indeed aware that it was at a great price
that the English had achieved liberty, it was in oceans
of blood, he says, a little rhetorically, that the English had
overthrown a despotic authority, but they do not think that
this was too high a price to pay for the establishment of good
laws. Other nations may have shed men's blood, but the
blood which they shed had only been the cement of their
slavery. The French, he says, think that the government of
England is more stormy than the sea which surrounds it,
and that is true; when the king raised the storms, and tried

to make himself the master of the vessel of which he was only the pilot.

The French civil wars had been longer and more cruel than those of England, but none of them had liberty as its aim; and Voltaire describes in contemptuous terms the attempted revolution of the Fronde. Cardinal Retz had neither reason nor purpose as a rebel, and seemed to have raised a civil war almost for his amusement; while the Parliament of Paris did not know what it wanted; and he sums up the character of French civil wars in a famous epigram. The civil wars of the time of Charles VI were cruel, those of the League were abominable, that of the Fronde was merely ridiculous. Finally, and with a singular audacity, he contrasts the war against Charles I of England, in which he was defeated in open battle, taken captive, tried and condemned at Westminster, with the assassinations of Henry III and Henry IV of France.[1]

So far for the eighth 'Lettre'. In the ninth he goes on to examine, in larger if not always very accurate terms, the history of the political development of England, and to point out something of what seemed to him the nature of the political authority which had gradually taken shape there.

Voltaire like other French writers whom we have considered was aware of the tradition of liberty in the Middle Ages, and he admits that kings did not then possess an absolute authority; but the people, he thinks, were still little more than slaves. And here we see that his criticisms begin to be directed not only against kings, but against the nobles. He speaks of the feudal nobles of the Middle Ages as little more than brigands, and he describes them as sub-tyrants who disputed with the kings the plunder of the people.

He treats the people as not only the most numerous, but also as the most virtuous part of mankind; it was composed of those who study the laws and the sciences, of the merchants and artisans; and yet they were regarded by the nobles of the Middle Ages as mere animals below the level of human nature; and he thinks that it had been a happy thing that the authority of these petty brigands had been

[1] Voltaire, *Lettres Philosophiques*, viii (ed. Bengesco).

destroyed in France by the legitimate authority of the kings, and in England by the legitimate authority of the kings and the people.

We may well feel that we are approaching the time when the 'Tiers État' was to be looked on as the really important part of the French nation.

Voltaire goes on to trace the rise of the people to power in England. Something, he thinks, was represented by the provisions of Magna Carta, but only a little; and it is to the period of the Tudors that he attributes the development of the liberty of the people, when the House of Commons grew steadily in power. With a singular penetration he notices that the new nobility created by the Tudors had little of the importance or power of the older baronage. They had indeed titles which seemed to imply a local and territorial importance, but actually they had nothing of the kind; the Duke of Dorset, for instance, had a title which seemed to mean much, actually it meant nothing, he did not own an inch of land in Dorsetshire. The nobles had indeed some authority in Parliament, but they had none outside of it; and even in Parliament, while the House of Lords was first in rank, and could reject a money Bill passed by the House of Commons, it could not modify it. He evidently thought that it was this which had brought it about that every man in England paid taxes, according to his means, and it was to this that he attributed the prosperity of the peasants in England, as compared with those in France.[1]

It was some thirty years later that Voltaire brought out the *Dictionnaire Philosophique*, and in some of its articles we find references to political institutions. In the article on 'Patrie' he remarks that all States were originally Republics, and that this was true of Europe as well as of other parts of the world, until the rise of the kinglets of Etruria and Rome. Eight of these republics without kings continue to this day, while Poland, Sweden, and England may be regarded as republics under a king. For four thousand years men had discussed the question which was the best form of government; the rich prefer an aristocracy, the people a democracy; it is only the kings who prefer a monarchy. Why

[1] Ibid. ix.

is it then, he asks, that almost all the world is governed by monarchies. The true reason is that men are only rarely worthy to govern themselves.

In the article on 'États' he represents a member of the Council of Pondicherry as discussing with a Brahmin the nature and advantages of various forms of government, and at last he asks the Brahmin under which he would prefer to live. The Brahmin answers: under that government where men obey only the laws. In the article on 'Tyrannie' he defines the tyrant as a sovereign who knows no law except his own caprice.

The historical judgements of Voltaire which we have been considering are summary, and are open to criticism; but here is at least something remarkable and noteworthy. For Voltaire was holding up to the admiration of France and Europe the political constitution of England as that which had succeeded in defending the liberty of the people, not only as against the king, but as against the nobles, and the effects of his arguments can be plainly seen, not only in political theory, but in the development of the political order of Europe.

If it was Voltaire who was the first to draw the attention of France and Europe to the constitutional development which had grown up in England upon the foundation of the medieval principles of law and government, it was Montesquieu who, in his famous work *De l'Esprit des Lois*, published in 1748, set out the structure of this constitution as representing in fact as well as in principle the resolute will of a nation to establish political liberty.

Montesquieu's treatment of the foundation of a true political order turns upon two principles, the supremacy of law and the maintenance of liberty, and his definition of monarchy and despotism is noticeable. A monarchy, he says, is a State in which one man governs, but according to fixed and established laws, while a despotism is that where one man rules according to his own will and caprice, and without law.[1] To this he adds in a later passage, when he said that in the despotic State the prince could himself act as

[1] Montesquieu's *De l'Esprit des Lois*, ii. 1.

judge, but he could not do this in a monarchy.[1] These were, as we have seen, the first principles of medieval society; the king is under God and the law, Bracton had said in the thirteenth century; and the feudal law was clear and constant in the judgement that the lord, even if he were the king, could not be judge in a dispute between himself and his vassal; and the independence of the Courts of Law, as against the king, was a fixed principle, not only in England, but also in France.

When Montesquieu turns to the discussion in detail of the nature of liberty, he finds this embodied in the English Constitution. He introduces the subject with a short chapter, in which he asks what liberty means, and points out that in democracies the people might seem to be able to do whatever it wished, but political liberty does not consist in doing whatever one wishes. In a State, that is a society which has laws, liberty consists in being able to do what one ought to wish, and in the absence of constraint to do what one ought not to wish. Liberty is the right to do what the laws permit. Democracy and aristocracy are not, merely as such, free States; liberty can only be found in the *État Modéré*, but it is not always found even always in it, for its power may be abused. What is needed is a constitution in which power is checked by power.[2] This brings him to his examination of the English Constitution, for, as he says, while different nations have different objects, there is one nation which has taken for its direct object political liberty, that is England.[3]

It is thus that Montesquieu comes to his famous discussion of the three powers which exist in every political society, and which, as he contends, must be kept distinct from each other if the society is to preserve its political liberty.

If, he says, the legislative power is united to the executive, whether this is embodied in a monarch or in a senate, there cannot be liberty, for the monarch or senate may make tyrannical laws and execute them tyrannically; and similarly there can be no liberty if the judicial power is not separated from the legislative and executive. He adds that most of the kingdoms of Europe were tempered (*modérés*), for even

[1] Ibid. vi. 5.   [2] Ibid. xi. 3, 4.   [3] Ibid. xi. 5.

while the prince held the legislative and executive power, he left the judicial power in the hands of his subjects; and he refers to Turkey, where the Sultan held all the three powers, as a horrid despotism.[1] He adds that the judicial power should not be given to a *Sénat permanent*, but should be exercised by persons drawn from the body of the people, and that in serious cases the accused should have the right to challenge the judges. (A note refers to Athens, but I should conjecture that this is probably also a reminiscence of the English jury system.)[1]

It must not, however, be imagined that Montesquieu thought that the mere separation of the powers was enough to constitute a condition of political liberty. He is equally emphatic in asserting that in a free State every man who is considered to have a free spirit (*une âme libre*) should be governed by himself, and therefore the people as a body should have the legislative power; but, as this is impossible in large States, and very inconvenient even in small, the people must act through representatives, and these should be chosen by local election. All the citizens should have a voice in the election of representatives, except those who are held not to have a will of their own.[1] Montesquieu adds that there should be a Second Chamber of hereditary nobles, as necessary for the protection of their special interests, but he limits their power with regard to finance to a negative voice.[1]

The executive authority should be placed in the hands of the monarch, for the function of the executive is action, which is best carried out by one person, and the executive should have power to negative the proceedings of the legislature, otherwise the legislature would have a despotic authority. The legislature should not have authority to stop the action of the executive, for the executive affairs constantly require immediate action; but it should have the right to inquire into the administration of the laws which it had made. It may not indeed proceed against the monarch, but it should have the right to proceed against and to punish the ministers who have given the monarch evil counsel. These should be tried by the House of Nobles.[1]

Montesquieu adds three observations, or what we may call

[1] Montesquieu's *De l'Esprit des Lois*, xi. 6.

practical rules, which should be followed under a free constitution. The executive authority should have no power to
impose taxation, but only to consent to it, or to forbid it.
The legislature should vote the necessary taxes only from
year to year, or it will lose control over the executive. It
should also decide from year to year on the armed forces
which it should entrust to the executive.[1]

Such were, as Montesquieu thinks, the principal elements
in the English Constitution, as illustrating what he had said
before, that there was one nation which had made the
establishment of political liberty its direct object.[2] Whether
the English actually possessed this liberty, was not, as he
says, for him to decide, it was enough to say that it was
established by their laws.[3] He was indeed careful to add
that he did not mean to depreciate other forms of government, or to suggest that the existence of this extreme
form of liberty should distress those who only enjoyed a
moderate form of it.

As we have seen in the last chapter, Montesquieu thought
that the medieval constitution of France, as of the other
kingdoms of Europe, had been monarchical, but tempered
by the authority of the community. He does not, at least in
this work, draw this out in an historical account of the representative assemblies of France, as Boulainvilliers had done,
nor does he directly say that it was by a reconstruction of
this system that the constitution of France should be reformed. It is, however, impossible to doubt the immense
effect produced in France, Europe, and America by his
admiring exposition of the forms and character of the
English Constitution, for this can be seen, not only in
the French Revolution, but in the whole reorganization of
European governments in the nineteenth century.

[1] Ibid. xi. 6.   [2] Ibid. xi. 5.   [3] Ibid. xi. 6.

III

THE AMERICAN REVOLUTION

IT is impossible in such a work as this to deal with the history of the great revolt which established the United States of America; or even to deal adequately with the principles of political liberty as embodied in the American Constitution. It is only possible to point out some of these principles as bearing upon our subject.

And first we must notice that the principles of the American Constitution had behind them a long history. They were obviously related to the political conceptions of the sixteenth and seventeenth centuries, but they were also continuous with the fundamental political principles of the Middle Ages: the conceptions of the supremacy of law and the self-government of the community. The law of medieval society was indeed the expression of the self-government of the community, for it was primarily the expression of the custom of the community, an authority not imposed upon it from without, but springing from its habit of life, and formed by its experience. And when in the later centuries of the Middle Ages men began to think of law as expressing a deliberate will and command, it was the will and command of the community. The phrase in which this was often expressed, 'Quod omnes tangit, ab omnibus approbetur', was not, as some ill-informed persons have thought, a mere tag from the Roman laws, but expressed an actual and working principle of the common life. Hooker's famous words, 'Laws they are not which public approbation hath not made so', were the proper expression, not of a merely personal opinion, but of the traditional mode of thinking and feeling of central and western Europe. And the positive law was supreme, subject always to the higher authority of the divine and natural law, not as impairing the liberty of the individual but as protecting it.

It is, however, true that more immediately the principles of the American Constitution are derived in large measure from John Locke's *Second Treatise on Civil Government*, and beyond Locke, from the post-Aristotelian philosophers, the

Roman jurists, and the Christian Fathers. The Declaration of Independence of 1776 said:

'We hold these truths to be self-evident, that all men are created equal, that they are endowed by their Creator with certain unalienable rights, that among these are life, liberty and the pursuit of happiness. That to secure these rights, governments are instituted among men, deriving their just powers from the consent of the governed.'

It seems evident that this statement is founded upon the principles which, as we have seen, had been set out by Locke; and we may specially remember some of Locke's words.

'To understand political power aright, and derive it from its original, we must consider what estate men are naturally in, and that is a state of perfect freedom to order their actions . . . within the bounds of the Law of Nature, without asking leave, or dependency upon the will of any other man. A state also of equality, wherein all the power and jurisdiction is reciprocal.'[1]

And, in a later chapter:

'Men, being, as has been said, by nature all free, equal and independent, no one can be put out of this estate, and subjected to the political power of another without his own consent, which is done by agreeing with other men to join and unite into a community for the comfortable, safe and peaceable living, one amongst another, in a secure enjoyment of their properties, and a greater security against any that are not of it.'[2]

The other principle, that is the supremacy of law, was also derived from the medieval tradition, but this had been greatly reinforced by Montesquieu, and indeed it was from his work that the form of the American Constitution, and its careful provision for the separation of the legislative, the executive, and the judicial powers, was in large measure derived.

The supremacy of law in the United States is embodied in the Federal Constitution of the United States of 1787. It is true that the Constitution might be amended, and the laws might be altered, but the authority of the legislature was carefully restrained and limited by the provisions of Article V. Changes could only be made with the consent of two-thirds of the House of Representatives, and of the Senate,

[1] Locke's *Second Treatise on Civil Government*, ii.
[2] Ibid. viii.

or by a Convention summoned on the application of two-thirds of the several States; and must further be ratified by three-fourths of the States. It is clear that the founders of the Constitution were anxious to make all attempts at changes in its fundamental laws difficult; and indeed this has proved to be the case in the experience of the United States.

The independent authority of the judicial power is carefully provided for in the First Section of the Third Article of the Constitution. 'The Judicial Power of the United States shall be vested in one Supreme Court, and in such inferior Courts as the Congress may from time to time advise and establish. The Judges both of the Supreme and inferior Courts shall hold their office during good behaviour.' By this clause two principles are established; first, that the rights and liberties of the citizens as defined by the Constitution are under the protection of the judicial power, and cannot, without great difficulty, be overridden even by the legislative authority, and second, that the judges of these courts are not subject to interference either by the executive or by the legislative power, for they cannot be deprived of their authority except by process of law.

This last provision was not, as far as I know, suggested by Locke; it was no doubt derived immediately from that most important clause of the Act of Settlement of 1701 which provided that the judges' commissions should for the future be made *quam diu se bene gesserint* (during good behaviour), and not *durante beneplacito* (at the King's pleasure); I should conjecture that this was also related to the doctrine of Montesquieu, that there could be no liberty in a political society unless the judicial power was separated from the legislative and executive powers. And it carried on the tradition which was so highly developed in medieval France of the independence of the judges of the *Parlement*.

The supremacy of the community over the executive is carefully provided for by that Clause of the Constitution (Article II, Section 4) which enacts that 'The President, Vice-President, and all civil officers of the United States shall be removed from office by an impeachment for, and conviction of, treason, bribery, and other high crimes and misdemeanours'. The direct and explicit enactment of such a rule was indeed of the highest importance, but it must not be thought that this was in principle an innovation. It is, I think, quite clear that this was constantly contemplated in medieval times, and was actually carried out in some famous cases. At least two emperors and one king of England had been formally deposed.[1]

The American Revolution and the character of the American Constitution gave an immense impulse to the development of political liberty in Europe, but its influence, perhaps, lay not even so much in its constitutional principles as in its achievement. It was the spectacle of the successful revolt of a great community against what it conceived to be the infringement of its liberty which had such a profound effect on Europe. The principles of political and individual liberty might be implicit in the historical tradition of European society, but it was another thing to see these principles clearly expressed and taking a concrete shape and form in a great national society.

[1] I may be allowed to refer to our *History of Mediaeval Political Theory,* vol. iii, part ii, chaps. 5 and 6; vol. iv, part i, chap. 8; vol. v, part i, chaps. 3 and 4; vol. vi, part i, chap. 4; part ii, chap. 3; part ii, chap. 3; part iv, chap. 2.

IV

BURKE

IT is at first sight paradoxical that Burke, whom we often
think of as the most determined enemy of the French
Revolution, should have also been, for England at least, the
most powerful and the most profound defender of the
American Revolution. But that is the truth; at least it is true
to say that by his great speeches and letters on the revolt of
the American Colonies he did more than any other man of
that time to develop and set forward the conception of
political liberty.

What did Burke mean by political liberty? And first we
must notice that he recognized that—

'The extreme of liberty (which is its abstract perfection, but its real
fault) obtains nowhere, nor ought to obtain anywhere. . . . Liberty
must be limited in order to be possessed. The degree of restraint, it is
impossible in any case to settle precisely. . . For liberty is a good to be
improved, and not an evil to be lessened. It is not only a private bless-
ing of the first order, but a vital spirit and energy of the State itself,
which has just so much life and vigour as there is liberty in it.'[1]

Freedom is not only something which the individual requires, but the real source and spring of the life of the State.
It was this spirit which Burke saw in the American Colonies.
'The people, who are to be the subjects of these restraints,
are descendants of Englishmen, and of an high and free
spirit,' Or again, 'In the character of the Americans, a love
of freedom is the predominating feature which marks and
distinguishes the whole; and, as an ardent is always a
jealous affection, your colonies become suspicious, restive,
and intractable whenever they see the least attempt to wrest
from them by force, . . . what they think the only advantage
worth living for. This fierce spirit of liberty is stronger in
the English colonies probably than in any other peoples of
the earth'.[3] Or again, 'If there be one fact in the world

[1] Edmund Burke, 'Letter to the Sheriffs of Bristol', *Works*, ed. 1803, iii.
185.
[2] Ibid., 'Observations on the present State of the Nation', *Works*, ii. 166.
[3] Ibid., 'Speech on Conciliation with America', *Works*, iii. 49.

perfectly clear it is, that the people of America is wholly
averse to any other than a free government, and this is
indication enough to any honest statesman, how he ought to
adapt whatever powers he finds in his hand to their case.'[1]
In his great speech on 'Conciliation', in 1775, he expressed
a profound judgement when he said 'freedom and not servitude is the cure of anarchy'.[2]

So far, then, we see that political freedom was to Burke a
thing not merely desirable, but the essential condition of all
living societies; and we must again ask—What did Burke
mean by political liberty?

We may begin by taking note of some remarkable words,
'If any man ask me what a free government is, I answer that,
for any practical purpose, it is what the people think so, and
that they, and not I, are the natural, lawful and competent
judges of the matter'.[3]   This may sound very paradoxical,
but a little reflection will show us that this is nothing but
the expression of a just historical sense that liberty, like
most profound conceptions of life, is a thing incapable of
definition, for it lives and moves with the movement of life
itself.

Some people may find this a little difficult, and we may
perhaps understand Burke's meaning more easily if we look
at some others of his observations on the relation of good
government to the temper of the political community.

'People must be governed in a manner agreeable to their temper and
disposition, and men of free character and spirit must be ruled with at
least some consideration to this spirit and character. The British
colonist must see something, which will distinguish him from the
colonists of other nations. Those reasonings which infer from the
many restraints under which we have already laid America, to our
right to lay it under still more, and indeed under all manner of restraints, are conclusive as to right, but the very reverse as to policy and
practice' (and a little further on), 'Whether all this (i.e. the supreme
authority of Great Britain and the American claim to normal freedom
from taxation) can be reconciled in legal speculation, is a matter of no
consequence.   It is reconciled in policy, and politicks ought to be

---

[1] Ibid., 'Letter to the Sheriffs of Bristol', *Works*, iii. 183.
[2] Ibid., 'Speech on Conciliation with America', *Works*, iii. 89.
[3] Ibid., 'Letter to the Sheriffs of Bristol', *Works*, iii. 183.

adjusted, not to human reasonings, but to human needs, of which the reason is but a part, and by no means the greater part.'[1]

This is again what is meant by one of Burke's most significant phrases, in his speech on 'Conciliation with America', in 1775.

'Sir, I think you must perceive that I am resolved this day to have nothing at all to do with the question of the right (i.e. the legal right) of taxation. I put it totally out of the question. It is less than nothing in my consideration. . . . It is not what a lawyer tells me, I may do, but what humanity, reason and justice tell me I ought to do.'[2]

In his 'Letter to the Sheriffs of Bristol' of 1777 Burke puts the principle of government for which he is contending in still plainer and larger terms.

'I must beg leave to observe that it is not only the insidious branch of taxation that will be resisted, but that no other given part of legislative rights can be exercised, without regard to the general opinion of those who are governed. That general opinion is the vehicle and organ of legislative omnipotence. Without this, it may be a thing to entertain the mind, but it is nothing in the direction of affairs. The completeness of the legislative authority of parliament over this kingdom is not questioned; and yet many things indubitably included in the abstract idea of that power, and which carry no absolute injustice in themselves, yet, being contrary to the opinions and feelings of the people, can as little be exercised, as if parliament in these cases had been possessed of no right at all. . . . In effect, to follow, not to force the public inclination; to give a direction, a form, a technical dress, and a specifick sanction, to the general sense of the community is the true end of legislation.'[3]

The truth is that Burke was turning from the doctrine that political liberty finds its essential character in the supremacy of law to a larger and more penetrating conception of the nature of an authority which lies behind the law, and even behind the legal authority of such a supreme body as the Parliament of Great Britain, and that is the living authority of the community.

The principle of the supreme authority of the law had indeed done good service to European civilization in the

[1] Edmund Burke, 'Observations on a Publication Intitled, "The present State of the Nation"', *Works*, ii. 166, 167, 170.
[2] Ibid., 'Conciliation with America', *Works*, iii. 74, 75.
[3] Ibid., 'Letter to the Sheriffs of Bristol', *Works*, iii. 179, 180.

resistance to the revolutionary attempt to set up an absolute authority in the ruler, but the law may be thought of under terms which give it the quality of the dead hand of the past, while political authority is the authority of a living and growing thing, that is the political community, living in the present, and looking forward to the future.

In the passages from the works of Burke which we have just cited he was dealing with the question of political liberty as related to the American Colonies. He had, however, already set out the same principle, that is the supremacy of the community, in terms related to the British Constitution itself. In his 'Thoughts on the Present Discontents' of 1770, he had said:

'The people will see the necessity of restoring publick men to an attention to the publick opinion, and restoring the constitution to its original principles. Above all, they will endeavour to keep the House of Commons from assuming a character which does not belong to it. They will endeavour to keep that House, for its very existence, for its power, and its privileges, as independent of every other, and as dependent on themselves as possible. This servitude is to the House of Commons (like obedience to the divine law) perfect freedom.'[1]

These are indeed strong words, and I am not sure whether their significance has been always sufficiently observed. For they represent very clearly the judgement of Burke as being, that in the last resort political liberty means, neither the supremacy of the law, nor the supreme authority of a representative assembly, but the supremacy of the community ('the people' he calls it). This was not indeed a wholly new principle, it was implied in the supreme authority of the custom of the community in medieval law, the living and growing custom. It had even found expression in the medieval use of the words of the Roman law: 'Quod omnes tangit, ab omnibus approbetur.' It had been from this developed by the sixteenth-century political writers like the Huguenots, by the Jesuit Mariana, by Althusius in Germany, and even by Hooker when he said of the kingdom of England, 'In Kingdoms therefore of this quality the highest Governor hath indeed universal dominion but with depen-

---

[1] Ibid., 'Thoughts on the causes of the Present Discontents', *Works*, ii. 342.

dence upon the whole entire body, over the several parts whereof he hath dominion; so that it standeth for an axiom in the case. The King is "major singulis, universis minor".[1] The conception was not wholly new, but I think it is true to say that Burke was giving it a new form and place in political thought. The judgements of the legislative body must correspond with the general sense of the community.

It was the same principle of the supreme authority of the community which was expressed by Burke in his treatment of the relation of the executive power to the legislature and to the community. Montesquieu had maintained that the executive and the legislative must be independent of each other. Burke does not indeed refer to Montesquieu, but in fact he maintains the opposite:

'One great end,' he says, 'of mixed governments like ours, composed of Monarchy, and of controuls on the part of the higher people and the lower, is that the prince shall not be able to violate the laws. This is useful indeed, and fundamental. But this, even at first view, is no more than a negative advantage, an armour merely defensive. It is therefore next in order and equal in importance, that the discretionary powers which are vested in the Monarch, whether for the execution of the laws, or for conducting the affairs of peace and war, or for ordering the revenue, should all be exercised upon publick principles and national grounds, and not on the likings or prejudices, the intrigues or policies, of a court. This I said is equal in importance to the securing a Government according to law. The laws reach but a very little way. Constitute governments how you please, infinitely the greater part of it must depend upon the exercise of the powers which are left at large to the prudence and uprightness of ministers of State. Even all the use and potency of laws depend on them. Without them, your Commonwealth is no better than a scheme upon paper, and not a living, acting, effective constitution. . . . Nothing, indeed, will appear more certain, on any tolerable consideration of this matter, than that every sort of government ought to have its administration correspondent to its legislature. If it should be otherwise, things must fall into a hideous disorder. The people of a free commonwealth, who have taken such care that their laws should be the result of general consent, cannot be so senseless as to suffer their executory system to be composed of persons on whom they have no dependence, and whom no proofs of

[1] Cf. 'Droit des Magistrats', ed. in *Mémoires de l'Estat*, ed. 1576, ii. 748, 776; Mariana, *De Rege*, i. 6, 8; Althusius, *Politica*, xxxviii. 127; Hooker, *Eccl. Polity*, viii. 2. 7.

the publick love and confidence have recommended to those powers upon the use of which the very being of the state depends.

The popular election of magistrates, and popular disposition of rewards and honours, is one of the first advantages of a free state. Without it, or something equivalent to it, perhaps the people cannot long enjoy the substance of freedom, certainly none of the vivifying energy of good government. The frame of our Commonwealth did not admit of such an actual election; but it provided as well, and (while the spirit of the constitution is preserved) better for all the effects of it than by the method of suffrage in any democratic state whatsoever. It had always, until of late, been held the first duty of Parliament, to refuse to support Government, until power was in the hands of persons who were acceptable to the people, or while factions predominated in the Court, in which the nation had no confidence.'[1]

It should be observed that Burke admitted that there were two forms under which the control of the executive by the community could be exercised, the election of magistrates, or the control of the executive by the legislature; it was the second which he saw as the method of the English Constitution; but by one method or another, he was clear that the executive should be controlled by the community. Political liberty, we then say, meant to Burke not only the supreme authority of the community as the source of all positive law, but also as the ultimate authority to which the executive government was responsible.

This principle of government was also not wholly new, but had a long history. The unhappy fate of so many royal favourites in the Middle Ages was due not only to the jealousy of the nobles, but also to other and more profound causes. The principle that the community as a whole should have part in the practical administration of its affairs found expression not only in the Provisions of Oxford in the thirteenth century, but in the parallel demands of the States General in France in the fourteenth century. It was in the middle of the fourteenth century that the history of the legal process for the removal and punishment of ministers of the Crown by way of impeachment began in England. And it should be observed that, as we have seen in the last chapter, ever Montesquieu, while he would not allow the legislature

[1] Ibid., 'Thoughts on the Present Discontents', *Works*, ii. 260–3.

to interfere directly with the action of the executive, accorded
to it the right to inquire into the administration of the laws
which it had made, and to proceed against and punish
ministers who had given the king evil counsel.[1]

The principle of the control of the executive by the community was not new, but Burke's dogmatic assertion of it,
while it was no doubt directly due to the circumstances of
the moment, was something like a new and deliberate assertion of an important element of political liberty as he saw it
in the Constitution of England.

It is, I think, evident that Burke's approach to the subject
of political liberty was different from that of most earlier
and contemporary political thinkers, and that he actually
made new and most important contributions to the conception of the subject.

Other thinkers, like Locke, had dealt with it under the
terms of the Stoic and Patristic theory of the primitive and
inalienable liberty of the human personality and had concluded from this that political authority was founded upon
a voluntary agreement to establish a society which all should
obey. This conception, though we all know that it was unhistorical, had a great importance in the development of
the principle of liberty. We know, indeed, that the origins
of political society cannot be found in a world of autonomous
or independent individuals, for the primitive world was a
world of groups, yet it represents the principle that the
formation and purposes of society are to liberate the human
personality.

Others had very justly argued that the development of
absolute monarchies in the sixteenth and seventeenth centuries was plainly contradictory to the historical character of
Western society, after the fall of the Roman Empire in the
West; that the first principle of all Western societies had
been the supremacy of law, and that the law was the expression of the life and custom of these societies.

Burke, however, in these works with which we have been
dealing treats precedent with the same contempt as Milton,
refuses to admit that even the laws of the past are to be taken
as determining the liberties of the present, and in the words

[1] Cf. p. 156.

we have cited describes political liberty as that which the people think to be liberty—an audacious paradox, but a true one. And, what is equally noticeable, he thinks of the people as being supreme both over the legislative and executive power. It was therefore in accordance with his most profound convictions that he defended the revolt of the American Colonies against what he conceived to be the unjustifiable attempt of the mother country to destroy their liberty.

V

THE FRENCH REVOLUTION AND CONDORCET

WE are approaching that great Revolution which moved the European world even more profoundly than the American. It would be absurd in a few and necessarily superficial words to attempt to express the character and meaning of that great upheaval. We can only recognize that whether men thought of it in the terms of that rapture with which the young Wordsworth greeted it—

> Bliss was it in that dawn to be alive.
> But to be young was very heaven!

or in the terms of the passionate loathing of Burke in his later writings, the Western world was shaken to its foundations.

Liberty, Equality, and Fraternity were the watchwords with which the Revolution placarded the walls of France, and whatever may have been the disappointments and disillusionments of the succeeding time, they still possess the souls of the Western world, and we know that so far as there has been, or is to be any reality of social and political progress, it is under these terms that we must look for it.

They were not indeed new terms. The later Hebrew prophets and the Stoics had proclaimed the liberty of the individual personality, the great cities of Greece and the Republic of Rome had laid the foundations of political liberty, and the Stoics and the Christian religion had taught men something of the universal equality and brotherhood of man.

And these principles had never been wholly forgotten in the Middle Ages; in spite of the criminal religious intolerance of the Church, and the temporary successes of the monarchical absolutisms of the seventeenth and eighteenth centuries. 'Successes' I have called them, but so far from being successful these monarchical absolutisms were, by the end of the eighteenth century, breaking down by the weight of their own incompetence.

The French Revolution was, in part, the result of this incompetence, but we are here concerned with it primarily as an attempt to recover that political liberty which had in France been almost lost during the preceding centuries, but had never even in France been wholly forgotten.

It would be impossible in such a work as this to attempt to give, even in summary form, an outline of this revolution, and I have selected—as some may think, somewhat arbitrarily—three writers to illustrate this, as representing the continuity of the conception of political liberty. These three writers are Condorcet, Thomas Paine, and Jean Jacques Rousseau.

Of these three, it is plain that Rousseau is by far the most important, and though he wrote before the Revolution, he will be treated last, because his treatment of liberty is much more profound than that of the others.

We turn therefore to Condorcet, and we find ourselves dealing with a man who was occupied mainly with practical proposals for the reform of the system of government in France, and was influenced primarily by the constitutional traditions of medieval France, while in matters of theory he derives mainly from Locke.

The first of his works with which we are here concerned is one on the influence of the American Revolution in Europe, written in 1786, and the very title is significant.

It is interesting to observe that when in this work he sets out to enumerate the Rights of Man, he states them in concrete rather than abstract terms. The Rights of man are—First, the security of his person, that is, security from violence, security in the exercise of his faculties, for he should enjoy the free use of these in all things which do not conflict with the rights of others. Secondly, the security and free enjoyment of his property. Thirdly, inasmuch as certain actions must be subjected to general regulations, and certain penalties must be imposed upon the men who attack the rights of others by force or fraud, these regulations and penalties must be embodied in general laws which apply to all citizens, and must be interpreted and enforced by impartial persons. Fourthly, the right to take his part, directly,

or by his representatives, in legislation and in all actions
done in the name of the society.[1] Condorcet, however, adds
that this is an ideal which should be aimed at; actually many
men are still so much under the influence of ignorance and
prejudice that its complete realization may for the present
be impracticable.

It is interesting to compare this statement of the 'Rights
of Man' with the 'Rights of the Nation' which Condorcet
set out a few years later in a treatise on the Instructions
which should be given by the Provinces to their representatives at the States General of 1789.

What, he asks, is the first 'Right' whose recognition the
nation should demand? It is the legislative authority. What
is the nature and extent of the legislative authority? Inasmuch as the general will is the law, the legislative authority
in its entirety belongs to the nation. He stops to ask how
the national society has been formed, and says that men were
too feeble when isolated to resist the dangers by which they
were surrounded, and they have therefore entered into a
contract, in which every individual person has promised to
help the society with all his power, while the society is
to employ all its power to help the individual. Returning to
the authority of the national society, he says that it is always
and only governed by itself, and has the right of rejecting
any authority which does not proceed from itself; it enacts
and changes the laws which it makes, and entrusts their
execution to one or more of its members.[2]

So far Condorcet was speaking in the terms of a general
theory of political authority, but he goes on to relate this to
the historical traditions of France. The (executive) authority
had been in France, from the beginnings of its institution,
placed in the hands of the prince, and his person is sacred,
because his authority is legitimate (i.e. in accordance with
law), and because in him are deposited all the powers of the
citizens to enforce the laws. Thus, in the French monarchy,
the nation declares the general will, the general will makes

[1] Condorcet, 'De l'Influence de la Révolution de l'Amérique sur l'Europe',
Works, ed. 1804, xi. 240–2.

[2] Ibid., 'Reflexions sur les Pouvoirs et Instructions à donner par les
Provinces à leur Députés aux États Generaux', Works, ed. 1804, xii. 374–6.

the law, and the law makes the prince and the executive power.

Such, Condorcet says, is the royal authority, as determined by our ancestors, and our historical monuments testify that the nation consented to recognize the monarch as an integral part of the legislative authority, and Condorcet cites the famous words of the 'Edictum Pistense' of 864: 'Lex fit consensu populi et constitutione regis.'[1]

There is indeed nothing to surpise us in this, for, as we have seen in earlier chapters, the tradition of the earlier character of the French constitutional system had never been forgotten, and had been frequently restated in the seventeenth and eighteenth centuries. It is important to notice that what Condorcet calls the 'Rights of the Nation' were, in his judgement, founded not only upon general and abstract principles, but upon a still living tradition.

The second of the 'Rights' which the nation should demand is, according to Condorcet, the individual personal freedom of the citizens; it is the principle of the supremacy of law as the protection of liberty which he was asserting, but now in very concrete terms. Condorcet was asserting the traditional principle of medieval law, that no man's liberty should be infringed, unless he is charged with some definite crime, and the particular form of this abuse which he attacked was the 'Lettres de Cachet'. These he describes as the worst of the abuses from which France had suffered. They had arrested, he says, the progress of enlightenment, they had prevented men from knowing what were their rights, from defending themselves, and from helping each other. They had for centuries shaken the courage and frustrated the efforts of those bodies whose duty it was to oppose the levying of illegal taxes. They had struck down those who had wished to defend the oppressed against the rapacity of ministers. They had been used by bishops to repress religious opinions, by governors of Provinces to satisfy their jealousy or their revenge. All had bowed under their yoke. The presidents of Estates had not blushed to threaten their deliberations with the exercise of this arbitrary power.[2]

---

[1] Ibid. xii. 378.   [2] Ibid. xii. 380.

We are not here concerned with the question how far
there may or may not have been some exaggeration in Condorcet's denunciations, what is important is to notice that
he was restating the first principle of medieval law, as we can
see it in Magna Carta, in the continual protests and demands
of the Cortes of Castile, and even in the declaration of the
Parliament of Paris in 1648;[1] the principle of all civilized
countries, that no man can be imprisoned without due
process of law.

The third 'Right' of the nation follows naturally upon the
second, it is that no man may be judged except in accordance
with the law, and by lawful judges who may not modify the
law, even by their interpretation of it.

The fourth 'Right' is that the nation should control the
levy and expenditure of the taxes, by means of the elected
representatives of the provinces.

The fifth 'Right' is that the ministers should be responsible for their actions, and liable to be tried for them in the
proper courts.

The sixth 'Right' is the fixed periodical meeting of the
States General, for, if all authority is in the nation, it must
have the right to meet when and where it wishes. In former
ages these General Assemblies were held in the month of
May; it is for the nation to determine their frequency; for
the executive power will always tend to become arbitrary
unless it is carefully supervised.[2]

Condorcet concludes by saying that the first duty of the
States General will be to embody these 'Rights' in a Charter
(i.e. a written Constitution) which will serve always to remind the prince and the people of their mutual obligations.

It is, I think, very important to observe, especially for
our purpose in this work, that Condorcet's assertion of
political liberty, while it was founded in part upon abstract
and general principles, was at least as much based upon the
traditions of medieval society, and an appeal to the history
of French institutions, and especially upon the French
traditions of the supremacy of the law, and the embodiment
of the national authority in its representative system.

[1] Cf. p. 65 of the present work.   [2] Condorcet, Works, xii. 313–90.

VI

THOMAS PAINE

IT is interesting to turn from Condorcet to Thomas Paine, from the Frenchman to the Englishman, and to find that, contrary to a frequent conception, it is the Englishman who is commonly occupied with the general or abstract principles of political liberty, while the Frenchman was concerned rather with the revival of what he conceived to be the historical forms of the political liberty of the French people. There is, however, nothing surprising in this when we take account of the obvious fact that Paine was practically restating, with some modifications, the political principles of Locke; and this, not only with reference to the origin of free governments, but also with reference to what he conceived to be the necessary limits of all political authority; for, like Locke, Paine maintained that the State possessed no absolute and unlimited power. Paine, like Locke, was not only asserting the political liberty of the free community; he was also, and equally, defending the liberty of the individual against the tyranny of the community.

The career of Paine was certainly interesting: by birth an Englishman, a citizen of the United States by his residence there, a citizen of France by the election of the National Convention, and a member of that Convention. He had become famous by his little treatise entitled *Common Sense*, published in 1776, which had greatly helped to give expression and form to the demand for the independence of the States, in terms intelligible and direct.

We are here concerned more immediately with two of his later works, the *Dissertations on Government* of 1786, and the *Rights of Man* of 1791. For our purpose we shall find it most convenient to notice first the principles of the later work, and we shall see at once that the political theories of Paine were clearly derived from those which Locke had inherited from the Middle Ages.

'Men', Paine says, 'are all of one degree, and consequently all men are born equal, and with equal Natural Rights. . . . Natural Rights are those which appertain to man in right of his existence. Of this kind are all the intellectual rights, or rights of the mind, and all those rights of acting as an individual for his own comfort and happiness, which are not injurious to the natural rights of others.'[1]

This conception of equality has no doubt become a revolutionary force in modern times, but it was not a new doctrine. We have only to compare the words of Paine with those of Locke:

'To understand political power aright, and to derive it from its original, we must consider what estate all men are naturally in, and that is a state of perfect freedom to order their actions, and dispose of their possessions and persons as they think fit, within the bounds of the law of nature, without asking leave or depending upon the will of any other man. A State also of equality, wherein all the power and jurisdiction is reciprocal, no one having more than another, there being nothing more evident than that creatures of the same species and rank, promiscuously born to the same advantages of nature, and the use of the same faculties, should also be equal one amongst another, without subordination or subjection.'[2]

This was not a doctrine invented by Locke; it was the doctrine of the post-Aristotelian philosophers, as we can see in Cicero and Seneca, the jurists of the Roman Empire, the Christian Fathers, and the medieval jurists.[3]

Paine no doubt describes the proper conditions of human life under the terms of 'Rights', while Locke uses the tradition of the 'Law of Nature', but their meaning is substantially the same. 'The State of Nature', Locke says, 'has a law of nature to govern it, and reason, which is that law, teaches all mankind who will but consider it, that being all equal and independent, no one ought to harm another in his life, liberty or possessions.' In the next paragraph, indeed, Locke speaks of these rules of the law of nature as constituting 'rights'.[4]

What is then the relation of these 'Rights' to the authority of political society? Paine's answer is clearly parallel to, if

[1] T. Paine, 'Rights of Man', *Works*, ed. 1894, ii. 304–6.
[2] Locke, *Second Treatise on Government*, i. 2.
[3] e.g., Cicero, *De Legibus*, i. 10, 12; Seneca, *De Beneficiis*, iii. 18, &c.; *Digest*, i. 1. 4; i. 5. 4; Ambrose, *De Joseph Patriarcha*, iv; Gregory the Great, *Expositio Moralis*, xxi. 15; Sachsenspiegel, iii. 421; Beaumanoir, *Coustumes du Beauvoisis*, xlv. 1453.
[4] Locke, *Second Treatise on Government*, ii. 6, 7.

not identical with, that of Locke; it is that, while the rights belong to men as such, it is not in their power to secure all of these by their own efforts.

'The natural rights,' Paine says, 'which he retains are all those in which the power to execute is as perfect in the individual as the right itself. Among this class, as is before mentioned, are all the intellectual rights, or rights of the mind, consequently religion is one of those rights. The natural rights which are not retained are all those in which, though the right is perfect in the individual, the power to execute them is defective. They answer not his purpose. A man, by natural right has the right to judge in his own cause, and, so far as the right of the mind is concerned, he never surrenders it; but what availeth it him to judge, if he hath not the power to redress? He therefore deposits this right in the common stock of society, and takes the arm of society, of which he is a part, in preference to and in addition to his own.'[1]

Paine in this passage attributes the necessity of a political society to the lack of power in the individual to maintain his natural rights, while Locke treats it as originating in the confusion and discord that would arise if men were to be judges in their own cases. 'I easily grant', he says, 'that civil government is the proper remedy for the inconvenience of the state of nature, which must certainly be great when men may be judges in their own case.'[2]

The difference is possibly of some importance, but the actual conclusion is the same, namely, that the execution of the laws of nature, or the rights of man, cannot be secured without the creation of some common power to protect and enforce them. Paine sums up the conclusions of the passage just quoted by saying:

'From these premises two or three certain conclusions will follow: First, That every civil right grows out of a natural right: or, in other words, is a natural right exchanged. Secondly, that civil power properly considered as such is made up of the aggregate of that class of the natural rights of man which becomes defective in the individual in point of power, and answers not his purpose, but, when collected to a focus, becomes competent to the purpose of every one. Thirdly, That the power produced from the aggregate of individual rights, imperfect in power in the individual, cannot be applied to invade the natural

[1] Paine, 'Rights of Man', *Works*, ii. 1307.
[2] Locke, *Second Treatise on Government*, ii. 13.

rights which are retained in the individual, and in which the power to
execute is as perfect as the right itself.'[1]

Political authority is not and cannot be, in Paine's judgement, anything more than the authority to protect the
natural rights of man, and this is practically the same principle as that of Locke, with which we have dealt in an earlier
chapter. The legislative authority of a political society is
not an absolute or arbitrary authority, for the society can
have no more authority than the individuals, who formed
the society, possessed by the law of nature, before they
entered into society.[2]

This principle is so important that it is well to observe
that Paine had already set it out, though in different terms,
in his earlier work, the 'Dissertations on Government, published in 1786. He begins indeed by setting out the doctrine,
derived ultimately no doubt from Bodin, that

'Every government, let its form be what it may, contains within
itself a principle common to all, which is that of a sovereign power, or
a power over which there is no control, and which controls all others.
. . . In republics, such as that established in America, the sovereign
power, or that power over which there is no control, and which
controls all others, remains where nature placed it—in the people; for
the people in America are the fountain of power. . . As the repository
where the sovereign power is lodged is the first criterion of distinction,
so the second is the principle on which it is administered.

'A despotic government knows no principle but will. Whatever
the sovereign wills to do, the government admits him the inherent
right, and the uncontrolled power of doing. He is restrained by no
fixed rule of right and wrong, for he makes the right and wrong himself, and as he pleases. . . . Having already shown what a despotic
government is, and how it is administered, I now come to show what
the administration of a republic is. The administration of a republic is
supposed to be directed by certain fundamental principles of right and
justice, from which there ought not to be any deviation; and whenever
any deviation appears, there is a kind of stepping out of the republican
principle, and an approach to the despotic one. . . . When a people
agree to form themselves into a republic (for the word republic means
the common good, or the good of the whole, in contradistinction to the
despotic form, which makes the good of the sovereign, or of one man,

---

[1] Paine, 'Rights of Man', *Works*, ii. 307.
[2] Locke, *Second Treatise on Government*, xi. 135.

the only object of the government), when, I say, they agree to do this, it is to be understood, that they mutually resolve and pledge themselves to each other, rich and poor alike, to support and maintain this rule of equal justice among them. They therefore renounce, not only the despotic power, but the despotic principle, as well of governing as of being governed by mere will and power, and substitute in its place a government of justice.

'By this mutual compact, the citizens of a republic put it out of their power, that is, they renounce as detestable, the power of exercising, at any future time, any species of despotism over each other, or doing a thing not right in itself, because a majority of them have strength of numbers sufficient to accomplish it.

'In this pledge and compact lies the foundation of the republic, and the security to the rich, and the consolation to the poor is, that what each man has is his own, that no despotic sovereign can take it from him, and that the common cementing power which holds all the parts of the republic together, secures him likewise from the despotism of numbers, for despotism may be more efficiently acted by many over few than by one man over all. . . . The sovereignty of a despotic monarch assumes the power of making wrong right, or right wrong as he pleases or as it suits him. The sovereignty of a republic is exercised to keep right and wrong in their proper and distinct places, and never suffers the one to usurp the place of the other. A republic, properly understood, is a sovereignty of justice in contradistinction to a sovereignty of will!'[1]

These are indeed important principles of government; they were indeed not new, for they are in substance the same as those of Locke, and the doctrines of Locke were chiefly derived from the medieval tradition that all laws whether of the State or the Church which were contrary to the laws of nature were *ipso facto* null and void. This means that there is not and cannot be an absolute or arbitrary sovereignty, and it is very important to notice that Paine repudiated the sovereignty of the majority as emphatically as he did that of the monarch.

We have considered Paine's conception of the nature and limitations of political authority, and we must turn to the question how, in his judgement, the political societies had come into being.

---

[1] Paine, 'Dissertations on Government', *Works*, ii. 133–41.

'It will be proper,' he says in the *Rights of Man*, 'to take a review of the several sources from which governments have arisen, and on which they have been founded. These may all be comprehended under three heads. First Superstition, Secondly Power, Thirdly, the Common Interests of Society and the Common Rights of Man.

'When a set of artful men pretended, through the medium of oracles, to have intercourse with the Deity, as familiarly as they now march up the backstairs in European courts, the world was completely under the government of Superstition. . . .

'After these a race of conquerors arose, whose government, like that of William the Conqueror, was founded in power, and the sword assumed the name of a sceptre. Governments thus established last as long as the power to support them lasts; but that they might avail themselves of every engine in their favour, they united fraud to force, and set up an idol which they called Divine Right. . . . When I contemplate the natural dignity of man, when I feel (for nature has not been kind enough to me to blunt my feelings) for the honour and happiness of its character, I become irritated at the attempt to govern mankind by force and fraud, as if they were all knaves and fools, and can scarcely avoid disgust at those who are thus imposed upon.'[1]

Paine evidently thought that in fact many of the Governments of mankind had been founded by illegitimate and repulsive methods, and he contrasts them with the legitimate and rational source of political authority.

'The fact therefore must be that the individuals themselves, each in his own personal and sovereign right, enter into a compact with each other to produce a government; and this is the only mode in which governments have a right to arise, and the only principle on which they have the right to exist.'[2]

Political authority is then, in the conception of Paine, founded upon a contract between men to set up a government to which, subject to the conditions which we have considered, they promise to render obedience. This is, of course the doctrine of Locke:

'Men being, as we have said, by nature all free, equal, and independent, no one can be put out of this estate and subjected to the political power of another, without his own consent, which is done by agreeing with other men to join and unite into a community for the comfortable, safe and peaceable living, one amongst another, in a

[1] Ibid., p. 309.
[2] Paine, 'Rights of Man', *Works*, ii. 308.

secure enjoyment of their properties, and a greater security against any that are not of it.'[1]

This was also the doctrine of Hooker:

'To take away such mutual grievances, injuries and wrongs, there was no way, but only by growing into composition and agreement amongst themselves, by ordaining some kind of government public, and by yielding themselves subject thereunto; that, unto whom they granted authority to govern, by them the peace, tranquillity and happy estate of the rest might be procured.'[2]

[1] Locke, *Second Treatise on Government*, viii. 95.
[2] Hooker, *Eccles. Polity*, i. 10.

VII

ROUSSEAU

IT would be impossible in a work of this kind to deal with all the aspects of Rousseau's political work, and we limit ourselves to two of his most important contributions to political thought. The first of these was his emphatic repudiation of the long tradition of the Stoics and the Christian Fathers that men in their primitive condition lived in a happy and innocent anarchy, and that the development of the coercive political societies was primarily the result, as it was also the remedy for the vices into which they had fallen. As against this Rousseau maintained that it was only by means of the great coercive authority of the State that they had become men.

This means that after nearly two thousand years Rousseau was restating the Aristotelian doctrine that man is by nature, not only a social, but a political being, or, to put it in other terms, that the political society is not merely a remedy for men's vices, but the necessary condition of all progress.

It is true that the Aristotelian principle had been apprehended by St. Thomas Aquinas in the thirteenth century, but it is also clear from the political literature of the sixteenth and seventeenth centuries that even the great influence of St. Thomas was not strong enough to prevail over the long philosophical and theological tradition. It is true that something of this survived in the extravagant individualism of the radical or extreme liberalism of the earlier part of the nineteenth century, and in the police theory of the State, but practically it was dying, if not dead, and we are once again Aristotelians.

This is the first and in some ways the most fundamental meaning of the *Contrat Social*, and is admirably stated in the eighth chapter of the First Book.

'Ce passage de l'état de nature a l'état civil produit dans l'homme une changement trés remarquable, en substituant dans sa conduite la justice a l'instinct, et donnant à ses actions la moralité qui leur manquoit auparavant. . . . Quoiqu'il se prive dans cet état de plusieurs avantages qu'il tient de la nature, il en regagne de si grands, ses facultés s'exercent

et se développent, ses idées s'étendent, ses sentiments s'ennoblissent, son
âme tout entière s'élève à tel point que si les abus de cette nouvelle
condition ne le dégradoient souvent au-dessous de celle dont il est sorti,
il devrait bénir sans cesse l'instant heureux qui l'en arracha pour jamais,
et qui, d'un animal stupide et borne, fit un être intelligent et un
homme.'[1]

We may render this: The transition from the state of nature
to the political condition brings about a very noteworthy
change, by substituting justice for mere instinct, and gives
to man's actions that moral character which before they
lacked. It is true that he loses some advantages which belonged to him by nature, but he gains more, his faculties
are developed, his conceptions enlarged, his feelings are
ennobled to such an extent, that if the evils of the new
condition did not often degrade him below the level of that
from which he came, he would never cease to bless that
happy moment which changed him from a stupid and
limited animal, and made him an intelligent being and a
man.

It should be noticed that there is a certain ambiguity
about Rousseau's use of the term 'state of nature', but it is
clear that he looks upon this as a merely animal condition,
not a human one at all, it is only in the political society that
he becomes a man.

Rousseau had begun the first chapter of the *Contrat
Social* by saying that man is born free, and yet is everywhere
in chains; and it has sometimes been thought by careless
readers that Rousseau meant that this was a lamentable
thing; but this was not his meaning at all, for he goes on
to say that he thinks that he could explain that this is
legitimate. It is legitimate, because man to be man must
live under the rational and intelligible authority of his
fellow men in the great community of the State.

It may seem paradoxical to say that Rousseau's first contribution to the conception of liberty in the *Contrat Social*
was, that men should live under authority, but that is what
he meant. It is worth while to remind ourselves that it was
only a few years later that Burke, in his 'Letter to the
Sheriffs of Bristol', writing in 1777 said, 'The extreme of

[1] Rousseau, *Contrat Social*, i. 8.

liberty (which is its abstract perfection, but its real fault) obtains nowhere, nor ought it to obtain anywhere. . . . Liberty too must be limited in order to be possessed.'[1] I think that his meaning is substantially the same as that of Rousseau, neither of them identified liberty with anarchy.

The truth is that Burke's conception of the real nature of political society was fundamentally the same as that of Rousseau, he also was an Aristotelian. There is a well-known passage in his *Reflections on the French Revolution* which will serve to illustrate this.

'It (the State) is to be looked on with other reverence; because it is not a partnership in things subservient only to the gross animal existence of a temporary and perishable nature. It is a partnership in all Science; a partnership in all Art, a partnership in every virtue; and in all perfection. As the end of such a partnership cannot be obtained in many generations, it becomes a partnership not only between those who are living, but between those who are living, those who are dead, and those who are to be born.'[2]

I do not know that there is any reason to think that Burke was acquainted with the *Contrat Social*. We may feel sure that in many respects he would have violently differed from Rousseau, but they are at one in repudiating the narrow conception of the origins and functions of the State held by the post-Aristotelians, and we can be sure that it would have been impossible for Burke as well as Rousseau to accept the meagre political theory of the early nineteenth-century radicals.

It may be thought that the difference between the traditional conception of the nature and functions of the State and that which is characteristic of Rousseau and Burke was little more than formal. It is true that while the medieval political thinkers formally accepted the doctrine that the State was primarily an organ for correcting the vices of human nature, in fact medieval society did not limit its actions to this.

And yet it is also true that the doctrine represented by Rousseau and Burke has had an immense effect upon the development of the social and political conceptions and

[1] Cf. p. 162.
[2] Burke, 'Reflections on the French Revolution', *Works*, ed. 1803, 184.

actions of the nineteenth century. The long struggle between the exaggerated individualism of the older economists
and the rising tide of social reform is the best illustration of
this.

It is true that the economists have seen the error of their
ways, but the pseudo-scientific application of the theory of
the struggle for existence, as determining progress or
development in the animal world, to the conditions of human
life and progress, had, and has still, a great influence among
the half-educated members of society.

We come then to the second great contribution of
Rousseau to the conception of liberty, and this lies in his
argument that man can be under authority and yet remain
free. This is the meaning of the great paradox of the sixth
chapter of the first book of the *Contrat Social*: 'Trouver une
forme d'association qui défende et protége de toute la force
commune la personne et les biens de chaque associé, et par
laquelle chacun, s'unissant à tous, n'obeisse pourtant qu'à
lui-même, et reste aussi libre qu'auparavant.[1] That is, we
want to find a form of society which will protect, with all
the common power, the person and goods of each member,
and in which the individual will unite himself to all the
members of the society, and yet will only obey himself, and
will remain as free as he was before.

An extravagant paradox, some will perhaps say, but that
depends upon what Rousseau meant by liberty, and what
is the authority which the men who form the political society
promise to obey.

By liberty Rousseau, as he says in the last paragraph of
the eighth chapter of the same book, does not mean the
right to do whatever the caprice or passion of the individual
may at any moment lead him to desire, but obedience to
the law which he has prescribed to himself. Obedience to
the first is slavery, obedience to the second is liberty.[2]

The authority which a man, in forming the political
society, promises to obey, is what Rousseau calls the
'General Will'. Rousseau says a number of things about
this, and I confess that I do not feel that his words are

[1] Rousseau, *Contrat Social*, i. 6.   [2] Ibid. i. 8.

always as clearly consistent as one could wish. It is, however, possible to say what Rousseau did not mean by the 'General Will'. It is not to be identified with the 'Will of all', for the 'Will of all' may be wrong, while the 'General Will' is always right.[1] Rousseau therefore did not mean that the will of the people, even of the whole community, at any given moment is always right, for the whole community may be carried away by some panic or caprice. The whole community therefore does not possess any absolute sovereign power.

The 'General Will' is a will which is in all those who form the political society; and it is upon this unanimity that it is founded.

It may be suggested that this conception of unanimity is impossible. I should myself venture to say that it is common sense. It is surely obvious that in any society, which is to continue, there must be agreement on some general principles of life which all the members of the society share when they are in their normal state of mind, even though the same men, when moved by some overpowering passion, may desire and do what is contrary to it. All men in a political society may normally agree in condemning and punishing murder or fraud, but the same men as individuals, or even as a whole, under the influence of some violent temptation or passion, may commit murder or fraud; and one may therefore say that, when a member of such a society is punished for committing such actions, he is punishing himself, he is obeying his own normal and rational will. He is free for he is being coerced by himself.

It is not necessary to multiply examples, the principle is clear, that is, that a political society is founded upon a certain homogeneity and unanimity, and that the authority of the society, except in matters of mere convenience, does not really extend beyond this. The authority of a political society is not, in the end, a mechanical thing, but the expression of a living unity, and we can see this in history.

Perhaps the most arresting example to us in England may be found in the history of the relations of England and Ireland. After some eight centuries of tragic conflict, we

---

[1] Rousseau, *Contrat Social*, ii. 3.

have at last recognized that for some reason or another the attempt to treat the two nations as homogeneous has broken down, and we recognize that the 'General Will' of the Irish, to use Rousseau's phrase, is different from that of the English.

Rousseau then, with whatever inconsistencies in language, has set out a principle on which an intelligible conception of political liberty and political authority is founded; the principle that freedom does not mean anarchy, but a rational subordination of the individual to the rational authority of a coercive society, in and through which alone he is a man; but this authority is limited by the principles of life which are common to himself and the other members of the society. That is, to put it in other terms, there is no arbitrary or absolute sovereign in a political society.

In the conception of the Stoics, of the Roman jurists, of the Christian Fathers, of the medieval political thinkers, as also in Hooker, and in Locke, this limiting authority was represented by the theory of the supremacy of the natural law, that is of the principles of life which men must rationally recognize as lying behind and controlling all positive law, and all political action. By Rousseau this limiting authority is conceived of as lying in the common principle of a homogeneous society.

The two principles are not identical, but they are parallel and they are rational and intelligible.

VIII

WHO ARE MEMBERS OF THE POLITICAL COMMUNITY?

IN this work we have been dealing with the history of the conception of political liberty under the terms of the authority of the political community over those persons to whom its immediate government is entrusted, but we have not considered the question who are the full members of the community. It may seem to us strange, but it is clear that till the middle of the eighteenth century the question was not generally present to men's minds, and that it was only in the nineteenth century that it was dealt with practically.

This does not mean that the question had not been raised earlier, and we should be omitting an important aspect of the development of the history of the conception of political liberty if we did not deal with some examples of this.

The question was raised at the 'General Council of Officers' of the Army held at Putney in October 1647 in the course of a discussion of the meaning of some clauses of the document known as 'The Agreement of the People':

'The Paper called the Agreement read.. Afterwards the first Article read by itself.' Commissary Ireton said: 'The exception that lies in it is this. It is said "The People of England etc. . . ., they are to be distributed according to the number of the inhabitants," and this doth make me think that the meaning is, that every man that is an inhabitant is to be equally considered, and to have an equal voice in the election of representatives, those persons that are for (i.e. to form) the General representative; and, if that be the meaning, then I have something to say against it. . . .'[1]

'Mr. Peters. We judge that all inhabitants that have not lost their birthright should have an equal voice in election.

'Colonel Rainborough. I desired that those that had engaged in it (should speak) for really I think that the poorest hee that is in England hath a life to live as the greatest hee; and therefore truly, Sir, I think it is clear that every man that is to live under a Government, ought first

[1] *The Clarke Papers*, ed. Firth, i. 299.

by his own consent, to put himself under that Government, and I doe think that the poorest man in England is not at all bound in a strict sense to the Government that he hath nor had a voice to put himself under. . . .

'Commissary Ireton. That's (the meaning of) this, (according to the number of the inhabitants). Give me leave to tell you, that if you make this the rule I think that you must fly for refuge to an absolute natural Right, and you must deny all Civil Right. . . . For my part I think that noe person has a right to an interest or share in the disposing or determining of the affairs of the Kingdom, and in chusing those that shall determine what laws we shall be ruled by heere, noe person hath a right to this, that hath not a permanent fixed interest in the Kingdom . . . that is, the persons in whom all land lies, and those in Corporations, in whom all trading lies. This is the most fundamental Constitution of this Kingdom, which, if you doe not allow, you allow none at all. . . .

'Colonel Rainborough. Truly, Sir, I am of the same opinion as I was. . . . I doe heare nothing at all that can convince me why any man that is borne in England ought not to have his voice in election of Burgesses. . . . I doe think that the maine cause why Almighty God gave man reason, itt was that they should make use of that reason, and that they should improve itt for that end and purpose that God gave itt them.'[1]

It is very interesting to observe how clearly we have here the statement of a fundamental difference of opinion between Ireton on the one hand and Peters and Rainborough on the other. Ireton understood that the 'Agreement of the People' claimed that 'every inhabitant' should have an equal voice in the election of representatives to sit in Parliament, and that this claim was founded upon an appeal to 'an absolute Natural Right' and the repudiation of 'all Civil Right'; meaning by this the political right as determined by existing law. Ireton formally and dogmatically repudiated this, and maintained that no one had a right to a share in the political authority who had not a permanent fixed interest in the kingdom as an owner of land, or as a member of a 'Corporation' 'in which all trading lies'. This, he said, was 'the most fundamental Constitution of the Kingdom'. That is, if we put this into our own words, that no one had a right to elect the representatives

[1] Ibid., pp. 300–4.

of the community in Parliament who was not a landowner, large or small, or a member of what he calls a 'trading Corporation'. That is, he maintained that the right to a voice in the control of the public affairs of the country belonged only to those who owned property in one form or another.

Rainborough, on the contrary, maintained that 'the poorest hee that is in England had a life to live as the greatest hee', and that it was only with his own consent that he could be put under any government, and, what is perhaps specially worth noting, he relates this to the fact that God gave man reason. It is interesting to notice that he puts the right to a share in the government of the country on the same ground as Cicero had put his doctrine of human equality, namely that man was possessed of reason.[1]

How far, and from what sources, this emphatic demand that all men should have a share in electing the representatives in whose hands the control of government should rest, had already developed, I do not pretend to be in a position to say. For the present it must suffice to notice the fact that this demand was raised in the middle of the seventeenth century.

There is little evidence that the question was formally raised again till we come to the work of Major Cartwright, with which we shall deal presently, but there are indications that it was present in some ways to men's minds. Locke, for instance, while he does not deal with it directly, does, in an interesting passage to which we have drawn attention, point out the absurdity of leaving the right to send representatives to the legislature to boroughs whose population had practically disappeared.

More significant, however, than this is the fact that some at least of the important French political writers of the eighteenth century felt it necessary to explain and justify the exclusion of some men from any direct share in the election of the members of the legislature.

Montesquieu, in the *De l'Esprit des Lois*, declares that in a free State every man who is considered to have a free spirit (*une âme libre*) should be governed by himself, and therefore

[1] Cf. p. 189.

the people as a body should have the legislative power, but, as this is impracticable, the people must act through their representatives, chosen by local election. All citizens should have a voice in these elections, except those who are not thought to have a will of their own.[1]

Montesquieu does not define the exact meaning of this exception; he does not like Ireton relate it directly to the ownership of property. We may perhaps suggest that it was because he was conscious of a difficulty that he puts his views into these rather abstract terms.

Condorcet in his work on the influence of the American Revolution in Europe, published in 1786, enumerates the 'Rights of Men', and, as the fourth of them, he says that every man has the right to take his part, directly, or through his representative, in legislation, and in all actions done in the name of the political society; this is a necessary consequence of the natural and primitive equality of man, and men should aim at its attainment.[2]

Condorcet was thinking, not of a property qualification for the franchise, but of the need of knowledge and intelligence in those who were to obtain the full powers and rights of citizens, and looked forward to the time when these conditions might be fulfilled.

Major Cartwright's little work entitled *The Legislative Rights of the Community Vindicated* (second edition published in 1777) seems to me to demand more careful consideration than it has always received. It is important not merely because Cartwright demands the extension of the franchise to all men of mature years, but even more because of the grounds on which he puts the contention. Cartwright's arguments are directed primarily against the notion that the right to take part in electing the representatives of the Commons to Parliament should be dependent on the ownership of property. These representatives are, he says, to be in a special manner

'the guardians of public freedom, in which the poor surely as well as

[1] Montesquieu, *De l'Esprit des Lois*, xi. 6.

[2] Condorcet, 'De l'Influence de la Révolution d'Amérique sur l'Europe', *Works*, ed. 1804, xi. 241–2.

the rich, have an interest. . . . Their poverty is surely the worst of all reasons for stripping them of their natural rights; let us rather reconcile to them the many hardships of their condition, by showing that it does not degrade them below the nature of man. If they have not wherewithall to gratify their pride, let them at least retain the dignity of human nature; by knowing they are free, and sharing in the privileges inseparable from liberty.'[1]

Cartwright adds ingeniously that Locke had argued that 'every man has a property in his own person, the labour of his body and the work of his hands, we may say are properly his'. And he also very reasonably says that the labouring man has to pay taxes like other men, and that it is the fundamental principle, upon which our liberties depend, that no man should be taxed but with his own consent, given either by himself or his representatives in Parliament.[2]

These, however, are not the really important grounds of his contention.

'But after all,' he says, 'surely it is not property—it cannot be the precarious possession of clay fields, and piles of brick and stone; nor of sheep and oxen, nor of guineas and shillings, and bankbills—nor indeed of any other species of property, which truly constitutes freedom. No, doubtless it is the immediate gift of God to all the human species, by adding free will to rationality, in order to render them beings, which should be accountable for their actions. All are by nature free, all are by nature equal; freedom implies choice; equality excludes degrees in freedom. All the Commons, therefore, have an equal right to vote in the elections of those who are to be the guardians of their liberties; and none can be entitled to more than one vote. . . . My own conception of the truth obliges me to believe that personality is the sole foundation of the right of being represented; and that property has, in reality, nothing to do in the case. . . . "It may be alledged", says Beccaria, "that the interests of commerce and property should be secured; but commerce and property are not the end of the social compact, but the means of obtaining that end", so that, by making property the object of representation, "we make", according to him, "the end subservient to the means, a paralogism in all science, and particularly, in all politics".'[3]

It is obviously of great importance to notice that in

[1] John Cartwright, *The Legislative Rights of the Community Vindicated*, i. 35 (ed. 1777, pp. 28, 30).
[2] Ibid., Sect. 38 (pp. 30, 31).   [3] Ibid., Sect. 39, 41, 42 (pp. 31–2).

Cartwright's judgement the possession of property has nothing to do with the right of representation, but that this arises from the fact that men are equal in virtue of their possession of reason; Cartwright was restating the contention of Cicero and Colonel Rainborough that it is the possession of reason which makes men equal. He expressed the same conception in other terms when he maintained that 'personality' was the sole foundation of the right of being represented. Here indeed was a large and sweeping contention. We need not suppose that Cartwright had a complete conception of the meaning of personality, indeed he would be a courageous person who would say that we have one to-day. But it is certainly important that the appeal to the principle that equality was founded upon the possession of reason, which had been approved in theory for nearly two thousand years, was at the end of the eighteenth century finding a new application in relation to political freedom.

These principles of Cartwright's were clearly conceived and stated, and in the nineteenth century they have been more or less carried out in all countries which are governed by constitutional methods, but, though it may seem paradoxical, it was only some of the revolutionary leaders in Europe and America who seem to have at that time appreciated the real significance of the question.

It is very noticeable that so able and powerful a leader of the American Revolution as John Adams seems clearly to have thought that those who were to elect the members of the Representative Assemblies, should be qualified by the possession of some property, particularly in land. In an important letter addressed by him in May 1776 to John Sullivan he says: 'It is certain in theory, that the only moral foundation of government is the consent of the people. But to what extent shall we carry this principle?'

Adams begins by excluding women and children, and goes on:

'Is it not equally true, that men in general, in every society, who are wholly destitute of property, are also too little acquainted with public affairs to form a right judgment, and too dependent upon other men to have a will of their own? If this is a fact, if you give to every man who

has no property, a vote, will you not make a firm encouraging provision for corruption, by your fundamental law? Such is the frailty of
the human heart, that very few men who have no property, have any
judgment of their own. They talk and vote as they are directed by
some man of property, who has attached their minds to his interest. . . .
Harrington has shown that power always follows property. This I
believe to be as infallible a maxim in politics, as that action and reaction
are equal in mechanics. Nay, I believe that we may advance a step
further and affirm that the balance of power in a society, accompanies
the balance of property in land.'

Adams was indeed democratic in his aspirations, for he
goes on to say:

'The only possible way then of pressing the balance of power on the
side of equal liberty and public virtue, is to make the acquisition of land
easy to every member of society, to make a division of the land into
small quantities, so that the multitude may be possessed of landed
estates. If the multitude is possessed of the balance of real estate, the
multitude will have the balance of power, and in that case the multitude will take care of the liberty, virtue and interest of the multitude,
in all acts of government.'[1]

John Adams was clearly anxious that the great body of
the people should have their part in the election of representatives, but he was also clear that the right to this must
depend upon the possession of property in some form. It
is therefore noteworthy that in the 'Report of a Constitution
for the Community of Massachusetts', which is supposed
to have been drafted by John Adams in 1779, it was provided that the electors to the House of Representatives
should have freehold property to the value of £3 a year, or
personal estate to the value of £60.[2]

When we turn to the debate in the 'Federal Convention'
held at Philadelphia in 1787, we find that it was proposed
by Gouverneur Morris that in the Articles of the Constitution, dealing with the qualification of the voters for the
Lower House of Congress, a provision should be inserted
confining the suffrage to freeholders. After considerable
debate this was rejected, and in the Constitution of the

[1] John Adams, *Works*, ed. 1854, ix. 375, 376.
[2] 'The Report of a Constitution or form of Government for the Community of Massachusetts', Part II, Sect. III, Art. 3 (ibid., vol. iv).

United States of 1787, ratified in 1788, it was laid down that 'the electors in each State should have the qualification requisite for the election of the most numerous branch of the State Legislature', that is, it was practically left to each State to determine who should be the electors for the Lower House of Congress.[1] It is evident that opinion in the United States was still divided on the whole question.

It should, on the other hand, be observed that one of the most illustrious of American statesmen was clearly dissatisfied, at least some years later. In 1816 Jefferson wrote to S. Kerchival:

'The question you propose on equal representation has become a party one, in which I wish to take no public share.... At the birth of our republic I committed that (i.e. my) opinion, to the world in the draft of a Constitution annexed to the "Notes on Virginia", in which provision was inserted for a representation permanently equal. The infancy of the subject at that moment, and our inexperience of self-government occasioned gross departures in that draft from genuine republican canons.... But inequality of representation in both Houses of the Legislature, is not the only republican heresy in this first essay of our revolutionary patriots at forming a Constitution. For, let it be agreed that a government is republican in proportion as every man composing it has his equal voice in the direction of its concerns (not indeed in person, which would be impracticable beyond the limits of a city or small township, but) by representatives chosen by himself and responsible to him at short periods, and let us bring to the test of that every branch of our Constitution.

In the legislature, the House of Representatives is chosen by less than half the people, and not at all in proportion to those who do choose.... The true foundation of republican government is the equal right of every citizen in his person and property, and in their management. Try by this, as a tally, every provision of our Constitution, and see if it hangs directly on the will of the people. Reduce your legislature to a convenient number for free but orderly discussion. Let every man who fights or pays, exercise his just and equal right in their election. Submit them to approbation or rejection at short intervals....

I have thrown out these, as loose heads of amendment, for consideration and correction; and their object is to secure self-government by the republicanism of our Constitution, as well as by the spirit of the people, and to nourish and perpetuate this spirit. I am not among those

[1] 'Constitution of the United States', Art. I, Sect. II. 1.

who fear the people. They, and not the rich, are our dependence for continued freedom.'[1]

Jefferson's meaning is clear, that is that he was gravely dissatisfied with the limitations of the existing electoral rights in the United States, and it is interesting to find from a letter of 1824 that he was acquainted with Cartwright and his works.[2]

As I have already said, I do not deal with the development of these principles in the nineteenth century. It is enough for our present purpose to observe that it has only been slowly recognized that full political freedom requires that every person of mature age should have an equal place in the ultimate authority which controls the legislative system.

[1] Thos. Jefferson, *Memoirs, Correspondence*, &c., ed. 1826, iv. 293 ff.
[2] Ibid. 403.

IX

THE RELATIONS OF ECONOMIC AND POLITICAL FREEDOM

WE have so far been considering the development of liberty mainly under the terms of the political freedom of the community, that is in relation to the development of constitutional or democratic government, but also with some reference to the freedom of the individual in political society, freedom of action, freedom of thought and speech.

We must, however, recognize that men find themselves confronted by economic forces, some of which are beyond control, while others can be controlled, not indeed by the individual, but in some measure at least by the collective action of groups, or by that of the political society as a whole. Economic freedom cannot be achieved by mere anarchy, but only by a reasonable control.

The modern development of this control belongs indeed to the nineteenth century, and lies therefore beyond the scope of this work, but the necessity for this has arisen out of economic conditions which had developed rapidly during the latter part of the eighteenth century, though they can be recognized as existing in much earlier times. In the Middle Ages the control of the economic conditions of human life had indeed been highly developed, but it is clear that by the end of the eighteenth century the forms of this had ceased to be adjusted to the needs of society and the changes in economic conditions, and it is therefore not surprising that the latter part of the century witnessed a great revolt against the older economic and industrial system. It was thought by many that the triumphant individualism of thought should find its counterpart in the form and methods of economic life.

That at any rate was what happened, and many thought that it was in liberty from collective control that economic progress and prosperity were to be found. It is indeed probable that the removal of restraints upon individual economic liberty may have contributed to the increased total

wealth of the Western nations, but it produced other and
disastrous results, and the natural reaction rapidly followed.

European society has found that the abolition of restraints
does not mean that men have yet attained freedom. The
individual has found himself very helpless. It may seem
merely paradoxical to say that individual freedom can only
be found by the collective action of organized groups, or
by that of the political society, but this is obviously true, as
a little observation and reflection will make clear. The truth
is that the failure to recognize this arises from a complete
misunderstanding of the relation of the individual to society.

The isolated individual is economically helpless, and
almost impotent. It is regrettable that so many seem to
have forgotten the significance of the treatment of this
subject by Adam Smith, to have forgotten that it is only
under the terms of the co-operative principle of the division
of labour that economic progress is possible.[1] It is a lamentable absurdity that so much attention has been paid to the
fact of competition, and comparatively little to the fact and
principle of co-operation, for it needs no argument to show
that all economic progress rests upon co-operation. Co-
operation is not merely an ideal, but is the necessary condition of economic life. In fact, however, the recognition of the
co-operative character of economic society has been almost
overwhelmed by the clamour and violence of competition,
and we are compelled to recognize that in their economic
relations men have found anarchy where we should hope to
find a rational order.

We can trace two methods by means of which men in
the nineteenth century have endeavoured to move towards
economic liberty. The one has been by the effort to
strengthen the economically weaker members of the community by combination among themselves, the method of
the trade unions, the co-operative and the friendly societies;
the other by the extension of the legal control of the political
community over economic conditions.

It is the anarchy of industrial relations which lies behind
the history of the combinations of the wage-earners which
we call trade unions. They generally indeed serve other

[1] Adam Smith, *Wealth of Nations*, i, chaps. 1 and 3.

purposes also, such as the insurance of their members against various accidents of life, but their real function is to maintain and improve their standards of life in face of the pressure of the employers, and behind the employers, against the real or imagined pressure of economic forces.

The trade unions represent the principle of co-operation for mutual help among the wage-earners, a great and generous conception, but it is also true that they represent the existence of what is meant by the 'Class War'; an ugly phrase, but the phrase is not as ugly as the fact. It is well expressed by Adam Smith's observation on one aspect of the conditions which determine the rate of wages, 'What are the common wages of labour, depends everywhere upon the contract made between these two parties whose interests are by no means the same. The workmen desire to get as much, the masters to give as little as they can.' Adam Smith adds, 'It is not, however, difficult to foresee which of the two parties must upon all ordinary occasions have the advantage in this dispute, and force the other into compliance with his terms.'[1]

Trade unions came into existence to meet these facts, and represent the reasonable judgement that, while the isolated wage-earner is normally weaker than the employer, his power may be greatly increased by combination with others in the same position. We are not here concerned to deal with the various methods by which the trade unions have during the nineteenth century striven to protect the standard of life and to improve the conditions of work of their members. The history of these has been set out specially in the masterly works of Sidney and Beatrice Webb, the *History of Trade Unionism*, and *Industrial Democracy*. We are not concerned to maintain that the trade unions have always been right or wise in their actions. What is important is that we should understand that the trade unions have been endeavouring to protect the liberty of their members against the apparently overpowering force of the employers. They have been, and are still, the protectors of liberty, for they have stood between their members and the anarchical tyranny of economic power.

[1] Ibid. i. 8.

It is, however, true that what they have been doing in one way has been fundamentally the same as that which the State has been doing in another. For the real meaning of the great system of the Factory Acts has been the protection of the economic liberty of the economically weaker members of the community. It is very significant that the great system of the Factory Acts of the nineteenth century began with legislation intended to secure some reasonable conditions of life and work for the children sent from the workhouses into the factories. These children had not even the protection of parents, and it was the principle behind the Act that the State should at least in some degree act in the place of the parents.

And again, if it is asked why it was thought necessary to impose such a system of compulsion upon the factory owners, when at least some of the wiser employers had acted wisely without this compulsion, the answer is that it was argued, rightly or wrongly, that it was difficult, if not impossible, for them to maintain better conditions in face of the competition of less scrupulous employers. The legal compulsion of the Act was a method of liberty both for the children and for the better employers.

It was, however, not very long before it was discovered that the children whose parents were living required the same protection as the children from the workhouses, and the next Factory Act extended the protection to all child workers in certain factories. The Act was needed not merely to protect the children, but also their parents against the pressure of poverty which compelled them to send their children into the factories. It was only slowly that it came to be recognized that the same circumstances compelled the extension of the Acts to women, and to the protection of the safety even of men.

It is unnecessary for our purpose to enumerate the stages of the development of Industrial Legislation, but it is well to observe that the development was for many years opposed not only by interested persons, but by many of those who considered themselves to be the defenders of individual liberty. They were unable to see that this apparent liberty which they defended was often meaningless, and that the

Factory Acts were emancipating human beings from the unrestrained and brutal coercion of blind economic forces.

It is thus that it has come to be recognized by all those who think seriously that the achievement of freedom does not mean merely the repeal of the older system of law which in course of time had proved to be a hindrance to economic freedom; for the repeal of these older laws made room, not only for freedom, but also for anarchy, the anarchy of a blind struggle of economic forces in which almost inevitably those who were weaker were overpowered by those who were stronger; and the consequences can be seen in the disastrous conditions of many of the wage-earning classes, as they were set out in the reports of the Inspectors of Factories specially about the middle of the nineteenth century.

Economic anarchy is not freedom, but only a peculiarly lamentable subjection of human beings to irrational forces. Freedom can only be attained by the subjection of these forces to moral and rational control. To say that the wage-earner is free because he is at liberty to give or to withhold his services is merely a fantastic foolishness. So far as he has achieved liberty it has been normally under the shelter of the great co-operative organizations of the trade unions, or by the regulations of the industrial legislation of the community. Economic liberty cannot be achieved by the isolated individual, but only by co-operation, and under the shelter of the collective control of the political community.

We are thus brought back to the nature of political liberty, that is to the supremacy of law and the common will, for our experience has shown us that there is no safety for liberty in the most well-meaning patriarchal absolutism, but only in following the venerable maxim that what concerns all should be determined by all.

No sensible person will maintain that the whole community is always wise or right; it is liable to be carried away by sophistry, or passion, or panic, just as the individuals who compose it. Aristotle, however, said that in his judgement, though the individual members of a community may be inferior to some one wise man, the multitude is a better judge of many things than any one man, and less

4718

O

liable to be corrupted.[1] It is not always remembered that
Machiavelli, who will not easily be charged with sentimen-
tality, contradicts the opinion of many historians that the
multitude are changeable and ungrateful, and maintains
that the people, as a whole if they accept the control of the
laws, is wiser, more prudent, and less variable than a prince;
a people which is well ordered will be more consistent, more
prudent than a prince, even a wise prince. The people is
much wiser than the prince in the appointment of magistrates, and is more constant in its opinions; there is more
excellence or energy [*virtù*] in the people than in the prince.[2]

It is these opinions which we think have been confirmed
by the experience of the modern world, and what we judge
to be true in the political order we think is also true of the
economic. That is the meaning of industrial democracy.
If the anarchy of economic society is to be transformed into
a rational and moral order, it must be done by the rational
control of the community, and it is only under such a
control that men can hope to achieve economic freedom.
Industrial democracy will not necessarily prove any more
perfect or infallible than political democracy, but there is
no reason why it should be less so, if it is properly organized
and works through similar machinery.

Individual energy is no doubt an invaluable element not
only in economic life, but in all forms of life, but, in the
economic as in the political, it must be controlled by and
subjected to the common judgement, if it is not to become
a mere form of anarchy, as our experience has shown. It is
a mere absurdity to think that freedom in economic matters
is comparable with the inalienable freedom of the intellectual
or moral or artistic life; in these it is indeed true that
the individual personality requires for its development
freedom from the coercive control of the community,
but this is not true of the economic. It is indeed absurd to
think this, for it is obvious from our experience that economic society cannot work except under the shelter and
protection of the great legal and coercive system of political
society.

[1] Aristotle, *Politics*, iii. 15.
[2] Machiavelli, *Discorsi sopra la prima Decade di Tito Livio*, i. 58.

PART IV
CONCLUSION

AN attempt has been made in this work to trace the nature and development of the conception of political liberty in the Middle Ages, and in the seventeenth and eighteenth centuries, and it will, I hope, serve to correct the rather absurd notion that the pursuit of political liberty is a recent and merely modern thing.

It is true that between us and the ancient commonwealths of Greece and Rome there lies a period during which the progress of political liberty seemed to be arrested, and Western civilization seemed to have relapsed into a fundamentally barbaric system of absolutism; for the ancient Roman Empire had this character; and in the seventeenth century it might have seemed that this was about to recur. In another work, the *History of Mediaeval Political Theory in the West*, my brother and myself have endeavoured to examine the various elements of the political civilization in the Middle Ages at some length; here I only present a summary account of our conclusions. It seems to us to be clear that when we consider the development of medieval civilization we find that it represents a continual progress towards the control of the life of the community by the community itself.

We must also take account of the fact that it was just in those later centuries of the ancient world, when political freedom had seemed to disappear, that the conception of individual or personal liberty was greatly enlarged. We may think that Ezekiel's principle of individual responsibility, Cicero's dogmatic assertion of human equality, and Seneca's of the autonomy of human personality were expressed in rhetorical and exaggerated terms. And yet it is true that their phrases were the expression of a profound change in the fundamental principles of Western civilization, of the recognition that man is distinguished from other living beings above all by the fact that he is a rational and moral being who must determine his own life to ends which are rational and moral. The Christian religion found this conception in the world into which it came, and expressed it in the terms of the immediate relation and responsibility of the individual man to God.

If we attempt to express what had happened, we may say that, in some large and general terms, to the primitive and even to the ancient world the human group was in some senses more important than the individual, while to the modern world the individual personality has an immeasurable significance, and the group finds its value in the development of the individuals who form it.

It is indeed one of the paradoxes of history that, while in the period of the ancient Roman Empire the sense of political liberty seemed almost to disappear, the great system of the Roman law contributed much to develop the sense of the rights of the individual, as we can see in its protection of the slave, the woman, and the child against the arbitrary authority of the head of the family group. It is again true that much of this freedom of the individual was for a time lost in the decay of the Roman civilization, that the West may be said to have, in a large measure, fallen back into barbarism, and that the liberty of the individual was almost lost in the authority of the group. It is unhappily true that the Christian Church, not the Christian religion, was in a large measure responsible for this, for it forgot its own doctrine that the individual was responsible only to God in spiritual things. St. Augustine's unhappy defence of the persecution of those who differed from the Church was not indeed the sole cause of this, but it contributed much to it, as we can see from the treatment of religious persecution in the canon law.[1]

The Church did indeed in some sense defend spiritual liberty, that is its own independence, from the authority of the Temporal Power, but it did this only to put it more completely under the control of the Church itself. This is true not only of the medieval Church, but of the Reformed Churches. It was not till the eighteenth and nineteenth centuries that the Western world recovered from this ruinous error.

What was then the medieval conception of political liberty? It meant above all the supremacy of justice, that

[1] Cf. Gratian, *Decretum*, Part II, Causa XXIII, Quaestio IV.

is justice as embodied in the natural law, and in the positive laws of the community; that is it meant the reign of
law as distinguished from the dominion of the mere caprice or arbitrary authority of the ruler. The political community of the Middle Ages felt itself free when its
customary franchises and liberties were protected by the
positive laws.

If it is asked, what were these laws, and who made them,
the answer is that for many centuries they were not normally and consciously made at all, but represented the
immemorial custom of the community, local or general. It
is indeed very significant that even as late as the sixteenth
century an important English jurist, St. Germans, when he
analysed the various forms of the laws of England, dogmatically laid it down that all forms of English law, with
one exception, were the expression of the customs of the
community, as recognized, not made, by the judges or by the
local authority of the different parts of the country, which
he calls the *Patria*. It is only when these were not adequate
that he admitted a place for the Statutes of Parliament.[1]

The laws which expressed the liberties of the English
people were not properly speaking made by any superior
authority, but expressed the habit of life of the community.
This was also the normal principle of all the great medieval
jurists like Bracton in England, Beaumanoir in France, the
authors of the *Siete Partidas* in Castile, as well as of the great
canon lawyers like Gratian. Here is indeed a conception which
is wholly different from that of the ancient Roman Empire,
that the will of the prince had the force of law. To the
people of the Middle Ages the prince was under the law, like
everyone else. Here was the first foundation of political liberty.

We cannot determine precisely the time when there first
appeared in the medieval world the doctrine that the laws
could be made or changed by the rational and deliberate
human will. We may find something of this in the terms
of the 'Edictum Pistense' of A.D. 864, when it describes the
laws as made *consensu populi et constitutione regis*,[2] and this
certainly corresponds with the theory and practice of the

[1] St. Germans, *Dialogus de Fundamentis Legum Angliae*, iv. 8.
[2] *Mon. Germ. Historica*, Leg. Sect. ii, vol. ii. 273.

centuries from the thirteenth. Here we find a more developed conception of political liberty in the Middle Ages. The political community was free in so far as the law expressed its will and consent, a conception very far removed from that of the sixth century, when Justinian claimed that he was the sole legislator.[1] The words which are so often cited in the thirteenth and fourteenth centuries, 'Quod omnes tangit, ab omnibus approbetur', may have had little significance in the ancient Empire, but in the Middle Ages they meant what they said, for the law of the community was made by the community, and was binding on the ruler just as much as on the community.

Here is, I think, one explanation of the profound distrust of the Roman law which was so marked not only in England, but throughout western and central Europe.

The first principle of the political system of the Middle Ages was the supremacy of law, but this was not a merely abstract principle, but found a practical form in the medieval rule that this authority was embodied in courts of law which were independent of the prince. This is the meaning of the famous clause of Magna Carta (39) that no free man can be taken or imprisoned even by the king except by the legal judgement of his peers, or 'by the law of the land'; and it must be remembered that this was not a merely English rule. Indeed we find it asserted by Alfonso IX of Castile and León in 1188, and repeated emphatically by the Cortes of Valladolid in 1299; and it was laid down in the Assizes of Jerusalem, and by so great a feudal jurist as Beaumanoir in France, that in cases between the lord and his vassal, the lord had no place, even in his own court. It was the principle of the authority of the court, even as against the king, which was dogmatically asserted in France and England by Gerson and Fortescue in the fifteenth century, and by De Seyssel in France in the sixteenth century.

It would be difficult to find a sharper contrast with this than the assertion of some Italian Roman lawyers of the fourteenth and fifteenth centuries that the king could do what he pleased above the law, against the law, and outside of the law.[2]

[1] *Code*, i. 14. 12. [2] Jason de Magno, *Comm. on Digest*, i. 4. 1.

⌐The discovery of a method by which the law might be
deliberately adapted to changing conceptions and circumstances in the life of the great political communities was of
almost equal importance. This method was that of the
representative system, and it must be clearly understood
that this was not in any way peculiar to England; it was
developed in Spain at least a hundred years earlier than in
England, and throughout central and western Europe in
the thirteenth and fourteenth centuries.⌐
⌐There is still current a curious misconception about the
nature and functions of these representative bodies, as
though these were limited to the control of taxation. The
truth is that while this was an important element in their
authority, their function was from the first much larger.
The first meeting of the States General in France was called
to deal with the great questions raised in the conflict
between Philip the Fair and Pope Boniface VIII in 1302.
Questions of legislation and of war and peace were to be
submitted to the Cortes of León in 1188, when the representatives of the cities were for the first time present.⌐ What
is true of the first meetings of the representative councils is
true also of their proceedings in the fourteenth and fifteenth
centuries.
⌐Indeed it was perhaps the most important characteristic
of the representative system that it provided a method by
which the control of the community could be extended
from one public concern to another, as the political conditions demanded. As early as the thirteenth and fourteenth
centuries it began to assert a right to control in some
measure the administrative system, or, to put it more accu-
rately perhaps, to claim authority to deal with those persons
who were the advisers and agents of the Crown, and to
demand their expulsion or punishment when their actions
seemed to be contrary to the public interest.⌐No doubt the
responsibility of Ministers to the modern House of Commons is a long way off from the Provisions of Oxford in the
thirteenth century, and the English impeachments of the
fourteenth century, or from the demands of the States
General in France in 1355–8 for the removal of the evil
counsellors of the Crown; but⌐the principle which was

asserted was the same, namely that the community should in some measure control not merely legislation and finance, but the administrative system.⁊ It is indeed curious to notice how the 'Song of Lewes', which belongs to about the same time as the 'Provisions of Oxford', anticipates the later development:

> Ex hiis potest colligi, quod communitatem
> Tangit quales eligi ad utilitatem
> Regni recte debent, qui velint et sciant
> Et prodesse valeant, tales regis fiant
> Et conciliarii et coadjutores.[1]

⟨ Further the actual character of political authority in the Middle Ages was founded not only on monarchy, but on a complex of authorities. It is very significant that St. Thomas Aquinas should have looked upon the best form of government as that in which the community in its various parts should be represented⟩ 'talis vero est omnis politia bene commixta ex regno, in quantum unus praeest; et aristocratia, in quantum multi principantur secundum virtutem; et ex democratia, id est potestate populi, in quantum ex popularibus possunt eligi principes; et ad populum pertinet electio principum.'[2] He thought that the prototype of this was to be found in the government of Israel by Moses and his successors.

We cannot indeed tell how far St. Thomas was aware of the actual constitutional experiments of his time, but in his treatment of the representative principle and the elective method he comes very near to the actual experiments which were being made in Spain, in England, and elsewhere. The government which he praised was a mixed government; it is well, he says in the earlier part of the passage just cited, that all should have some part in the government. 'Quorum unum est, ut omnes aliquam partem habeant in principatu.'

⟨ Such then were the traditions of the proper nature of government and of political liberty which the Middle Ages handed on to the modern world—the doctrine of the final

---

[1] *Carmen de Bello Lewensi*, ed. Kingsford.
[2] St. Thomas Aquinas, *Summa Theologica*, i. 2. 105. 1.

authority of justice, or the natural law, to which all positive law must conform, against which all positive law was null and void; the principle that the supreme authority in the community was the positive law, which was first embodied in the custom of the community, and later in the will of the community as expressed in and through the representative assemblies.

To put the matter in other terms, we may say that the political freedom of the community was embodied in a mixed government, in which the king had normally an important place, but in which also the whole community had its part.

It is true that in the sixteenth, seventeenth, and eighteenth centuries there grew up in theory, and in large measure in fact, a system of absolute monarchy. In England, in Holland, and in some smaller countries alone was this development successfully resisted; but it is of the first importance to observe that this absolutism was felt by many in other countries, even in France and Spain, to be an innovation; and the medieval conception of a limited monarchy survived. So far from its being true that the defenders of political liberty were asserting a new principle, it was rather true that they were restating the essential principles of government of the Middle Ages. If these were now expressed in more controversial, more dogmatic, more general terms than had generally been used in the Middle Ages, this was because in the sixteenth, and even more in the seventeenth century, the defenders of political liberty were confronted by a new and dogmatic assertion of the absolute authority of the prince, as for instance by Bodin in France, without any definite reason given, or in England by James I on the ground that his political authority rested upon conquest, or as in France and England because it was said that the authority of the Prince proceeded directly from God, the doctrine asserted by the English 'Convocation Book', and in France by Bossuet.

What was, however, more important was, that these theories of absolutism were being translated into the terms of a practical absolutism, which was checked in England, but established in France, and from France passed into

O*

most of the continental countries. What actually happened
is fairly clear; but it has not, I think, been sufficiently observed that the development was looked upon by many, not
only in England, but throughout Europe, with alarm and
disapprobation. It is hardly necessary to speak of opinion
in England, we have seen something of the attitude of great
English political thinkers from Hooker and Milton to
Halifax and Locke, and it is no wonder that the absurd
arguments of the defenders of absolute monarchy failed
ignominiously to carry any conviction. It is no doubt true
that the case for absolute monarchy, as expressed in the
eccentric foolishness of James I's *True Law of Free Monarchies*, or in Filmer's *Patriarcha*, could hardly have been put
in worse terms, but the Revolution of 1688 cut the controversy short in England.

In most of the continental countries on the other hand
the absolute authority of the prince was temporarily established, though we cannot say that its literary defenders
made a much better case than in England; Bossuet's arguments were not indeed quite so absurd in form as those of
Filmer, but in substance they were on much the same level.

The criticism of the absolutist theories was, on the other
hand, serious and well considered in France, in Spain, and
in other countries. In some respects perhaps the most
important criticism was rather implied than directly expressed; but even by the most cautious legal writers, like
Coquille and Loyseau in France, the new developments of
the royal authority were regarded as innovations, as modern
changes which were far removed from the traditional methods
of medieval governments; even when they seemed to be
prepared to acquiesce in the new authority, they were clear
that these developments were new. Coquille asserts that it was
Louis XI who had brought in these changes in government,
while Loyseau cites Commines on the control of taxation
by the States General. This was not peculiar to them,
the same judgement was expressed by Joly, Jurieu, and
Fénelon. Fénelon indeed did not merely express an opinion
on the past, but set out a practical policy for the future.
When we turn from France to Spain we find that Ribadeneyra and Saavedra looked upon the constitutional

authority of the Cortes as belonging to the normal tradition
of government in Spain.

⟨If we look at the general political principles set out by
French and Spanish writers, we must notice in the first
place that one of the most conservative of them, the Spanish
bishop and jurist, Covarruvias, lays down dogmatically that
all temporal authority is derived from the community itself,
and flatly repudiates the doctrine of the 'Divine Right' of
the king, as it was set out a little later in the English 'Convocation Book', and by Bossuet. /

⟨In the second place, Covarruvias, Ribadeneyra, and
Saavedra in Spain, Joly, Jurieu, and Fénelon in France, were
clear that the king or prince had no absolute authority, that
this is a characteristic of the tyrant, not of the legitimate
prince.⟩

⟨ In the third place, that the positive laws of the community
are supreme over the prince, is declared as firmly by
Ribadeneyra and Saavedra in Spain as by Joly and Fénelon
in France, and, that in cases between the prince and a subject,
the decision lies with the courts of justice and not with the
prince. There is nothing to surprise us in Joly's contention
that the royal authority rests upon a contract between the
prince and the people. /

Perhaps the most interesting observation is that made by
Saavedra, that no monarchy could endure unless it was
mixed and included the elements of aristocracy and democracy. Absolute power is tyranny, and the king who obtains
it achieves his own ruin. It is important to observe that this
is the same in substance as what Fénelon says in *Télémaque*.

It will be clear that the attempt to establish a system of
absolute monarchy was as drastically criticized by some
continental writers in the seventeenth century as in England.
It will be useful, however, to remind ourselves of the characteristics of two of the English defenders of liberty in the
seventeenth century, for in different ways they represented
some of the most important elements in the political thought
of the time. Halifax was by temperament moderate and
critical, and thought of himself as standing outside both the
great parties, the Whig and the Tory, which were taking
shape during the reign of Charles II. He warns the prince

that he will ruin himself if he disregards or violates the law, and holds that it was liberty alone which gave life reality. 'It is hard', he says, 'for a soul that doth not love liberty ever to raise himself towards another world, he taketh it to be the fountain of all virtue, and the only seasoning that giveth a relish to life'; and he found an embodiment of the union of law and liberty in the English parliamentary constitution.

Locke's *Second Treatise on Government* is very different. It is a carefully ordered statement of what he considered the most important principles of the origin and structure of political society. These were not strictly speaking new, for he was in large measure restating the most important elements in the political theory of Hooker and of the Middle Ages, but it must be observed that he was setting out not only the liberty and authority of the community against the ruler, but was as much concerned to defend the liberty of the individual as against the community. That is, he denied that the community had any absolute or arbitrary authority: he was contradicting the conception of an absolute authority in the State. This was not indeed a new conception, on the contrary it was perhaps the most important principle of the Middle Ages, and found its expression in the doctrine that all laws which were contrary to the natural law were *ipso facto* null and void.

When we turn to the conception of political liberty in the eighteenth century we shall do well to begin by observing the importance of the historical tradition that all political authority was derived from the community, and, not only derived from it, but that its authority had been actually embodied in an assembly which represented the whole community. This was illustrated at the very outset of the century in the work of Fénelon; and in a developed form in that of Boulainvilliers. It is indeed a very interesting thing to find in Boulainvilliers one of the earliest historical accounts of the States General in France.

There was, however, a new element in the development of political theory in this century, and that was the immense influence exercised on the Continent by two great events.

First the English Revolution of 1688, and the discovery by continental countries that the principles of a limited monarchy and a representative constitutional system were not merely traditions of the past, but actual realities. And secondly by the American Revolution in the later part of the century; the successful revolt of a great community against what it felt to be an arbitrary interference with its political freedom.

The influence of England was for practical purposes first seen in Voltaire's *Lettres Philosophiques*, no doubt in a popular, but nevertheless a singularly effective form. Voltaire was perhaps not a great political thinker, but he was a very shrewd observer, and the contrast between the political system of England and that of France as it had grown up in the seventeenth century could not have been more effectively shown. At any rate he made it plain that political liberty was not only a tradition but an actually existing thing. He saw England not as a backward and inefficient country, but as having achieved where other countries had failed. What Voltaire had begun Montesquieu continued in his famous exposition of what he considered to be the real character of the English Constitution, as protecting the liberty of the English people.

If this was the influence of the English Revolution, that of the American was probably even greater in the second part of the eighteenth century, for it asserted and embodied not only the liberty of a great community, but, in the famous 'Declaration' of 1776, founded it upon the great tradition of the Middle Ages that all governments derived their authority from the community.

It would be difficult to overstate the immense influence of these great events in setting forward the liberation of Europe from the absurdities of the absolute monarchies. It is no doubt true that so profound a change in the political forms of European society could not be carried through in a few days, nor can we say that the process is yet complete, for there have been throughout the century reactionary movements, and these have indeed, even in the present day, assumed new and formidable expression.

To return, however, to the eighteenth century, it may

seem paradoxical to say that it was Edmund Burke, whom we usually think of as the most determined enemy of the French Revolution, who was the most penetrating and profound interpreter and defender of the American Revolution, but that is probably the truth. In his great speeches and letters on the revolt of the American Colonies he did more than anyone else in Europe to forward and develop the conception of political liberty.

We must recall some of his great paradoxes which we have already cited. 'If any man ask me what a free Government is, I answer that, for any practical purpose, it is what the people think so, and that they and not I are the natural lawful and competent judges of the matter.' And again, 'Politicks ought to be adjusted not to human reasoning, but to human needs, of which the reason is but a part, and by no means the greater part.' And again, 'In effect, to follow not to force the public inclination, to give a direction, a form, a technical dress, and a specific sanction to the general sense of the Community, is the end of legislation.'

We have throughout this work had occasion to observe that medieval political civilization found its most significant form in the principle of the supremacy of the law; Burke was maintaining that political liberty meant that it is the authority of a living and growing thing, that is the community, which is supreme. In another place he warned the House of Commons that it is the people, and not even the House of Commons, in which the supremacy resides. The law is great and august, but it may be dead, while it is the community which lives and grows; and a free government is one in which that life is embodied.

A dangerous doctrine, some will say, but all life is dangerous, and at any rate it was the doctrine of Burke, and it was in the name of this doctrine that he repudiated vehemently the claims that the English law and the English Parliament had any absolute authority over the American people.

It would be impossible in a few words to sum up the character and the results for France and for Europe of the French Revolution.

Liberty, Equality, and Fraternity were its watchwords,

revolutionary no doubt at that time and place, but not new conceptions. The later Hebrew prophets, and the post-Aristotelian philosophers had proclaimed the liberty and equality of human personality; Athens and the Roman Republic had laid the foundations of political liberty, while the Stoics and the Christian religion had taught the Western world something of the brotherhood of all the races of men; and these principles had never been wholly forgotten during the Middle Ages, nor even during the temporary success of the absolute monarchies of the seventeenth and eighteenth centuries, and these were now breaking down under the weight of their own incompetence.

The political liberty of the community was asserted, and its authority was established, but it was necessary that this authority should be limited, if the individual personality was to achieve its liberty. In medieval times this was represented by the principle that behind the authority of the positive law of the community, there was a greater and more august authority, that of the law of nature. Tom Paine may not have been a profound political thinker, but he showed a singular judgement when he translated the terms in which Locke had expressed this tradition into more modern ones:

'A man', Locke had said, 'cannot subject himself to the arbitrary power of another; and having, in the state of nature, no arbitrary power over the life liberty or person of another, but only so much as the law of nature gave him for the preservation of himself and the rest of mankind, this is all that he doth or can give up to the Community and by it to the legislative power, so that the legislature can have no more power than this. . . . Thus the law of nature stands as an eternal rule to all men, legislators as well as others.'[1]

Paine translates this:

'The administration of a republic is supposed to be directed by certain fundamental principles of right and justice. . . . They therefore (i.e. the people of a republic) renounce not only the despotic power, but the despotic principle, as well of governing as of being governed by mere will and power, and substitute in its place the government of justice. . . . By this mutual compact . . . they renounce as detestable the power of exercising at any future time any species of dominion over

[1] Locke, *Second Treatise of Government*, xi (par. 134).

each other, or anything not right in itself, because a majority of them may have strength sufficient to accomplish it . . . the common cementing power which holds all the parts of the republic together secures him (i.e. the individual) from the despotism of numbers, for despotism may be more effectively acted by many over few than by one man over others. The sovereignty of a republic is exercised to keep right and wrong in their proper and distinct place, and never suffers the one to usurp the place of the other. A republic, properly understood, is a sovereignty of justice, in contradistinction to a sovereignty of will.'[1]

Paine has substituted the terms, 'A sovereignty of justice' for Locke's 'Law of Nature', but the meaning is substantially the same. And it is of high importance to notice that Paine repudiated the conception of the absolute power of a majority as energetically as that of one man.

Rousseau begins his greatest political work by saying that man must be under authority, that is under the authority of the society to which he belongs, and this arises from the common agreement; but it is a limited authority, for it represents the unanimous will of those who form the society. This is what is meant by the supremacy of the general will.

Rousseau indeed contributed two great principles to the development of serious modern political thought. In the first place he restated the Aristotelian principle that the State is not merely a remedy for man's vices, as the post-Aristotelians and the Church Fathers had thought, but the necessary condition of all human life; the necessary condition, for without it man is a beast or a God.

This may seem a merely abstract conception, but it is, on the contrary, the foundation of all the living principles of human life and progress, and it is the same as that which Burke had expressed in those great words in which he describes the political society as a 'partnership in all perfection'.

It is true indeed that this conception has been by some unwise and hasty men perverted into the notion that the State has an absolute and unlimited authority over its members, and indeed Rousseau was not always very wise in the terms he uses, but his real meaning is very different.

The authority which a member of the political society is

[1] Cf. p. 178.

bound to obey is not the capricious will of the society, for liberty is not obedience to caprice or passion. It is obedience to a law which he has prescribed to himself. This is what he calls the 'General Will'. The 'General Will' is a will which is normally in all those who form the political society, it expresses a unanimity among its members, and the individual man is obeying himself when he obeys it. This may seem paradoxical, but it is really common sense, for without some such unanimity a human society is impossible. The whole society may be wrong, all those who form it may be wrong, but the general will is always right, that is, Rousseau might have added, that the individual man is free, for he is obeying himself when he obeys it.

Rousseau's conception is penetrating, but I am inclined to think that the older conceptions of the natural law, which Paine describes as the 'Sovereignty of Justice', with all their vagueness were more satisfactory.

The French Revolution may then be said to represent the continuity of political principles which can be recognized in the history of the Middle Ages, and in the seventeenth and eighteenth centuries. No doubt the absolute monarchies of the seventeenth and eighteenth centuries seemed for a time to have interrupted this continuity, but the interruption was superficial, abnormal, and short-lived. The older and more normal political principles overpowered the attempt to establish absolutism in England, and, even where they temporarily succeeded, the older tradition of the authority of the community survived. No doubt the French Revolution was violent, and in its very violence brought about a reaction to absolutism in the Empire of Napoleon. But this also was only temporary, and the normal development of the political civilization of Europe was resumed in the nineteenth century, nor is there any serious reason to think that this has ceased because some politically undeveloped countries have not been able to keep pace with it.

INDEX